P9-DFO-174

MEMOIRS OF
McCHEYNE

MEMOIRS OF McCHEYNE

PART I

Including His Letters and Messages

Edited By
ANDREW A. BONAR

With a Biographical Introduction
By
S. MAXWELL CODER

MOODY PRESS
CHICAGO

Printed in the United States of America

Lincoln Christian College

CONTENTS

Gift of Miss Marie E. Graham   February 1, 1972

42554

BIBLE MESSAGES

BIOGRAPHICAL INTRODUCTION

SCARCELY once in a century does such a remarkable volume appear as this collection of the letters, Bible messages, and other papers of Robert Murray McCheyne, originally compiled by Andrew A. Bonar. First published in 1844, it has been sought after and treasured by God's people everywhere as one of the greatest and most blessed spiritual classics of all time. Within twenty-five years after its first appearance, the book was in its one hundred sixteenth English edition, and its circulation in America was likewise phenomenal.

In spite of the almost countless editions in which the volume has been published during the past century, it has been practically unobtainable for many years. There is no reason for doubting that this scarcity is the result of the fact that those who are fortunate enough to possess copies regard them as almost priceless.

Why such a collection of papers, gathered together by a friend and published after McCheyne's death, should be so cherished by so many for so long a time, while the careful life work of other men of God has quickly passed into oblivion, cannot be understood apart from some knowledge of the life of this young minister of the Church of Scotland, who died at the age of twenty-nine.

Robert Murray McCheyne was born in Edinburgh on May 21, 1813, at a time when the first evidences of a spiritual awakening in Scotland were beginning to appear, following a period when orthodoxy and piety had sunk to such a low level that "the things which remained were ready to die." Among the secret preparations of God for coming times of refreshing from on high was the birth of this youngest son of Adam McCheyne, writer to the signet, for he was destined to be recognized as one of God's greatest gifts to His Church in many generations, and to be known long after his death as "the saintly Mc-Cheyne."

That brilliance of intellect which was later to make him an accomplished Hebrew and Greek scholar was evident at the early age of four, when he taught himself to name and write all the letters of the Greek alphabet, as a means of recreation. Within the next year he achieved eminence among his school fellows because of his progress in English, and the sweetness and correctness of his powers of recitation.

McCheyne entered the high school in his eighth year, and matriculated at Edinburgh University when he was fourteen, in November, 1827. There he repeatedly distinguished himself as a versatile student, especially in poetical exercises. He was awarded a special prize by Professor Wilson for a poem, "On the Covenanters." He is described as having been of a tall, light form, full of elasticity and vigor as a young man; ambitious, yet noble in his disposition, disdaining everything like meanness or deceit. Some would have regarded him as exhibiting many traits of a Christian character; but his susceptible mind had not, at that time, a relish for any higher joy than the refined gaieties of society, and for such pleasures as the song and the dance could yield.

Although he never knew the date of his new birth, he possessed a definite assurance that it had taken place. It was characteristic of his ministry that such assurance did not prevent deep and lifelong searchings and longings for greater holiness of life.

In the winter of 1831 he commenced his studies in the Divinity Hall where Thomas Chalmers was Professor of Divinity and David Welsh, Professor of Ecclesiastical History. Those who recall the important movements within the Church of Scotland at this period, and the places of leadership these men occupied, will realize that this four-year course afforded no ordinary advantages to McCheyne for enlarging his understanding and deepening his spiritual life.

From the day of the death of Robert's eldest brother, David, his senior by eight or nine years, his friends observed a change. His diary contains numerous allusions to the effect the passing of this godly and well-beloved brother had upon young McCheyne, who was eighteen years of age at the time. One year later, he wrote, "On this morning last year came the first overwhelming blow to my worldliness; how blessed to me, Thou, O God, only knowest, who hast made it so." Again to a friend, he penned the lines, "Pray for me, that I may be made holier and wiser—less like myself, and more like my heavenly Master; that I may not regard my life, if so be I may finish my course with joy. This day eleven years ago, I lost my loved and loving brother, and began to seek a Brother who cannot die."

Together with Edward Irving, Andrew and Horatius Bonar, and other ardent young souls, McCheyne met frequently for prayer, Bible study and exercises in the Hebrew and Greek Scriptures. When Dr. Chalmers heard of the simple literal way in which the words of Scripture were taken by these young believers, he said, "I like these literalities." A study of any of McCheyne's sermons reveals how profound was his respect for the exact language of the written Word of God, whether he was speaking of the return of the Lord, or of the obligation resting upon believers to reach the lost about them for Christ. These young men also set apart an hour or two every week for visiting the careless and needy in the most neglected portions of the town. They stirred each other up to faithfulness in this ministry, in such hours as might otherwise have been given to recreation. His diary reveals the state of mind of young McCheyne during these years of preparation.

"*May 21.* This day I attained my twenty-first year. Oh, how long and how worthlessly I have lived, Thou only knowest! *Neff* died in his thirty-first year; when shall I?"

"*October 17.* Private meditation exchanged for conversation. Here is the root of the evil—forsake God and He forsakes us."

"*November 21.* If nothing else will do to sever me from my sins, Lord, send me such sore and trying calamities as shall awake me from earthly slumbers. It must always be best to be alive to Thee, whatever be the quickening instrument. I tremble as I write, for Oh! on every hand do I see too likely occasions for sore afflictions."

On December 31, 1832, McCheyne summed up twelve months of progress. "God has in this past year introduced me to the preparation of the ministry—I bless Him for that. He has helped me to give up much of my shame to name His name, and be on His side, especially before particular friends— I bless Him for that. He has taken conclusively away friends that might have been a snare—must have been a stumbling block—I bless Him for that. He has introduced me to one Christian friend, and seals more and more my amity with another—I bless Him for that."

The consciousness of some sin caused him to write, "Somewhat overcome. Let me see: There is a creeping defect here. Humble, purposelike reading of the Word omitted. What plant can be unwatered and not wither?"

His diary gives evidence of unsparing self judgment.

"*June 4.* Evening almost lost. Music will not sanctify, though it make feminine the heart."

"*June 22.* Omissions make way for commissions. Could I but take effective warning! A world's wealth would not make up for that saying, 'If any man sin, we have an advocate with the Father.' But how shall we that are dead to sin live any longer therein?"

"*August 13.* Clear conviction of sin is the only true origin of dependence on another's righteousness, and therefore (strange to say!) of the Christian's peace of mind and cheerfulness."

"*September 8.* Reading Adams' *Private Thoughts.* Oh, for his heart-searching ability! Ah me! On what mountains of pride must I be wandering, when all I do is tinctured with the very sin this man so deplored; yet where are my wailings, where my tears, over my love of praise?"

"*November 14.* I fear the love of applause or effect goes a great way. May God keep me from preaching myself instead of Christ crucified."

"*February 23, (1834).* Rose early to seek God and found Him whom my soul loveth. Who would not rise early to meet such company? The rains are over and gone. They that sow in tears shall reap in joy."

Wrote Andrew Bonar of his friend, "During his first years of his college course, his studies did not absorb his full attention; but no sooner was the change in his soul begun, than his studies shared in the results. A deeper sense of responsibility led him to occupy his talents for the service of Him who bestowed them. There have been few who, along with a devotedness of spirit that sought to be ever directly engaged in the Lord's work, have nevertheless retained such continued and undecaying esteem for the advantages of study. While attending the usual literary and philosophical classes, he found time to turn his attention to theology and natural history. And often in his days of most successful preaching, when, next to his own soul, his parish and his flock were his only care, he has been known to express a regret that he had not laid up in former days more stores of all useful knowledge; for he found himself able to use the jewels of the Egyptians in the service of Christ. His previous studies would sometimes flash into his mind some happy illustration of divine truth, at the very moment when he was most solemnly applying the glorious gospel to the most ignorant and vile."

His own words will best show his estimate of study, and at the same time the prayerful manner in which he felt it should be carried on. "Do get on with your studies," he wrote to a young student in 1840. "Remember you are now forming the character of your future ministry in great measure, if God spare you. If you acquire slovenly or sleepy habits of study now, you will never get the better of it. Do everything in its own time. Do everything in earnest; if it is worth doing, then do it with all your might. Above all, keep much in the presence of God. Never see the face of man until you have seen His face who is our light, our all. Pray for others; pray for your teachers and fellow students." To another he wrote: "Beware of the atmosphere of the classics. It is pernicious indeed; and you need much of the south wind breathing over the Scriptures to counteract it. True, we ought to know them; but only as chemists handle poisons—to discover their qualities, not to infect their blood with them." And again: "Pray that the Holy Spirit would not only make you a believing and holy lad, but make you wise in your studies also. A ray of divine light in the soul sometimes clears up a mathematical problem wonderfully. The smile of God calms the spirit, and the left hand of Jesus holds up the fainting head, and His Holy Spirit quickens the affections, so that even natural studies go on a million times more easily and comfortably."

Vacation time, for McCheyne and such of his intimate friends as remained in town, was not regarded as a period of complete cessation from study. Once every week they spent a morning together for the purpose of investigating some point of systematic theology, and stating to each other the amount and result of their private reading. During another summer they studied unfulfilled prophecy each week at an early morning hour. As they said, "Though our views differed much on particular points, we never failed to get food for our souls in the Scriptures we explored." These discussions were so profitable that the young men formed the habit of gathering together at half past six each Saturday morning during the school term, to study whatever might cast light on the Word of God.

A young man with such unusual intellectual powers, with which were associated a love for study and a remarkably accurate memory, might have become noted for scholarship, had it not been for the fact that he regarded the winning of souls as his chief task. He made every talent he possessed subsidiary to the single desire of awakening those who were dead in trespasses and sins. He prepared his soul for what he regarded as the terrible and awful responsibility of ministering the Word of God, "by much prayer, and much study of the Word of God; by affliction in his person; by inward trials and sore temptations; by experience of the death of corruption in his own heart, and by discovery of the Saviour's fullness and grace. He learned experimentally to ask, 'Who is he that overcometh the world but he that believeth that Jesus is the Son of God?' (I John 5:5)."

Robert Murray McCheyne was licensed to preach by the Presbytery of Annan, on July 1, 1835. After preaching in various places for several months, during which many began to perceive the peculiar sweetness of the Word on his lips, he became assistant to Mr. John Bonar in the united parishes of Larbert and Dunipace, near Stirling, on November 7, 1835. His preaching was the giving out of his own inward life, the unfolding of his own soul's experience as he grew in grace and in the knowledge of his Lord and Saviour. He began each day by singing Psalms at an early hour. This was followed by the reading of the Word for his own sanctification. He found a mine of spiritual riches in the *Letters of Samuel Rutherford.* Other favorites of his were Baxter's *Call to the Unconverted,* and *The Life of David Brainerd,* by Jonathan Edwards.

He studied both the Old and New Testaments regularly, determined to "examine the most barren chapters to collect the good for which they were intended." His desire to have every possible help to holiness led him to seek the fellowship of more advanced believers. In a letter to a friend he compared these contacts with other Christians to the necessity for keeping his pocket watch corrected by consultation with the trustworthy and proved clocks in the church steeples. He wrote, "And just so I sometimes think it may be with that inner watch, whose hands point not to time but to eternity. By gradual and slow changes the wheels of my soul lag behind, or the springs of passions become too powerful; and I have no living timepiece with which I may compare, and by which I may amend my going. You will say that I may always have the Son, and so it should be; but we have many clouds which obscure the Son from our weak eyes."

After only a few weeks of ministry, a heart condition and an irritating cough made it necessary for him to be laid aside from public duty. He said to Mr. Bonar, "I hope and pray that it may be His will to restore me again to you and your parish, with a heart tutored by sickness, to speak more and more as dying to dying." Again, "Paul asked, 'What wilt thou have me to do?' and it was answered, 'I will show him what great things he must *suffer* for my name's sake.' Thus it may be with me. I have been too anxious to do great things. The lust of praise has ever been my besetting sin; and what more befitting school could be found for me than that of suffering alone, away from the eye and ear of man?"

Those who observed Mr. McCheyne's ministry closely were aware that he gave out not merely living water, but living water drawn from the springs that he had himself drunk of. He reproached himself for what he called any bitter speaking of the gospel. "Surely it is a gentle message, and should be spoken with angelic tenderness, especially by such a needy sinner." Meeting a fellow pastor on one occasion, he asked what his friend's last Sabbath subject had been. The reply was "The wicked shall be turned into hell." On hearing this awful text, McCheyne asked, "Were you able to preach it *with tenderness?*"

His diary contains the cry, "Oh, when will I plead, with my tears and inward yearnings, over sinners! Oh, compassionate Lord, give me to know what manner of spirit I am of! Give me Thy gentle Spirit, that neither strives nor cries. Much weariness, want of prayerfulness, and want of cleaving to Christ." "Since Tuesday have been laid up with illness. Set by once more for a season to seal my unprofitableness and cure my pride. When shall this self-choosing temper be healed? 'Lord, I will preach, run, visit, wrestle,' said I. 'No, thou shalt lie in thy bed and suffer,' said the Lord. Today missed some fine opportunities of speaking a word for Christ. The Lord saw I would have spoken as much for my own honor as His, and therefore shut my mouth. *I see a man cannot be a faithful minister, until he preaches Christ for Christ's sake*—until he gives up striving to attract people to himself, and seeks only to attract them to Christ. Lord, give me this! Tonight some glimpses of humbling, and therefore some wrestling in social prayer. But my prayers are scarcely to be called prayers."

When a friend died, he bewailed, "Oh, how I repent of our vain controversies when we last met, and that we spoke so little of Jesus. Oh, that we had spoken more one to another! Lord, teach me to be always speaking as dying to dying."

McCheyne's advice to a young man about Bible reading is most instructive as to his own prayer life. "You read your Bible regularly, of course; but do try and understand it, and still more to *feel* it. Read more parts than one at a time. For example, if you are reading Genesis, read a Psalm also; or if you are reading Matthew, read a small bit of an Epistle also. *Turn the Bible into prayer.* Thus, if you were reading the First Psalm, spread the Bible on the chair before you, and kneel, and pray, 'O Lord, give me the blessedness of the man'; 'let me not stand in the counsel of the ungodly.' This is the best way of knowing the meaning of the Bible, and of learning to pray."

After ten months' ministry at Larbert and Dunipace under Mr. John Bonar, McCheyne was unanimously called to become pastor of a new church, St. Peter's in Dundee, where his congregation amounted from the beginning to about eleven hundred hearers. He was ordained on November 24, 1836. From that time on, there was abundant evidence that God had answered his prayer, "Lord, may Thy grace come with the laying on of the hands of the Presbytery." His very first sermon as a pastor was the means of awakening souls, as he afterwards learned, and evidently every message he ever gave served to deepen the impression he made upon his people.

The details of the manner of McCheyne's life, and of the way he conducted himself as a minister of the gospel, have for a hundred years been studied by other Christian workers who have longed to see God's blessing resting upon them as it rested richly upon every part of the service of this young man of God.

He resolutely secured time for devotion before breakfast each day, believing that three chapters from the Bible were little enough food for his soul at the beginning of each day. He refused to give to his people on the Lord's day anything which had not cost him much of diligent application in study, meditation, and prayer. When asked by a friend about his view of how one should prepare for the pulpit, he called attention to Exodus 27:20: *"Beaten oil—beaten oil for the lamps of the sanctuary."* He greatly admired the words of Jeremy Taylor, "If thou meanest to enlarge thy religion, do it rather by enlarging thine ordinary devotions than thy extraordinary." While McCheyne did set apart special seasons for prayer and fasting, the real secret of his soul's prosperity lay in the daily enlargement of his own heart in fellowship with God. On one Sunday his diary carried the comments, "Very happy in my work. Too little prayer in the morning. Must try to get early to bed on Saturday, that I may 'rise a great while before day.' "

McCheyne introduced a regular Thursday evening prayer meeting at his church, at a time when the mid-week service was a rarity. It was his custom to begin such meetings by reading some great promise from Scripture, to be hidden in the hearts of his people. Prayer preceded and followed a twenty minute Bible study period, and then the young pastor read some history of revivals, with comments in passing.

He set apart another evening for a class for the young people of his congregation. Sunday schools he encouraged in all the districts of his parish. One of the secrets of the great success of his work among children is to be found in the qualifications upon which he insisted for every teacher. "She should be able to keep up in her scholars the fluency of reading, and the knowledge of the Bible and Catechism which they may have already acquired. She should be able to teach them to sing the praises of God with feeling and melody. But, far above all, she should be a Christian woman, not in name only, but in deed and in truth—one whose heart has been touched by the Spirit of God, and who can love the souls of little children. Any teacher who wanted this last qualification, I would look upon as a curse rather than a blessing—a center of blasting and coldness and death, instead of a center from which light and warmth and heavenly influence might emanate."

His method of preaching was an effort to emulate the ministry of the Apostles by expounding Scripture in his sermons. After announcing the subject of a discourse, he called attention to the context, then proceeded to bring out the doctrines of the text. A friend said, "The heads of his sermons were not the milestones that tell you how near you are to your journey's end, but they were nails which fixed and fastened all he said." He referred to himself as "just an interpreter of Scripture." Far from simply preaching Bible doctrine, he sought to preach Christ, from whom all doctrine shoots forth as rays from a center. Many spoke of the peculiar sweetness and holy unction of his preaching, which attracted visitors from far and wide.

Offers for his pastoral services which came from wealthier districts with much larger emoluments, McCheyne rejected, because he was convinced that he was in the will of God "among the noisy mechanics and political weavers of this godless town. He will make the money sufficient. He that paid His taxes from a fish's mouth will supply all my needs." It was his hope that "perhaps the Lord will make this wilderness of chimney tops to be green and beautiful as the garden of the Lord, a field which the Lord hath blessed!" God graciously fulfilled this yearning of His young servant's heart, but in an altogether unexpected way, as the fruit of much suffering and prayer.

Before the showers of heavenly blessing came which were to fall on St. Peter's Church at Dundee, McCheyne's ministry was greatly enlarged when he became, in 1837, Secretary to the Association for Church Extension in the County of Forfar, in which capacity he traveled all over that area, ministering the Word. He might have written much, and have gained a name by his writing; but he laid everything aside when put in comparison with preaching the gospel. He scarcely ever refused an invitation to preach on a weekday, and his visits were always longed for in other communities as times of special refreshment.

In our own day of laxity in church discipline, it is interesting to read a statement made by Robert Murray McCheyne at an ordination of elders. "When I first entered upon the work of the ministry among you, I was exceedingly ignorant of the vast importance of church discipline. I thought that my great and almost only work was to pray and preach. I saw your souls to be so precious, and the time so short, that I devoted all my time, and care, and strength, to labor in word and doctrine. When cases of discipline were brought before me and the elders, I regarded them with something like abhorrence. It was a duty I shrank from; and I may truly say it nearly drove me from the work of the ministry among you altogether. But it pleased God, who teaches His servants in another way than man teaches, to bless some of the cases of discipline to the manifest and undeniable conversion of the souls of those under our care; and from that hour a new light broke in upon my mind, and I saw that if preaching be an ordinance of Christ, so is church discipline. I now feel very deeply persuaded that both are of God—that two keys are committed to us by Christ: the one the key of doctrine, by means of which we unlock the treasures of the Bible; the other the key of discipline, by which we open or shut the way to the sealing ordinances of the faith. Both are Christ's gifts, and neither is to be resigned without sin."

One of the most notable characteristics of McCheyne, frequently remarked upon by his contemporaries, was the holy consistency of his daily walk. Knowing, as he did, that one idle word, one needless contention, one covetous act, could destroy in his people the effect of many a solemn expostulation and earnest warning, he was peculiarly circumspect in his everyday walk. As Andrew Bonar wrote about his friend, "We must not only speak faithfully to our people in our sermons, but live faithfully for them too. Perhaps it may be found that the reason why many who preach the gospel fully and in all earnestness are not owned of God in the conversion of souls, is to be found in their defective exhibition of grace in these easy moments of life. 'Them that honor me, I will honor' (I Sam. 2:30). It was noticed long ago that men will give you leave to *preach against* their sins as much as you will, if so be you will but be easy with them when you have done, and talk as they do, and live as they live. How much otherwise it was with Mr. McCheyne, all who knew him are witnesses."

His biographer mentions the reproach which McCheyne was obliged to bear, even while his holy walk and his heavenly ministry were manifestly raising the tone of Christians. "He was the object of supercilious contempt to formal, cold-hearted ministers, and of bitter hatred to many of the ungodly . . . . Very deep was the enmity borne to him by some, all the deeper, because the only cause of it was his likeness to his Master. But nothing turned him aside. He was full of ardor, yet ever gentle, and meek, and generous; full of zeal, yet never ruffled by his zeal; and not only his strength of first love (Rev. 2:4), but even its warm glow, seemed in him to suffer no decay. Thus he spent the first years of his ministry in Dundee. The town began to feel that they had a peculiar man of God in the midst of them."

Two deep impressions were preparing McCheyne during these years for an altogether different form of service. These were his intense interest in missions, and the decided impression on his own mind that his career would be short, often seen as he sealed his letters with this statement, "The night cometh."

At the close of 1838, his unremitting labor brought on a violent palpitation of the heart, which made it necessary for him to leave Dundee to seek rest and change of occupation. In Edinburgh, Dr. Candlish suddenly asked McCheyne one day what he would think of "being useful to the Jewish cause during his cessation from labor, by going abroad to make personal inquiries into the state of Israel?" The idea thus suddenly suggested led to the sending forth of a delegation from the Church of Scotland to the Jews of Europe and Asia, to inquire into their condition, and to report on the prospects and best means of calling their attention to the character and claims of the Lord Jesus Christ. It was a signal evidence of the high esteem and confidence in which Robert Murray McCheyne was held by his brethren that he was thus honored, in the twenty-fourth year of his age, and was chosen, in connection with three older ministers, as a member of the famous Mission of Inquiry.

The interest which this proposed journey excited in Scotland was very great. For some time, the condition of the people of Israel had been upon the hearts of godly ministers in Scotland. It was anticipated that there would be "an outpouring of the Spirit, when our church should stretch out its hand to the Jew as well as to the Gentile."

During the journey to Palestine McCheyne wrote, "For much of our safety I feel indebted to the prayers of my people, I mean the Christians among them, who do not forget us. If the veil of the world's machinery were lifted off, how much we could find is done in answer to the prayers of God's children." Although extremely weak and ill, McCheyne neglected not his own prayer life. While the tent was being erected at the end of a day's arduous journey, he would lie down on the ground under some tree, completely exhausted by the long ride. After lying almost speechless for half an hour, when the palpitation of his heart somewhat abated, he would propose that his friend Andrew Bonar, who was also a member of the party, and he should pray together. Often, at the point of death in a foreign land, feeling his faculties going, one by one, with every reason to expect that he would soon be with his God, McCheyne devoted himself to prayer for his people. He wrote to them, "When I got better, I used to creep out in the evenings about sunset. I often remembered you all then. I could not write, as my eyes and head were much affected; I could read but very little; I could speak very little, for I had hardly any voice; and so I had all my time to lay my people before God and pray for a blessing on them."

On one of those days when he was stretched on his bed, praying for his flock despite all his own suffering, a very remarkable revival began to be witnessed back in Dundee, under the preaching of Mr. W. C. Burns, who was supplying Mr. McCheyne's place in his absence. Beginning in Kilsyth, a great awakening took place which soon swept over Dundee. For some time there had been symptoms of deeper attention than usual at St. Peter's, and of real anxiety in some who had previously been careless. On Thursday evening after the usual weekly prayer meeting, Mr. Burns invited those to remain who felt the need of an outpouring of the Spirit. About a hundred remained; and at the conclusion of a solemn address to these anxious souls, suddenly the power of God seemed to descend, and all were bathed in tears. At a similar service next evening in the church, there was much melting of heart and intense desire after the Lord, and a vast number pressed into the after meeting with awful eagerness.

"It was like a pent-up flood breaking forth; tears were streaming from the eyes of many, and some fell on the ground groaning, weeping, and crying for mercy. Onward from that evening meetings were held every day for many weeks; and the extraordinary nature of the work justified and called for extraordinary services. The whole town was moved. Many believers doubted; the ungodly raged; but the Word of God grew mightily and prevailed. Instances occurred where whole families were affected at once. Other men of God in the vicinity hastened to aid in the work.

"When Mr. McCheyne arrived at the conclusion of his trip through Europe, the blessing was still continuing. He saw such evidence of the revival for which he had been praying as to make his heart rejoice. He had no envy because another instrument was so honored in the place where he himself had labored with many tears and trials. In true Christian magnanimity, he rejoiced that the work of the Lord was done, by whatever hand."

His people welcomed his arrival with the greatest joy. There was not a seat in the church unoccupied; people were crowded into every available space. Many were weeping; all were still and calm, intensely earnest to hear. On coming out of his church he found the road to his house crowded with old and young who were waiting to welcome him back. He discovered that many of those who were saved during the revival were numbered among those for whom he and others had prayed before he left them. Mr. McCheyne mentioned a pleasing result of the awakening, "I find many souls who were saved under my own ministry, whom I never knew of before. They are not afraid to come out now, it has become so common a thing to be concerned about the soul."

Robert Murray McCheyne returned from his mission to Israel at the end of the year 1839. In the spring of 1843, he visited the north of England on an evangelical mission, and made similar journeys to London and Aberdeenshire. On returning from the latter place, he was seized with a sudden illness. In visiting some people sick of the fever, he had caught the infection. The crisis came on March 24, 1843.

When it became known that his life was in danger, a weeping multitude assembled in St. Peter's. Next morning, at a quarter past nine, he expired, and all that day nothing was to be heard in the houses around but lamentation and great mourning, and, as a friend in that neighborhood wrote, "In passing along the high road, you saw the faces of every one swollen with weeping." McCheyne was buried by St. Peter's Church, where an imposing tombstone marks his grave.

Tributes to his greatness could be cited almost without number. A London pastor called him "altogether one of the loveliest specimens of the Spirit's workmanship." In the *Dundee Warder,* a tribute said, "Every note from his hand had a lasting interest about it; for his mind was so full of Christ, that, even in writing about the most ordinary affairs, he contrived, by some natural turn, to introduce the glorious subject that was always uppermost with him."

This calls attention to the greatest tribute which could ever have been paid to McCheyne, the manner in which God's people have received his collected letters and messages.

Of all the works of McCheyne,* the present collection of
papers is by far the most outstanding volume. Typical of the
high regard in which this work has always been held are these
quotations from a review of the original edition, which appeared in July, 1844, in *The Presbyterian Review and Religious
Journal,* an Edinburgh periodical.

"Such language could not have been prompted by an ordinary man. Robert Murray McCheyne! . . . That disentangled,
pilgrim look which showed plainly that he 'sought a city';—
the serene self-possession of one who walks by faith . . . that
aspect of compassion, in such unison with the remonstrating
and entreating tones of his melodious and tender voice—that
entire appearance as of one who had been with Jesus, and who
would never be right at home till, where Jesus is, there he
should also be.

"To know him was the best interpretation of any text. At
least, we have a clearer conception of what is meant by a hidden life, and a 'living sacrifice,' and can better understand the
sort of life which Enoch led, since we made the acquaintance
of Robert McCheyne.

"In his prayers he held such reverential and endearing communion with a reconciled God; he pressed so near the throne;
there was something so filial in his 'Abba, Father'; it was so
obvious even to lookers-on, that he was putting his petitions
and praises into the golden censer; so express, and urgent, and
hopeful were his supplications, that it was awakening to hear
him pray. It was enough to make some Christians feel, 'hitherto we have asked nothing in Jesus' name'; enough to prick

---

* His principal works are: 1. *Narrative of a Mission of Inquiry to the Jews*
(jointly with Andrew Bonar), Edinburgh, 1842. 2. *Expositions of the Epistles to
the Seven Churches of Asia,* Dundee, 1843. 3. *The Eternal Inheritance: the
Believer's Portion, and Vessels of Wrath Fitted to Destruction, Two Discourses,*
Dundee, 1843. 4. *Memoir and Remains of Robert Murray McCheyne* (edited by
Andrew A. Bonar), Edinburgh, 1843. 5. *Additional Remains, Sermons, and Lec-
tures,* Edinburgh, 1844. 6. *A Basket of Fragments, the Substance of Sermons,*
Aberdeen, 1849.

the hearts of prayerless worldlings. His preaching was a continuation of his prayers. In both he spoke from within the veil, his hand on the mercy seat, and his eye fixed on things invisible.

"To give this article a practical tendency, we may be allowed to mention what we believe to have been the secret of Mr. McCheyne's uncommon usefulness. . . . We are persuaded that next to his habitual dependence upon the Spirit of God, the occasion of his uncommon success was the consistency and conspicuousness of his Christian character. He lived in the eye of his people. Though his house had been a glass-fronted cabinet, they could scarcely have been more minutely cognizant of his movements and whole manner of life. They knew that his weekdays were but a sequel to his Sabbath. And what they saw him in the pulpit, they found him in his study and among his friends, by the wayside, and in their own houses."

In an American edition published in Philadelphia in 1844, Samuel Miller, of the Theological Seminary at Princeton, New Jersey, wrote an introduction in which he said, "Such a spirit ought to be studied deeply and recommended as widely as possible. . . . I consider that the appearance and the popularity of such works as this Memoir are a pledge that the gracious King of Zion will revive us. . . . Surely the contemplation of such a portrait as that presented in this Memoir ought to fill us with humiliation and shame. . . . I write these lines, and recommend this work . . . under the deep impression that we cannot pray for a greater blessing to our beloved Church, than that the mantle of this holy man may rest upon all our pastors and elders, exciting them to the zeal, the unceasing diligence, and the entire consecration to their Master in heaven which were so conspicuous in his short course."

Alexander Whyte, in a preface to a centenary edition of this notable work which was being published in Edinburgh in 1913, spoke of "that great spiritual classic, Andrew Bonar's *Memoir of McCheyne*. I am constantly hearing of the great good that book has been the means of doing, especially to ministers, and not seldom to ministers far removed from the communion to which McCheyne and Bonar belonged. . . . Depend upon it, this wonderfully fresh and fruitful book will have a new lease of life given it from this year." There is every reason to believe that Alexander Whyte's words will find another fulfillment in our own generation, as this present edition goes forth.

S. MAXWELL CODER.

LETTERS

LETTERS

To Rev. R. MacDonald, Blairgowrie

Written when first laid aside by that illness which afterwards led him to take a trip to Palestine.

Edinburgh, January 12, 1839

THE VERY DAY I received your kind letter, I intended to have written you that you might provide some one to stand in my place on Monday evening next. I am ashamed at not having answered your kind inquiries sooner, but am not very good at the use of the pen, and I have had some necessary letters to write. However, now I come to you. This is Saturday, when you will be busy preparing to feed the flock of God with food convenient. Happy man! It is a glorious thing to preach the unsearchable riches of Christ! We do not value it aright till we are deprived of it. Then Philip Henry's saying is felt to be true—that he would beg all the week in order to be allowed to preach on the Sabbath day.

I have been far from alarmingly ill; my complaint is all unseen, and sometimes unfelt. My heart beats by night and day; but especially by night, too loud and too strong. My medical friends have tried several ways of removing the trouble, hitherto without complete success. As long as it lasts, I fear I shall be unfit for the work of the ministry. But I do hope that God has something more for me to do in the vineyard, and that a little patient rest, accompanied by His blessing, may quiet and restore me. Oh! my dear friend, I need it all to keep

this proud spirit under. Andrew Bonar was noticing the providence of "Elijah in the wilderness" being my alloted part at
our next meeting. I read it in the congregation the Sabbath
after, with an envious feeling in my own heart, though I did
not like to express it, that I would now be sent a like day's
journey to learn the same lessons as the prophet—that it is not
the tempest, nor the earthquake, nor the fire, but the still small
voice of the Spirit that carries on the glorious work of saving
souls.

Andrew will be with you on Monday, and I am almost
tempted to send this tonight to the post office; but it is not
right to encourage the Sabbath mail, so will defer it till Monday. May you have a time of refreshing from the presence of
the Lord! May He be the third with you who joined the two
disciples on the way to Emmaus, and made their hearts burn
by opening to them the Scriptures concerning Himself. I
hope your evening meeting may be as delightful as the last.
May your mind be solemnized, my dear friend, by the thought
that we are ministers but for a time; that the Master may
summon us to retire into silence, or may call us to the temple
above; or the midnight cry of the great Bridegroom may break
suddenly on our ears. Blessed is the servant that is found
waiting! Make all your services tell for eternity; speak what
you can look back upon with comfort when you must be
silent.

I am persuaded that I have been brought into retirement
to teach me the value and need of prayer. Alas! I have not
estimated aright the value of near access unto God. It is
not the mere daily routine of praying for certain things that
will obtain the blessing. But there must be the need within,
the real filial asking of God the things which we need, and
which He delights to give. We must study prayer more. Be
instant in prayer. You will be thinking my affliction is teaching me much, by my saying these things. Oh! I wish it were so.

Nobody ever made less use of affliction than I do. I feel the assaults of Satan most when I am removed into a corner; every evil thought and purpose rushes over my soul, and it is only at times that I can find Him whom my soul loveth.

Monday, January 14, 1839—I now sit down to finish this, and send it away. I am much in my usual today, perhaps, if anything, a little better. Still I have a hope at present of resuming my labors. Will you give me a Sabbath-day's labor? I had no intention of asking you when I began this; but I feel that I had better not close it without asking this favor. I would fain be back, but I do not feel that I would be justified in so doing. When I give a short prayer in the family, it often quite knocks me up. I heard of my people today: they are going on as well as can be expected. Death is busy among them, and Satan too. I try to lean then all on Him who entrusted them to me. I did hear of your brother's illness, and sympathized with you in it, though I heard no particulars. Write me particularly how he is. I hope and believe that he has an anchor within the veil, and therefore we need not fear for him whatever storms may blow. Remember me to him when you write him or see him. May we both be made better men, and holier, by our affliction.

Take care of your health. Redeem the time, because the days are evil. Does the work of God still go on among your people? There is a decided improvement in the ministers here—more prayer and faith and hope. There are marks of God's Spirit not having left us. Remember me to Gillies and Smith, your fellow laborers. May their names be in the Book of Life.

To Mrs. Thain, Heathpa·

During the continuance of the same ...

Ea:nburgh·   .ary 9, 1o59

I WAS HAPPY to receive your and Mr. Thain's kind letter. It is very cheering to me, in my exile from my flock, to hear of them. I send you a short line, as I am not good at writing. I am glad you are keeping pretty well, and still more that your spiritual health seems to prosper. The spring is advancing—I feel already the softness of the wind—so that we may hope the winter is past, the rain over and gone. I know the summer revives you, and the doctor gives me good hope that it will revive me. In spiritual things, this world is all wintertime so long as the Saviour is away. To them that are in Christ there are some sweet glistenings of His countenance, there are meltings of His love, and th· sweet song of the turtledove when His Holy Spirit dwells in the bosom; still it is but wintertime till our Lord shall come. But then, "to you that fear his name, shall the Sun of righteousness arise with healing in his wings." And if before He comes we should go away to be where He is, still we shall enter into a world of perpetual summer—we shall behol His glory which the Father gave Him.

I feel much better than usual today; but I have retrns of my beating heart occasionally. Jesus stands at the door and knocks, and sometimes I think the door will give way before His gentle hand. I am bid to try the seawater hot bath, which I hope will do me good. I have good hope of being restored to my people again, and only hope that I may come in the fullness of the blessing of the gospel of Christ, that this time of silent musing may not be lost.

I am thankful indeed at the appointment of Mr. Lewis. I hope he has been given in answer to prayer, and then he will be a blessing. We must pray that he may be furnished from on high for his arduous work. I have great hope that he will be the means of raising many more churches and schools in our poor town—I mean poor in spiritual things.

I hope Mr. Macdonald was happy, and made others so. "Apollos watered." May great grace be upon you all.

———

To Mrs. Thain

Before going forth on the mission to Israel.

Edinburgh, March 15, 1839

YOU WILL think me very unkind in breaking my word to Mr. Thain, in not writing you in answer to your kind letter by him. But I did too much the week he was in Edinburgh, and fairly knocked myself up, so that I had just to lay aside my pen and suffer quietly. My friendly monitor is seldom far away from me, and when I do anything too much he soon checks me. However, I feel thankful that I am better again this week, and was thinking I would preach again. This is always the way with me. When my heart afflicts me, I say to myself: Farewell, blessed work of the gospel ministry! happy days of preaching Christ and Him crucified! winning jewels for an eternal crown! And then again, when it has abated, I feel as if I would stand up once more to tell all the world what the Lord of Glory has done for sinners.

You have sent me a pocket companion [a Bible] for Immanuel's land. I shall indeed be very happy to take it with me, to remind me of you and your kind family, at the time when I am meditating on the things that concern our everlasting peace. All my ideas of peace and joy are linked in with my Bible; and I would not give the hours of secret converse with it for all the other hours I spend in this world.

Mr. M—— is the bearer of this, and I have told him he

is to call on you with it. He is one much taught of God, and though with much inward corruption to fight against, he still holds on the divine way a burning and shining lamp.

I knew you would be surprised at the thought of my going so far away; and, indeed, who could have foreseen all that has happened? I feel very plainly that it is the Lord's doing, and this has taken away the edge of the pain. How many purposes God has in view of which we know nothing! Perhaps we do not see the hundredth part of His intentions towards us in sending me away. I am contented to be led blindfold; for I know that all will redound, through the thanksgiving of many, to the glory of our heavenly Father. I feel very plainly that towards many among my people this separation has been a most faithful chastisement. To those that liked the man but not the message, who were pleased with the vessel but not with the treasure, it will reveal the vanity of what they thought their good estate. To some, I hope, it has been sent in mercy. To some, I fear, it has been sent in judgment.

Above all, none had more need of it than myself; for I am naturally so prone to make an ill use of the attachment of my people, that I need to be humbled in the dust, and to see that it is a very nothing. I need to be made willing to be forgotten. Oh! I wish that my heart were quite refined from all self-seeking. I am quite sure that our truest happiness is not to seek our own—just to forget ourselves—and to fill up the little space that remains, seeking only, and above all, that our God may be glorified. But when I would do good, evil is present with me.

I am not yet sure of the day of my going away. There is to be a meeting on Monday to arrange matters. Andrew Bonar and Dr. Black can hardly get away till the first week of April; but I may probably go before to London next week. I know you will pray for me in secret and in the family, that

I may be kept from evil, and may do good. Our desire is to save sinners—to gather souls, Jew or Gentile, before the Lord come. Oh, is it not wonderful how God is making people take an interest in the Jews! Surely the way of these kings of the East will be soon prepared.

I shall be quite delighted if J—— is able to take a small part in the Sabbath school. She knows it is what I always told her—not to be a hearer of the Word only, but a doer. It is but a little time, and we shall work no more here for Him. Oh, that we might glorify Him on the earth! I believe there are better ministers in store for Scotland than any that have yet appeared. Tell J—— to stay herself upon God. Jesus continueth ever, He hath an unchangeable priesthood. Others are not suffered to continue by reason of death.

You expected me in Dundee before I go; but I dare not. You remember Paul sailed past Ephesus—he dared not encounter the meeting with his people. Indeed, I do not dare to think too much on my going away, for it often brings sadness over my spirit, which I can ill bear just now. But the will of the Lord be done.

Kindest regards to you all. Christ's peace be left with you. I shall remember you all, and be glad to write you a word when I am far away.

———

To Miss Collier, Dundee

How his silence may be useful to his people and himself.

Edinburgh, March 14, 1839

I FEEL IT very kind your writing to me, and rejoice in sending you a word in answer by my excellent friend Mr. Moody. Indeed, I was just going to write to you when I received yours, for I heard you had been rather poorly, and

I was going to entreat of you to take care of yourself; for you do not know how much my life is bound up in your life, and in the life of those around you who are likeminded. I feel it quite true that my absence should be regarded by my flock as a mark that God is chastening them; and though I know well that I am but a dim light in the hand of Jesus, yet there is always something terrible where Jesus withdraws the meanest light in such a dark world.

I feel that to many this trial has been absolutely needful. Many liked their minister naturally, who had but little real relish for the message he carried. God now sifts these souls, and wants to show them that it is a looking to Jesus that saves, not a looking to man. I think I could name many to whom this trial should be blessed. Some also who were really on the true foundation, but were building wood, hay, and stubble upon it, may be brought to see that nothing would truly comfort in the Day of the Lord but what can stand the hour of trial. You yourself, my dear friend, may be brought to cleave much more simply to the Lord Jesus. You may be made to feel that Christ continueth ever, and hath an unchangeable priesthood; that His work is perfect, and that infinitely; and poor and naked as we are, we can appear only in Him—only in Him.

But if the trial was needed by my people, it was still more needed by *me*. None but God knows what an abyss of corruption is in my heart. He knows and covers all in the blood of the Lamb. "In faithfulness thou hast afflicted me." It is perfectly wonderful that ever God could bless such a ministry. And now, when I go over all the faults of it, it appears almost impossible that I can ever preach again. But then I think again, who can preach so well as a sinner—who is forgiven so much, and daily upheld by the Spirit with such a heart within! I can truly say that the fruit of my long exile has been, that I am come nearer to God, and long more for perfect holiness, and for the world where the people shall be all righteous. I do long to be free from self, from pride, and ungodliness; and I know where to go, "for all the promises of God are yea and amen in Christ Jesus." Christ is my armory, and I go to Him to get the whole armor of God—the armor of light. My sword and buckler, my arrows, my sling and stone, all are laid up in Jesus. I know you find it so. Evermore grow in this truly practical wisdom. You have a Shepherd; you shall never want.

What effect my long absence may have on the mass of unconverted souls I do not know. I cannot yet see God's purposes towards them: perhaps it may be judgment, as in the case of Ephesus, Revelation 2:5; perhaps it may be in mercy, as in the case of Laodicea, Revelation 3:19; or perhaps there are some who would not bend under my ministry, who are to flow down as wax before the fire under the ministry of the precious fellow laborer who is to succeed me. William Burns, son of the minister of Kilsyth, has for the present agreed to supply my place; and though there is a proposal of his being sent to Ceylon, I do hope he may be kept for us. He is one truly taught of God—young, but Christ lives in him. You know he comes of a good kind by the flesh.

Another reason of our trial, I hope, has been God's mercy to Israel. There is something so wonderful about the way in which all difficulties have been overcome, and the way opened up, that I cannot doubt the hand of Jehovah has been in it. This gives me, and should give you, who love Israel, a cheering view of this trial. The Lord meant it for great good. If God be glorified, is not this our utmost desire? Oh, it is sweet, when in prayer we can lay ourselves and all our interests, along with Zion, in the hands of *Him* whom we feel to be *Abba!* And if we are thus tied ourselves in the same bundle with Zion, we must resign all right to our-

selves, and to our wishes. May the Lord open up a way to His
name being widely glorified on the earth even before we die!

I know you will pray for us on our way, that our feet may
be beautiful on the mountains of Israel, and that we may
say to Zion, "Thy God reigneth." Pray that your poor friend
may be supplied out of His riches in glory, that he may not
shrink in hours of trial, but endure hardness as a good soldier
of Jesus Christ. I will remember you when far away, and
pray God to keep you safe under the shadow of the Redeemer's wings till I come again in peace, if it be His holy
will. Dr. Black and Andrew Bonar have both consented to go.
I shall probably be sent before to London next week, to open
the way. I am not very strong yet; often revisited by my warning friend, to tell me that I may see the New Jerusalem before
I see the Jerusalem beneath. However, I have the sentence of
death in myself, and do not trust in myself, but in God,
who raises the dead.

I saw Mrs. Coutts yesterday, in good health, and full of
spirit. She almost offered to go with us to Immanuel's Land.
I fear the Pastoral Letters are not worth printing; but I
shall ask others what they think. Farewell for the present.
The Lord give you all grace and peace.

To the Rev. W. C. Burns

On his agreeing to undertake the charge of St. Peter's, during Mr. McCheyne's
absence in Palestine.

Hill Street, Edinburgh, March 22, 1839

BECAUSE I TRUST I may now reckon you among the
number in the truest sense, I haste to send you a line
in answer to your last. I am glad you have made up your
mind to begin your spiritual charge over my flock on the first
week of April. The Committee has resolved that I leave
this on Wednesday next, so that you will not hear from me

again till I am away. Take heed to *thyself*. Your own soul is your first and greatest care. You know a sound body alone can work with power; much more a *healthy soul*. Keep a clear conscience through the blood of the Lamb. Keep up close communion with God. Study likeness to Him in all things. Read the Bible for your own growth first, then for your people.

Expound much; it is through *the truth* that souls are to be sanctified, not through *essays upon the truth*. Be easy of access, apt to teach, and the Lord teach you and bless you in all you do and say. You will not find many companions. Be the more with God. My dear people are anxiously waiting for you. The prayerful are praying for you. Be of good courage; there remaineth much of the land to be possessed. Be not dismayed, for Christ shall be with thee to deliver thee. Study Isaiah 6, and Jeremiah 1, and the sending of Moses, and Psalm 51:12, 13, and John 15:26, 27, and the connection in Luke 1:15, 16.

I shall hope to hear from you when I am away. Your accounts of my people will be a good word to make my heart glad. I am often sore cast down; but the eternal God is my refuge. Now farewell; the Lord make you a faithful steward.

———

Pastoral Letters to the Flock of St. Peter's

First Pastoral Letter

View of what God has done, how it should affect them.

Edinburgh, January 30, 1839

TO ALL OF YOU, my dear friends and people, who are beloved of God, and faithful in Christ Jesus, your pastor wishes grace and peace from God the Father, and Christ Jesus our Lord.

As several of you have expressed a desire to hear from me, and as He who at first sent me to you to bear witness of the Lord Jesus has for many weeks withdrawn me, and still lays His afflicting but gentle hand on me, it has seemed good to me, not without prayer, to write to you from week to week a short word of exhortation. May the Holy Spirit guide the pen, that what is written may be blessed to your comfort and growth in grace!

God is my record how greatly I long after you all in the bowels of Jesus Christ; and the walls of my chamber can bear witness how often the silent watches of the night have been filled up with entreaties to the Lord for you all. I can truly say with John, "that I have no greater joy than to hear that my children walk in the truth"; and though many of you were in Christ before me, and were living branches of the true Vine before I was sent into the vineyard, yet, believe me, it is true of you also, I have no greater joy than to know that you are more and more filled with the Holy Ghost, and bear more and more fruit to the glory of God the Father. "Herein is the Father glorified, that you bear much fruit."

You remember what Paul, when he was a prisoner of the Lord, wrote to the Philippians (1:12), "I would that ye should understand, brethren, that the things which happened unto me have fallen out rather unto the furtherance of the gospel." I am very anxious that you and I should understand the very same, in the things which have happened unto me, that we may vindicate God in all His dealings with us, and "not despise the chastening of the Lord." I know too well that there are many amongst you who would feel it no grievance if all the Lord's ministers were taken out of the way. Ah! how many are there who would rejoice if they were forever left to sin unreproved, and to do what was right in their own eyes! Still I am quite sure that to you, "who have obtained like precious faith with us," to you who are the Lord's people, the present is a season of affliction, and you feel, as Naomi felt, that the hand of the Lord is gone out against us. My present object in writing to you is shortly to persuade you that "it is well"—"the Lord doeth all things well"—and that it may be really for the furtherance of the gospel among you. In many ways may this be the case.

First, with respect to myself. It does not become me here to show what benefit it may be to me. Suffice it to say that it has been a precious opportunity in which to reflect on the sins and imperfections of my ministry among you. A calm hour with God is worth a whole lifetime with man. Let it be your prayer that I may come out like gold, that the tin may be taken away, and that I may come back to you, if that be the will of God, a better man, and a more devoted minister. I have much to learn, and these words of David have been often in my heart and on my lips, "I know that thy judgments are right, and that thou in faithfulness hast afflicted me" (Ps. 119:75). Ministers are God's tools for building up the gospel temple. Now you know well that every wise workman takes his tools away from the work from time to time, that they may be ground and sharpened; so does the only-wise Jehovah take His ministers oftentimes away into darkness and loneliness and trouble, that He may sharpen and prepare them for harder work in His service. Pray that it may be so with your own pastor.

Second, with regard to you, my dear brothers and sisters in the Lord, this time of trial is for your furtherance. Does not God teach you, by means of it, to look beyond man to the Saviour, who abideth ever? Is not God showing you that ministers are earthen vessels, easily broken, and fit only to be cast aside like a broken pitcher out of mind? Is He not bidding you look more to the treasure which was in them, and which flows in all its fullness from Christ? It is a sad

error into which I see many Christians falling, that of leaning upon man, mistaking friendship toward a minister for
faith in the Son of God.

Remember that before Moses was sent to deliver Israel, his
hand was made leprous, as white as snow, to teach them that
it was not the might of that hand that could deliver Israel
(Exod. 4:6, 7). It has been the fault of some of you to
lean too much on man. Now God is teaching you that, though
the *cistern* may break, the *fountain* abides as open and full
and free as ever—that it is not from sitting under any particular
ministry that you are to get nourishment, but from being vitally
united to Christ. Ministers "are not suffered to continue by
reason of death, but *Christ,* because He continueth ever,
hath an unchangeable priesthood" (Heb. 7:23, 24).

Third, with regard to those among you who are almost,
but not *altogether,* persuaded to be Christians, does not this
providence teach you to make sure of an interest in Christ
without delay? You thought you would have the Saviour held
up to you for an indefinite number of Sabbaths, little thinking that your Sabbaths and mine are all numbered. Many a
time you have said to me in your heart, "Go thy way for
this time; when I have a more convenient season I will call
for thee." You did not think that a time might come when
you may call for your teachers, and they be silent as the grave.

I find many godly people here are looking forward to a
time when God's faithful witnesses shall be put to silence,
and anxious souls shall wander from sea to sea, seeking the
Word of God, and shall not find it. Be entreated, O wavering
souls, to settle the question of your salvation *now.* Why halt ye
between two opinions? It is most unreasonable to be undecided
about the things of an endless eternity, in such a world
as this, with such frail bodies, with such a Saviour stretching
out His hand, with such a Spirit of love striving with you.
Remember you are flesh—you will soon hear your last sermon.

"I call heaven and earth to record this day against you, that I have put before you life and death, blessing and cursing: therefore choose life, that both thou and thy seed may live" (Deut. 30:19).

Fourth, there is another class who are not of you, and yet are on every hand of you, of whom I have told you often, and now tell you, even weeping, that they are the enemies of the cross of Christ, whose god is their belly, who glory in their shame, who mind earthly things. Ah! you would not believe if I were to tell you the great heaviness and continual sorrow that I have in my heart for you, and yet I hope my absence may be blessed even to you. Just think for a moment, if God were to remove your teachers one by one, if He were to suffer the church of our covenanted fathers to fall before the hands of her enemies, if He were to suffer Catholicism again to spread its dark and deadly shade over the land, where would you be?—you that despise the Sabbath, that care little for the preached Word, you that have no prayer in your families, and seldom in your closets, you that are lovers of pleasure, you that wallow in sin! You would have your wish then: you would have your silent Sabbaths indeed— no warning voice to cry after you—no praying people to pray for you—none to check you in your career of wickedness— none to beseech you not to perish. Learn from so small a circumstance as the absence of your stated minister what may be in store for you, and flee now from the wrath to come. "It may be ye shall be hid in the day of the Lord's anger" (Zeph. 2:3).

Finally, my brethren, dearly beloved and longed for, my joy and crown, abide all the more in Christ because of my absence, and maintain a closer walk with God, that when I return, as God gives me good hopes now of doing, I may rejoice to see what great things God has done for your souls. God feeds the wild flowers on the lonely mountainside, without

the help of man, and they are as fresh and lovely as those
that are daily watched over in our gardens. So God can
feed His own planted ones without the help of man, by the
sweetly falling dew of His Spirit. How I long to see you
walking in holy communion with God, in love to the brethren,
and burning zeal for the cause of God in the world! I will
never rest, nor give God rest, till He make you a lamp that
burneth—a city set upon a hill that cannot be hid. Now
strive together with me, in your prayers to God for me, that
I may come unto you with joy by the will of God.

The grace of our Lord Jesus Christ be with you. My love be
with you all in Christ Jesus. Amen.

SECOND PASTORAL LETTER

Past times of privilege reviewed—privileges still remaining.

Edinburgh, February 6, 1839

TO all of you, my dear flock, who have chosen the good
part which cannot be taken away, your pastor wishes grace,
mercy, and peace, from God our Father and the Lord Jesus
Christ.

The sweet singer of Israel begins one of his psalms with
these remarkable words: "I will sing of mercy and judgment;
unto thee, O God, will I sing." This is the experience of
all God's servants in time of trouble. Even in the wildest
storms the sky is not all dark; and so in the darkest dealings
of God with His children, there are always some bright tokens
for good. His way with us of late has been "in the sea, and
his path in the deep waters." Yet some of you may have felt
that His own hand was leading us like a flock (Ps. 77:19, 20).
One great token of His loving-kindness has been the way
in which He has supplied the absence of your stated minister.
Ordained messengers, men of faith and prayer, have spoken

to you from Sabbath to Sabbath in the name of the Lord. Awakening, inviting, comforting messages you have had; and even your meetings on Thursday evenings He has continued to you; the gates of the house of prayer, like the gates of the city of refuge, have been as open to you as ever, inviting you to enter in and behold by faith what Jacob saw in Bethel, "the ladder set on earth, and the top of it reaching into heaven," inviting you to meet with Him with whom Jacob wrestled till the breaking of the day.

Think how often, in times of persecution, the apostles were constrained to leave the seed they had sown, without leaving anyone to water it but "the Lord on whom they believed." (See Acts 13:50, 52, and 14:23, and 16:40.) How often, in times of persecution in the Church of Scotland, our faithful pastors had to leave their few sheep in the wilderness, without any human shepherd to care for their souls, commending them to God and to the Word of His grace! These times may come again. God may be preparing us for such fiery trials. But He hath not yet dealt so with us. He that tempers the wind to the shorn lamb, and "who stays his rough wind in the day of his east wind," has mingled mercy with judgment; and even when He humbles us, gives us cause for praise. "Oh, that men would praise the Lord for his goodness, and for his wonderful works to the children of men!"

Another mark of His loving-kindness to us is His suffering me to pray for you. You remember how the apostles describe the work of the ministry, Acts 6:4, "We will give ourselves continually to prayer, and to the ministry of the word." Now, God is my record that this has been my heart's desire ever since my coming among you. I have always felt myself a debtor to you all, both to the wise and to the unwise; so as much as in me is I have been ready to preach the gospel unto you; but God has for a time withdrawn me from that part of the work amongst you. To me that grace is not now given to preach among you the unsearchable riches of Christ. (Oh, how great a grace it is! how wonderful that it should ever have been given to me!) Still He allows me to give myself unto prayer. Perhaps this may be the chief reason of my exile from you, to teach me what Zechariah was taught in the vision of the golden candlestick and the two olive trees, (Zech. 4:6), that it is not by might, nor by power, but by *His Spirit,* obtained in believing, wrestling prayer, that the temple of God is to be built in our parishes. I have hung my harp upon the willow, and am no more allowed "to open to you dark sayings upon the harp," nor "to speak of the things which I have made touching the King," who is "fairer than the children of men."

Still my soul does not dwell in silence. I am permitted to go in secret to God, my exceeding joy; and, while meditating His praise, I can make mention of you all in my prayers, and give thanks for the little flock, who, "by patient continuance in welldoing, seek for glory, and honor, and immortality." "If I forget thee, O Jerusalem, let my right hand forget her cunning; if I do not remember thee, let my tongue cleave to the roof of my mouth, if I prefer not Jerusalem above my chief joy."

I feel it is another gift of grace that I am suffered to write to you. You remember how often the apostles cheered and strengthened the disciples, when absent from them, by writing to them.[1] What a precious legacy of the Church in all ages have these epistles been! every verse like a branch of the Tree of Life, bearing all manner of fruit, and the leaves for the healing of the nations. You remember how holy Samuel Rutherford, and many of our persecuted forefathers in the Church of Scotland, kept the flame of grace alive in their deserted parishes by sending them words of counsel,

---

[1] II Corinthians 7:12; Galatians 6:11; I Thessalonians 5:27; Hebrews 13:22; I Peter 5:12; II Peter 1:12-15; 3:1; John 1:4; Jude 3.

warning, and encouragement, testifying, not face to face, but with ink and pen, the gospel of the grace of God. I do feel it a great privilege that this door is open to me, and that, even when absent, I can yet speak to you of the things pertaining to the kingdom.

"This second epistle, beloved, I now write unto you, in both which I stir up your pure minds by way of remembrance; yea, I think it meet, so long as I am in this tabernacle, to stir you up by putting you in remembrance."

I. Abide in Him, little children, whom I have always preached unto you, that when He shall appear we may have confidence and not be ashamed before Him at His coming. Let every new sight of your wicked heart, and every new wave of trouble, drive your soul to hide in Him, the Rock of your salvation. There is no true peace but in a present hold of the Lord our Righteousness.

II. Enjoy the forgiveness of sins—keep yourselves in the love of God. If you abide in Christ, you shall abide in His love: your joy let no man take from you. "These things write we unto you that your joy may be full."

III. Be ye clean that bear the vessels of the Lord. "He that saith he abideth in him ought himself also so to walk even as he walked." Ah, how many falls will I have to mourn over when I return, if God send me back to you, how many unseemly quarrellings and miscarriages among you that are God's own, how many unlovely tempers among those who follow Him who is altogether lovely! Oh, take heed, do not give the enemy cause to blaspheme; naming the name of Christ, depart from all iniquity.

IV. Continue in prayer. How many messages have been carried to you publicly and from house to house, and yet how little success! I bless God for all the tokens He has given us, that the Spirit of God has not departed from the Church of Scotland—that the glory is still in the midst of her. Still the Spirit has never yet been shed on us abundantly. The many absentees on the forenoon of the Sabbaths, the thin meetings on Thursday evenings, the absence of *men* from all meetings for the worship of God, the few private prayer meetings, the little love and union among Christians—all show that the plentiful rain has not yet fallen to refresh our corner of the heritage. Why is this? This is the day of Christ's power—why are the people not made willing? Let James give the answer: "Ye have not, because ye ask not." "Hitherto ye have asked nothing in my name. Ask, and ye shall receive, that your joy may be full."

Finally, dear brethren, farewell. Day and night I long to come to you, but still God hinders me. Do not omit to praise Him for all the great grace He has mingled in our cup of bitterness. "Seven times a day do I praise thee because of thy righteous judgments." When passing through the waters He has been with us, and in the rivers they have not overflowed us; and, therefore, we may be sure that when we pass through the fire we shall not be burned, neither shall the flames kindle upon us.

Now, may the God of peace Himself give you peace always, by all means, and the grace of the Lord Jesus Christ be with your spirits. Amen.

THIRD PASTORAL LETTER

How God works by providences.

Edinburgh, February 13, 1839.

TO all of you, my dear friends and people, who are and shall ever be followers of the Lamb, whithersoever He goeth, your pastor again wishes grace and peace from God our Father, and the Lord Jesus Christ.

I long very much that this grace may again be given unto me to preach among you face to face "the unsearchable riches of Christ." "Oftentimes I purpose to come unto you, but am let hitherto." Still I feel it a great privilege that, even in my retirement, I can send you a word, to the end that you may be established. I feel as if one door was left open to me by the Lord. Believe me, it is the foremost desire of my heart that Christ may be glorified in you, both now and at His coming, that you may be a happy and a holy people, blessed and made a blessing. For the sake of variety, let me guide your thoughts to a passage of God's own Word, and there I will speak to you as if I were yet present with you, and half forget that you are not before me.

In Job 23:8-10 you will find these solemn words: "Behold, I go forward, but he is not there; and backward, but I cannot perceive him: on the left hand, where he doth work, but I cannot behold him: he hideth himself on the right hand, that I cannot see him. But he knoweth the way that I take: when he hath tried me, I shall come forth as gold."

You all know the afflictions which came upon Job. "He was a perfect and upright man," and the greatest of all the men of the East, yet he lost his oxen and his asses, his sheep and camels, and his ten children, in one day. Again, the breath of disease came upon him, and he sat down among the ashes. In all this Job sinned not with his lips. He blessed the hand that smote him: "What! shall we receive good at the hand of the Lord, and shall we not receive evil?"

And yet when his troubles were *prolonged,* he knew not what to think. Learn how weak the strongest believer is; a bruised reed, without Christ, we are, and can do nothing. When Job's brethren dealt deceitfully with him "as a brook," when he felt God hedging him in, and God's arrows drinking up his spirit—then clouds and darkness rested on his path, he could not unravel God's dealings with his soul; then he cried, "Show me wherefore thou contendest with me!" He longed to get an explanation from God: "Oh, that I knew where I might find him! that I might come even to his seat! Behold, I go forward, but he is not there; and backward, but I cannot perceive Him: on the left hand, where he doth work, but I cannot behold him: he hideth himself on the right hand, that I cannot see him." You have here, then, in the eighth and ninth verses, a child of light walking in darkness—an afflicted soul seeking, and seeking in vain, to know why God is contending with him.

Dear friends, this is not an uncommon case; even to some of you God's providences often appear inexplicable. I hear that God has been at work among you, and "his way is in the sea." He has tried you in different ways: some of you by the loss of your property, as He tried Job; some of you by the loss of dear friends; some by loss of health, so that "wearisome nights are appointed you"; some by the loss of the esteem of friends, aye, even of Christians. "Your inward friends abhor you." Perhaps more than one trouble has come on you at a time—wave upon wave, thorn upon thorn. Before one wound was healed, another came, before the rain was well away, "clouds returned." You cannot explain God's dealings with you, you cannot get God to explain them; you have drawn the Saviour's blood and righteousness over your souls, and you know that the Father Himself loveth you; you would like to meet Him to ask, "Wherefore contendest thou with me?" "Oh, that I knew where I might find him!"

My dear afflicted brethren, this is no strange thing that has happened unto you. Almost every believer is at one time or another brought to feel this difficulty: "God maketh my heart soft, and the Almighty troubleth me." Is it in anger, or is it in pure love, that He afflicts me? Am I fleeing from the presence of the Lord, as Jonah fled? What change would He have wrought in me? If any of you are thinking thus in your heart, pray over this word in Job. Remember the word in Psalm 46, "Be still, and know that I am God." God does many things to teach us that *He* is God, and to make us wait upon Him. And, still further, see in the tenth verse what light breaks in upon our darkness: "But he knoweth the way that I take: when he hath tried me, I shall come forth as gold."

Observe, *first,* "*He* knoweth the way that I take." What sweet comfort there is in these words: *He* that redeemed me— *He* that pities me as a father—*He* who is the only wise God— *He* whose name is love—"*He* knoweth the way that I take!"

The ungodly world does not know it; the world knoweth us not, even as it knew Him not. A stranger doth not intermeddle with the joys or sorrows of a child of God. When the world looks on your grief with unsympathizing eye, you feel very desolate. "Your soul is exceedingly filled with the scorning of those who are at ease." But why should you? He that is greater than all the world is looking with the intensest interest upon all your steps.

The most intimate friends do not know the way of an afflicted believer. Your spirit is lonely, even among God's children; for your way is hid, and the Lord hath hedged you in. Still be of good cheer, the Father of all, the best of friends, knows all the way that you take.

You do not know your own way. God has called you to suffer, and you go, like Abraham, not knowing whither you go. Like Israel going down into the Red Sea, every step is strange to you. Still, be of good cheer, sufferer with Christ! God marks your every step. "The steps of a good man are ordered by the Lord, and he delighteth in his way." *He* that loves you with an infinite, unchanging love, is leading you by His Spirit and providence. *He* knows every stone, every thorn in your path. Jesus knows your way. Jesus is afflicted in all your afflictions. "Fear not, for I have redeemed thee. I have called thee by my name, thou art mine. When thou passest through the waters, I will be with thee; and through the rivers, they shall not overflow thee. When thou walkest through the fire, thou shalt not be burned, neither shall the flame kindle upon thee."

Second, "When he hath tried me, I shall come forth as gold." This also is precious comfort. There will be an end of your affliction. Christians must have "great tribulation"; but they come out of it. We must carry the cross; but only for a moment, then comes the crown. I remember one child of God's saying, that if it were God's will that she should remain in trials a thousand years, she could not but delight in His will. But this is not asked of us: we are only called *"to suffer a while."* There is a set time for putting into the furnace, and a set time for taking out of the furnace. There is a time for pruning the branches of the vine, and there is a time when the husbandman lays aside the pruninghook. Let us wait His time; "he that believeth shall not make haste." God's time is the best time.

But shall we come out the same as we went in? Ah, no! "we shall come out like gold." It is this that sweetens the bitterest cup; this brings a rainbow of promise over the darkest cloud. Affliction will *certainly* purify a believer. How boldly he says it: "I shall come out like gold!" Ah, how much dross there is in every one of you, dear believers, and in your pastor! "When I would do good, evil is present with me." Oh that all the dross may be left behind in the furnace! What imperfection, what sin, mingles with all we have ever done! But are we really fruit-bearing branches of the true vine? Then it is certain that when we are pruned, we shall bear more fruit. We shall come out like gold. We shall shine more purely as "a diadem in the hand of our God." We shall become purer vessels to hold the sweet-smelling incense of praise and prayer. We shall become holy golden vessels for the Master's use in time and in eternity.

To the many among you who have no part nor lot in Christ, I would say, "See here the happiness of being a Christian in time of trouble." It is no small joy to be able to sing Psalm 46 in the dark and cloudy day. I have often told you, and now tell you when I am far from you, "We are journeying to the place of which the Lord hath said, I will give it you: come then with us, and we will do thee good, for God hath spoken good concerning Israel."

Finally, pray that your pastor may come out of his trials like gold. All is not gold that glitters. Pray that everything that is but glittering dross may be taken away, and that, if it be *His* will, I may come unto you like the fine gold of Ophir. "Continue in prayer, and watch in the same with thanksgiving, withal praying also for us, that God would open unto us a door of utterance to speak the mystery of Christ."

My chief comfort concerning you is, that "my God shall supply all your need according to his riches in glory by Christ Jesus." Brethren, farewell! Be perfect, be of good comfort, be of one mind, live in peace, and the God of love and of peace shall be with you.

The grace of the Lord Jesus Christ, and the love of God, and the communion of the Holy Ghost, be with you all. Amen.

Fourth Pastoral Letter

God the answerer of prayer.

Edinburgh, February 20, 1839.

TO all of you, my dear flock, who are chosen in Christ before the foundation of the world, to be holy and without blame before Him in love, your pastor again wishes grace and peace from God the Father and our Lord Jesus Christ.

There are many sweet providences happening to us every day, if we would but notice them. In the texts which ministers choose, what remarkable providences God often brings about! I have often felt this, and never more than now. Some of you may remember that the last chapter of the Bible which I read to you in the church was I Kings 19, where we are told of Elijah's going away into the wilderness for forty days and forty nights to the mount of God, where he was taught that it is not by the *wind,* nor the *earthquake,* nor the *fire,* that God converts souls, but by the still small voice of the gospel. May not this have been graciously intended to prepare us for what has happened?

Another providence some of you may have noticed. For several Thursday evenings before I left you I was engaged in explaining and enforcing the sweet duty of believing prayer. Has not God since taught us the use of these things? "Trials make the promise sweet." "Trials give new life to prayer." Perhaps some of us were only receiving the information into the head; is not God now impressing it on our hearts, and driving us to practice the things which we learned?

I do not now remember all the points I was led to speak upon to you, but *one,* I think, was entirely omitted—I mean the subject of answers to prayer. God left it for us to meditate on *now.* Oh, there is nothing that I would have you to be more sure of than this, that "God hears and answers prayer." There never was, and never will be, a believing prayer left unanswered. Meditate on this, and you will say, "I love the Lord, because He hath heard my voice and my supplication" (Ps. 116:1).

First, God often gives the very thing His children ask at the very time they ask it. You remember Hannah (I Sam. 1:10): she was in bitterness of soul, and prayed unto the Lord, and wept sore. "Give unto thine handmaid a manchild." This was her request. And so she went in peace, and the God of

Israel heard and granted her petition that she had asked of Him; and she called the child's name Samuel, that is, "Asked of God." Oh, that you could write the same name upon all your gifts! You would have more joy in them and far larger blessings along with them.

You remember *David*, in Psalm 138: *"In the day* that I cried thou answeredst me, and strengthenedst me with strength in my soul." You remember *Elijah*, I Kings 17:21, 22: "O Lord my God! I pray thee let this child's soul come into him again. And *the Lord heard the voice* of Elijah, and *the soul of the child came into him again*, and he revived."

You remember *Daniel*, 9:20, 21: *"While I was* speaking, and praying, and confessing my sin, and the sin of my people Israel, and presenting my supplication before the Lord my God for the holy mountain of my God; yea, whiles *I was speaking in prayer*, even the man Gabriel, being caused to fly swiftly, touched me about the time of the evening oblation." Oh, what encouragement is here for those among you who, like Daniel, are greatly beloved, who study much in the books of God's Word, and who set your face unto the Lord to seek by prayer gifts for the Church of God! Expect answers while you are speaking in prayer. Sometimes the vapors that ascend in the morning come down in copious showers in the evening. So may it be with your prayers.

Take up the words of David, Psalm 5:3: "My voice shalt thou hear in the morning; in the morning will I direct my prayer unto thee, and will look up." You remember, in Acts 12, Peter was cast into prison, "but prayer was made without ceasing of the church unto God for him." And, behold, the same night the answer surprised them at the door. Oh! what surprises of goodness and grace God has in store for you and me, if only we pray without ceasing! If you will pray in union to Jesus, having childlike confidence towards God, having the spirit of adoption, crying Abba within you, seeking

the glory of God more than all personal benefits, I believe
that in all such cases you will get the *very thing you ask, at
the very time you ask it.* Before you call, God will answer; and
while you are speaking, He will hear.

Oh, if there were twenty among you who would pray thus,
and persevere therein like wrestling Jacob, you would get
whatever you ask! Yea, the case of Daniel shows that the
effectual fervent prayer of one such believer among you will
avail much. "Delight thyself in the Lord, and he shall give
thee the desires of thine heart" (Ps. 37:4).

*Second, God often delays the answer to prayer for wise
reasons.* The case of the Syrophoenician woman will occur to
you all, Matthew 15:21-28. How anxiously she cried, "Have
mercy on me, O Lord, thou son of David! But Jesus answered
her not a word." Again and again she prayed, and got no
gracious answer. Her faith grows stronger by every refusal.
She cried, she followed, she kneeled to Him, till Jesus could
refuse no longer. "O woman, great is thy faith! Be it unto
thee even as thou wilt."

Dear praying people, "continue in prayer, and watch in
the same with thanksgivings." Do not be silenced by one refusal. Jesus invites importunity by delaying to answer. Ask,
seek, knock. "The promise may be long delayed, but cannot
come too late." You remember, in the parable of the impor-
tunate widow, it is said, "Shall not God avenge his own elect,
which cry day and night unto him, though he bear long with
them? I tell you that he will avenge them speedily" (Luke
18:1-8). This shows how you, who are God's children, should
pray. You should cry day and night unto God. This shows
how God hears every one of your cries, in the busy hour of
the daytime, and in the lonely watches of the night. He treasures them up from day to day; soon the full answer will
come down: "He will answer speedily." The praying souls
beneath the altar, in Revelation 6:9-11, seem to show the same

truth, that the answer to a believer's prayers may, in the adorable wisdom of God, be delayed for a little season, and that many of them may not be fully answered till after he is dead.

Again, read that wonderful passage, Revelation 8:3, where it is said that the Lord Jesus, the great Intercessor with the Father, offers to God the incense of His merits, with the prayers of *all saints*, upon the golden altar which is before the throne. Christ never loses one believing prayer. The prayers of every believer, from Abel to the present day, He heaps upon the altar, from which they are continually ascending before His Father and our Father; and when the altar can hold no more, the full, the eternal answer will come down.

Do not be discouraged, dearly beloved, because God bears long with you—because He does not seem to answer your prayers. Your prayers are not lost. When the merchant sends his ships to distant shores, he does not expect them to come back richly laden in a single day: he has long patience. "It is good that a man should both hope and quietly wait for the salvation of the Lord." Perhaps your prayers will come back, like the ships of the merchant, all the more heavily laden with blessings, because of the delay.

Third, God often answers prayer by terrible things. So David says in Psalm 65: "By terrible things in righteousness wilt thou answer us, O God of our salvation." And all of you who are God's children have found it true. Some of you have experienced what John Newton did when he wrote that beautiful hymn, "I asked the Lord that I might grow."[1] You prayed with all your heart, "Lord, increase my faith." In answer to this, God has shown you the misery of your connection with Adam. He has revealed the hell that is in your heart. You are amazed, confounded, abashed. You cry,

[1] *Olney Hymns,* Book iii, Hymn 36.

"O wretched man that I am, who shall deliver me from the body of this death?" You cleave to a Saviour God with a thousand times greater anxiety. Your faith is increased. Your prayer is answered by terrible things. Some of us prayed for a praying spirit, "Lord, teach us to pray." God has laid affliction upon us. Waves and billows go over us. We cry out of the depths. Being afflicted, we pray. He has granted our heart's desire. Our prayer is answered by *terrible things*.

Fourth, God sometimes answers prayer by giving something better than we ask. An affectionate father on earth often does this. The child says, Father, give me this fruit. No, my child, the father replies; but here is bread, which is better for you. So the Lord Jesus dealt with His beloved Paul, II Corinthians 12:7-9. There was given to Paul a thorn in the flesh, a messenger of Satan to buffet him. In bitterness of heart he cried, "Lord, let this depart from me." No answer came. Again he prayed the same words. No answer still. A third time he knelt, and now the answer came, not as he expected. The thorn is not plucked away—the messenger of Satan is not driven back to hell; but Jesus opens wide His more loving breast, and says, "My grace is sufficient for thee; for my strength is made perfect in weakness." Oh! this is something exceeding abundant above all that he asked, and all that he thought. Surely God is able to do "exceeding abundantly above all that we ask or think" (Eph. 3:20).

Dear praying believers, be of good cheer. God will either give you what you ask, or something far better. Are you not quite willing that He should choose for you and me? You remember that even Jesus prayed, "O my Father, if it be possible, let this cup pass from me!" That desire was not granted, but there appeared unto Him an angel from heaven strengthening Him, Luke 22:43. He received what was far better—strength to drink the cup of vengeance. Some of you, my dear believing flock, have been praying that, if it be God's will, I might be speedily restored to you, that God's name might be glorified; and I have been praying the same. Do not be surprised if He should answer our prayers by giving us something above what we imagined. Perhaps He may glorify Himself by us in another way than we thought. "Oh the depth of the riches both of the wisdom and knowledge of God! how unsearchable are his judgments, and his ways past finding out! For of him, and through him, and to him, are all things: to whom be glory forever. Amen."

These things I have written, that you may come boldly to the throne of grace. The Lord make you a praying people. "Strive together with me in your prayers to God for me." "I thank my God upon every remembrance of you, always in every prayer of mine for you all, making request with joy."

Now, the God of patience and consolation grant you to be likeminded one towards another, according to Christ Jesus. "The God of hope fill you with all joy and peace in believing; and the God of peace be with you all. Amen."

Fifth Pastoral Letter

What God has done, and the returns made: Isaiah 5:4.

Edinburgh, February 27, 1839.

TO all of you, my dear flock, who are washed and sanctified and justified in the name of the Lord Jesus, and by the Spirit of our God, your pastor again wishes grace, mercy, and peace.

This is now the fifth time I am permitted by God to write to you. If *you* are not wearied, it is pleasant and refreshing to me. I wish to be like Epaphras, Colossians 4:12: "Always laboring fervently for you in prayer, that you may stand perfect and complete in all the will of God." When I am hindered

by God from laboring for you in any other way, it is my heart's
joy to labor for you thus. When Dr. Scott of Greenock, a
good and holy minister, was laid aside by old age from preaching for some years before his death, he used to say, "I can
do nothing for my people now but pray for them, and sometimes I feel that I can do that." This is what I also love to
feel. Often I am like Amelia Geddie, who lived in the time
of the Covenanters, and of whom I used to tell you. The
great part of my time is taken up with bringing my heart
into tune for prayer; but when the blessed Spirit does help
my infirmities, it is my greatest joy to lay myself and you,
my flock, in His hand, and to pray that God may yet make
"the vine to flourish, and the pomegranate to bud."

If you turn to Isaiah 5:4, you will find these affecting words:
"What could have been done more to my vineyard, that I have
not done in it? wherefore, when I look that it should bring
forth grapes, brought it forth wild grapes?"

Consider these words, my dear people, and may the Spirit
breathe over them that they may savingly impress your souls.
These words are God's pathetic lamentation over His ancient
people, when He thought of all that He had done for them,
and of the sad return which they made to Him. We have
come into the place of Israel; the natural branches of the
good olive tree have been broken off, and we have been
grafted in. All the advantages God gave to Israel are now
enjoyed by us; and ah! has not God occasion to take up the
same lamentation over us, that we have brought forth only
wild grapes? I would wish every one of you seriously to
consider what more God could have done to save your soul
that He has not done. But, ah! consider again whether you
have borne grapes, or only wild grapes.

First, consider how much God has done to save your souls.
He has provided a great Saviour, and a great salvation. He
did not give man or angel, but the Creator of all, to be the

substitute for sinners. His blood is precious blood. His righteousness is the righteousness of God; and now "to him that worketh not, but believeth on him that justifieth the ungodly, his faith is counted to him for righteousness" (Rom. 4:5). Most precious word! Give up your toil, self-justifying soul. You have gone from mountain to hill; you have forgotten your resting place; change your plan: work not, but believe on Him that justifieth the ungodly. Believe the record that God hath given concerning His Son. A glorious, all-perfect, all-divine Surety is laid down at your feet. He is within your reach—He is nigh thee: take Him and live; refuse Him and perish! "What could have been done more for my vineyard, that I have not done in it?"

Second, again, consider the ordinances God has given you. He has made you into a vineyard. Scotland is of all lands the most like God's ancient Israel. How wonderfully has God planted and maintained godly ministers in this land, from the time of Knox to the present day! He has divided the whole land into parishes; even on the barren hills of our country He has planted the choicest vine. Hundreds of godly laborers He has sent to gather out the stones of it. God has done this for you also. He has built a tower in the midst of you. Have you not seen His own hand fencing you round, building a gospel tower in the midst of you, and a gospel wine press therein? And has He not sent me among you, who am less than the least of all the members of Christ, and yet "determined not to know anything among you save Jesus Christ and Him crucified?" Has not the Spirit of God been sometimes present in our sanctuary? Have not some hearts been filled there with gladness more than in the time that their corn and wine increased? Have not some hearts tasted there the "love that is better than wine?" "What could have been done more for my vineyard, that I have not done in it?"

Now let me ask, what fruit have we borne—grapes or wild

grapes? Ah! I fear the most can show nothing but wild grapes. If God looks down upon us as a *parish,* what does He see? Are there not still a thousand souls utter strangers to the house of God? How many does His holy eye now rest upon who are seldom in the house of prayer, who neglect it in the forenoon! How many who frequent the tavern on the Sabbath day! Oh! why do they bring forth wild grapes? If God looks upon you as *families,* what does He see? How many prayer-less families! How often, as I passed your windows, late at eve or at early dawn, have I listened for the melody of psalms, and listened all in vain! God also has listened, but still in vain.

How many careless parents does His pure eye see among you, who will one day, if you turn not, meet your neglected children in an eternal hell! How many undutiful children! How many unfaithful servants! Ah! why such a vineyard of wild grapes? If God looks on you as *individual souls,* how many does He see that were never awakened to real concern about your souls! How many that never shed a tear for your perishing souls! How many that were never driven to pray! How many that know not what it is to bend the knee! How many that have no uptaking of Christ, and are yet coldhearted and at ease! How many does God know among you that have never laid hold of the only sure covenant! How many that have no "peace in believing," and yet cry, "Peace, peace, when there is no peace!" (Jer. 8:11). How many does God see among you who have no change of heart and life, who are given up to the sins of the flesh and of the mind! And yet you "bless yourself in your heart, saying, I shall have peace, though I walk in the imagination of my heart, to add drunkenness to thirst" (Deut. 29:19).

Ah! why do you thus bring forth wild grapes? "Your vine is of the vine of Sodom, and of the fields of Gomorrah: your grapes are grapes of gall, your clusters are bitter" (Deut.

32:32). Ah! remember you will blame yourselves to all eternity
for your own undoing. God washes His hands of your destruction. What could have been done more for you that God
has not done? I take you all to record this day, if I should
never speak to you again, that I am pure from the blood of
you all. Oh barren fig trees, planted in God's vineyard, the
Lord has been digging at your roots; and if ye bear fruit, well;
if not, then ye shall be cut down (Luke 13:6-9).

Now I turn for a moment to you who are God's children.
I am persuaded better things of you, my dearly beloved, and
things that accompany salvation, though I thus speak. Yet
what need is there, in these trying times, to search your heart
and life, and ask what fruit does God find in me!

What fruit of *self-abasement* is there in you? Have you
found out the evil of your connection with the first Adam
(Rom. 5:19)? Do you know the plagues of your own heart
(I Kings 8:38)? the hell of corruption that is there (Jer. 17:
9)? Do you feel you have never lived one moment to His
glory (Rom. 3:25)? Do you feel that to all eternity you never
can be justified by anything in yourself (Rev. 7:14)?

Consider, again, what fruit there is of *believing* in you. Have
you really and fully taken up Christ as the gospel lays Him
down (John 5:12)? Do you cleave to Him as a sinner (I Tim.
1:15)? Do you count all things but loss for the excellency
of the knowledge of Him (Matt. 9:9)? Do you feel the
glory of His person (Rev. 1:17)? His finished work (Heb.
9:26)? His offices (I Cor. 1:30)? Does He shine like the
sun into your soul (Mal. 4:2)? Is your heart ravished with
His beauty (S. S. 5:16)?

Again, what fruit is there in you of *crying after holiness?*
Is this the one thing you do (Phil. 3:13)? Do you spend your
life in cries for deliverance from this body of sin and death
(Rom. 7:24)? Ah! I fear there is little of this. The most of
God's people are contented to be saved from the hell that is

without. They are not so anxious to be saved from the hell that is *within*. I fear there is little feeling of your need of the indwelling Spirit. I fear you do not know "the exceeding greatness of his power" to usward who believe. I fear many of you are strangers to the visits of the Comforter. God has reason to complain of you, "Wherefore should they bring forth wild grapes?"

Again, what fruit is there of *actual likeness to* God in you? Do you love to be much with God—"to climb up near to God (Gen. 5:22)—to love, and long, and plead, and wrestle, and stretch after Him?"[1] Are you weaned from the world (Ps. 131)—from its praise, from its hatred, from its scorn? Do you give yourselves clean away to God (II Cor. 8:5)—and all that is yours? Are you willing that your will should be lost in His great will? Do you throw yourselves into the arms of God for time and for eternity? Oh, search your hearts and try them; ask God to do it for you, and "to lead you in the way everlasting!" (Ps. 139:23, 24).

I am deeply afraid that many of us may be like the fig tree by the wayside, on which the hungry Saviour expected to find fruit, and He found none. Ah! we have been an ungrateful vine, minister and people! What more could God have done for us? Sunshine and shade, rain and wind, have all been given us; goodness and severity have both been tried with us; yet what has been returned to Him? Have curses or praises been the louder rising from our parish to heaven? Does our parish more resemble the garden of the Lord, or the howling wilderness? Is there more of the perpetual incense of believing prayer, or the "smoke in God's nose" of hypocrisy and broken sacraments?

I write not these things to shame you, but as "my beloved sons I warn you." If there be some among you, and some there are, who are growing up like the lily, casting forth their

---

[1] See *Brainerd's Diary*, Part 2, April 4.

roots like Lebanon, and bearing fruit with patience, remember "the Lord loveth the righteous." He that telleth the number of the stars taketh pleasure in you. "The Lord taketh pleasure in his people; he will beautify the meek with salvation." Keep yourselves in the love of God. Go carefully through all the steps of your effectual calling a second time.

The Lord give you daily faith. Seek to have a large heart. Pray for me, that a door of utterance may be opened to me. Remember my bonds. Pray that I may utterly renounce myself, that I may be willing to do and to suffer all His will up to the latest breath.

May you all obtain mercy of the Lord now, and in that day to which we are hastening. The grace of the Lord Jesus be with your spirits. Amen.

Sixth Pastoral Letter

Self-devotedness—what it ought to be.

Edinburgh, March 6, 1839.

TO all my dear flock over which the Holy Ghost hath made me overseer—to all of you who are of the Church of God, which He hath purchased with His own blood—your pastor wishes grace, mercy, and peace.

I thank my God without ceasing that ever I was ordained over you in the Lord. For every shower of the Spirit that ever has been shed upon us—for every soul among you that has ever been added to the Church—for every disciple among you whose soul has been confirmed during our ministry, I will praise God eternally. May this letter be blessed to you by the breathing of the Holy Spirit! May it teach you and me more than ever that we "are not our own, but bought with a price."

The most striking example of self-devotedness in the cause of Christ of which I ever heard in these days of deadness, was told here last week by an English minister. It has never been printed, and therefore I will relate it to you, just as I heard it, to stir up our cold hearts, that we may give ourselves to the Lord.

The awful disease of leprosy still exists in Africa. Whether it be the same leprosy as that mentioned in the Bible, I do not know, but it is regarded as incurable, and so infectious that no one dares to come near the leper. In the south of Africa there is a large lazarhouse for lepers. It is an immense space, enclosed by a very high wall, and containing fields, which the lepers cultivate. There is only one entrance, which is strictly guarded. Whenever anyone is found with the marks of leprosy upon him, he is brought to this gate and obliged to enter in, never to return. No one who enters in by that awful gate is ever allowed to come out again. Within this abode of misery there are multitudes of lepers in all stages of the disease. Dr. Halbeck, a missionary of the Church of England, from the top of a neighboring hill, saw them at work. He noticed two particularly sowing peas in the field. The one *had no hands,* the other *had no feet*—these members being wasted away by disease. The one who wanted the hands was carrying the other who wanted the feet upon his back, and he again carried in his hands the bag of seed, and dropped a pea every now and then, which the other pressed into the ground with his foot; and so they managed the work of one man between the two. Ah! how little we know of the misery that is in the world! Such is this prisonhouse of disease.

But you will ask, who cares for the souls of the hapless inmates? Who will venture to enter in at this dreadful gate, never to return again? Who will forsake father and mother, houses and land, to carry the message of a Saviour to these poor lepers? Two Moravian missionaries, impelled by a divine love for souls, have chosen the lazarhouse as their field of labor. They entered it never to come out again; and I am told that as soon as these die, other Moravians are quite ready to fill their place. Ah! my dear friends, may we not blush, and be ashamed before God, that we, redeemed with the same blood, and taught by the same Spirit, should yet be so unlike these men in vehement, heart-consuming love to Jesus and the souls of men?

I wish now to mention to you a proposal which deeply involves the happiness of you and me, and of which I believe most of you have already heard something. Oh that you would trace the Lord's hand in it! Oh that you would be still, and know that He is God! Let me go over some of the ways by which God has led us hitherto. When I came to you at the first, it was not of my seeking. I never had been in your town, and knew only one family in it. I did not ask to be made a candidate. I was quite happy where I was laboring in the Lord's work. God turned your hearts to ask me to settle among you. It was the Lord's doing. Since that day "ye know after what manner I have been with you at all seasons," and how, as far as God gave me light and strength, "I have kept nothing back that was profitable unto you, but have showed you, and have taught you publicly, and from house to house." Ye know also, some of you in your blessed experience, that God has given testimony to the word of His grace, so that "our gospel came not to you in word only, but in power, and in the Holy Ghost, and in much assurance."

It is indeed amazing how God should have blessed the Word when there was so much weakness and so much sin. But "who is a God like unto our God, that pardoneth iniquity, and passes by the transgressions of the remnant of his heritage?" We planted and watered, and God gave the increase. Ye are God's husbandry—ye are God's building. To Him be the glory.

You know also that I have had some painful trials among

you. The state of the mass of unconverted souls among you
has often made my heart bleed in secret. The coldness and
worldliness of you who are God's children has often damped
me. The impossibility of fully doing the work of a minister
of Christ, among so many souls, was a sad burden to me. The
turning back of some that once cared for their souls pierced
my heart with new sorrows.

Still I have had two years of great joy among you—unspeakable joy—in seeing souls added to the Church of such as shall
be saved. I may never be honored to preach again, yet still to
all eternity I shall praise God that He sent me to you: "For
what is our hope, or joy, or crown of rejoicing? Are not even
ye in the presence of the Lord Jesus Christ at his coming?
For ye are our glory and joy" (I Thess. 2:19, 20). And should
I lightly break up such a connection as this? Ah, no! My dear
friends, I do not need all your affectionate letters to persuade
me, that, if it were the Lord's will, my own vineyard is the
happiest place in the world for me to be. Again and again
other vineyards were offered to me, and I was asked to leave
you; but I never for a moment listened to one of them, for
ye were the seal of my ministry; and where could I be happier
than where the Lord had blessed me, and was still blessing
me?

But God sent another message to me. He laid a heavy
hand upon my body. I long struggled against it, but it was
too much for me. For two months I have been an exile from
you, and I have felt all the time like a widower, or like Jacob
bereaved of his children. My constant prayer was, that I might
be restored to you, and to the Lord's service. You prayed the
same; and when it was not answered, I cried, "Wherefore
contendest thou with me?" That word was sent in answer:
"My son, despise not thou the chastening of the Lord, neither
be weary of his correction" (Prov. 3:11). God seems plainly
to shut the door against my returning to you at present. I am

greatly better, yet still I am forbidden to preach. I am not even allowed to conduct the family devotions morning and evening; indeed, whenever I exert myself much in conversation, I soon feel the monitor within, warning me how frail I am.

In these circumstances, the General Assembly's Committee on the Jews has this day resolved that your pastor, accompanied by Dr. Black of Aberdeen, and my beloved friend Andrew Bonar of Collace,[1] should travel for the next six months, to make personal inquiry after the lost sheep of the house of Israel.

They propose that we should go without delay to the Holy Land—that we should then return by Smyrna, Constantinople, Poland, Germany, and Holland. Now I did not seek this appointment—I never dreamed of such a thing. "But he that hath the key of David, he that openeth and no man shutteth, and shutteth and no man openeth," He has thrown open this door to me, while He keeps the door of return to you still shut. My medical men are agreed that it is the likeliest method of restoring my broken health, and that I have strength enough for the journey. You know how my heart is engaged in the cause of Israel, and how the very sight of Immanuel's land will revive my fainting spirit. And if it be the will of God, I shall return to you, my beloved flock, to tell you all that I have seen, and to lead you in the way to the Jerusalem that is above.

I cannot tell you how many providences have been sent to me, every one convincing me that it is God's will and purpose I should go.

The most cheering one to me is, that a young man has nearly consented to fill my place, and feed your souls during my absence, who is everything I could wish, and who will make you almost forget that you want your own pastor. Nay, what

---

[1] Dr. Keith of St. Cyrus had not at that time joined the deputation.

ever happens, I hope you will never forget me, but remember me in your families, and remember me in your secret prayers. You are all graven on my heart—I never can forget you. How wonderful have been God's dealings with us! For many reasons He has sent this affliction on us—for sin in me, for sin in you; but also, I am persuaded, that He might seek after "the dearly beloved of his soul," that are now in the hand of their enemies. His way is in the sea; His name is Wonderful.

I grieve to write so much about myself. I had far rather speak to you of *Him* who "is fairer than the children of men." May you look beyond all ministers to *Him*—may He be your guide even unto death! Once again I hope to write before I leave my home and my country. Till then, may all grace abound toward you, and peace be upon Israel. Amen.

SEVENTH PASTORAL LETTER

Unexpected calls to labor—parting counsels to believers.

Edinburgh, March 13, 1839.

TO all of you who are my brethren, and my companions in tribulation, and in the kingdom and patience of our Lord Jesus Christ, your pastor wishes grace, mercy, and peace.

It gives me great joy to address you once more; and if I could only grave on your heart some of those words which make wise unto salvation, my time and labor would be amply repaid. The providences of every day convince me that I have followed not my own will, but God's, in leaving you for a time. If the Lord permit, I shall come to you again, and I trust more fully taught by the Spirit—a holier, happier, and a more useful minister. I did not know when I last preached to you that I was to be so long parted from you; and though I **felt a solemn** tenderness stealing over my soul which I could not well account for, and eternity seemed very near, and your souls seemed very precious, yet the Lord was "leading the blind by a way which we knew not." I have been searching God's Word to find examples of this, and I find them very many.

You remember *Abraham,* how he was living quietly in his father's house, in Ur of the Chaldees, when the Lord appeared to him, and said, "Get thee out of thy country, and from thy kindred, and from thy father's house, unto a land that I will show thee" (Gen. 12:1). And he went out, not knowing whither he went. You remember *Jacob:* his mother said unto him, "Arise, flee thou to Laban, my brother, to Haran, and tarry with him *a few days."* But the Lord meant it otherwise; and it was twenty years before Jacob came back again (Gen. 27:43, 44). You remember *Joseph:* his father sent him a message to his brethren: "Go, I pray thee, see whether it be well with thy brethren, and well with the flocks, and bring me word again" (Gen. 37:14). He expected to see him return in a few days; but God had another purpose with him. It was more than twenty years before he saw the face of Joseph again; till he said, "It is enough; Joseph my son is yet alive: and I will go and see him before I die."

You will find the same method of dealing in the New Testament. How little *Peter* knew that morning when he went up to the housetop to pray, that he was that very day to be sent away to open the door of faith to the Gentiles (Acts 10:9); and yet God said to him, "Arise, get thee down, and go with them, nothing doubting" (v. 20). Again, you remember *Barnabas* and *Saul,* how happily they were engaged with the brethren at Antioch, ministering to the Lord and fasting. Little did they think that the next day they would be sailing away to carry the gospel to other lands. As they ministered to the Lord and fasted, the Holy Ghost said, "Separate me Barnabas and Saul for the work whereunto I have called them. And when they had fasted and prayed, and laid their hands on them, they sent them away" (Acts 13:2, 13).

Once more, when Paul had preached the gospel in all the cities of Asia, and was come to Troas, on the seacoast, how little did he think that night when he laid his head upon his pillow, that by the next morning the swift ship would be carrying him across the seas, to bear the message of salvation to another continent! "A vision appeared to Paul in the night: there stood a man of Macedonia, and prayed him, saying, Come over into Macedonia and help us. And after he had seen the vision, immediately we endeavored to go into Macedonia, assuredly gathering that the Lord had called us for to preach the gospel unto them" (Acts 16:9, 10).

Now, has not God dealt with us in a similar manner? Although we are nothing in ourselves but evil and hell-deserving creatures, yet, when accepted in the Beloved, God cares for us. Oh! we err, not knowing the Scriptures, nor the power of God, when we think that God is indifferent to the least of all that are in Christ. We are fastened on the Redeemer's shoulder. We are graven on His breastplate, and that is on the Redeemer's heart. Surely He hath directed our steps. "O the depth of the riches both of the wisdom and the knowledge of God!" In other circumstances, I suppose, I would not have listened to this proposal. I could not have torn myself away had I been in strength and usefulness among you, and indeed the expedition probably would never have been thought of.

But God, who chose *Israel* to be His peculiar treasure, can easily open up ways when *His set time* is come. I parted from you only for a *few days;* but God meant otherwise, and He will make it His own fixed time. And now, behold, I know that there are some of you among whom I have gone preaching the kingdom of God, who "shall see my face no more." "He that keepeth Israel" may preserve your pastor under His almighty feathers. I know you will pray for me, as you have done in secret, and in your families, and in your meetings for prayer, "that the sun may not smite me by day, nor the moon by night"; but if I should come back again, will I find you all where I left you? Alas! I know it cannot be so. "For what is your life? It is even a vapor"; and God is still crying, "Return, return, ye children of men."

For some among you, I give thanks unto the Father that He hath made you meet to be partakers of the inheritance of the saints in light (Col. 1:12). There are some among you from whom I have learned more than I taught you, "who have been succorers of many, and of myself also" (Rom. 16:2), and who have often reminded me of corn, when it was fully ripe. Shall we be surprised if the Son of Man puts in the sickle? (Rev. 14:13, 16). Dear advanced believers, we may never meet again. I feel it almost wrong to pray that ye may be kept to comfort us on our return. It is wrong to grudge you "an entrance into perfect day," where you shall lay aside that body of death and sin which is your greatest grief; yet may the Lord spare you, and bless you, and make you a blessing, that ye may bear fruit in old age. Oh, fill up the little inch of time that remains to His glory; walk with God; live for God. Oh, that every thought, and word, and action might be in His favor, and to His praise! The Lord grant that we may meet again here, and with you be refreshed; but if not, may we meet where we shall walk with Christ in white. God, who knows my heart, knows it would be a hell to me to spend an eternity with unconverted, Christless souls; but to be with Christ and His people is heaven to me, wherever it is.

There are many young believers among you, whom I may never meet again. It is hard to think of parting with you; the mother feels it hard to part with the sucking child. It was my highest delight in this world to see you growing day by day— to see your sense of the plague in your own heart deepening —to see you cleaving to Christ with full purpose of heart—

to see your "peace widening like a river," and to see your love burning higher and higher toward the throne of God. You are in my heart to live and to die with me. Still *He* who at any time fed you by *me,* can as easily feed you by another. I commend you to the Lord, on whom you believe. Read II Peter 3:17; meditate over it, pray over it; beware lest ye also, being led away with the error of the wicked, fall from your own steadfastness; but grow in grace.

The only way to be kept from *falling* is to *grow.* If you stand still, you will fall. Read Proverbs 11:28, "The righteous shall flourish as a branch." Remember you are not a *tree,* that can stand alone; you are only "a branch," and it is only while you abide in *Him,* as a branch, that you will flourish. Keep clear your sense of justification; remember *it is not* your own natural goodness, nor your tears, nor your sanctification, that will justify you before God. It is Christ's sufferings and obedience *alone.* Seek to be made holier every day; pray, strive, wrestle for the Spirit, to make you like God. Be as much as you can with God. I declare to you that I had rather be one hour with God, than a thousand with the sweetest society on earth or in heaven. All other joys are but streams; God is the fountain: "all my springs are in Thee."

Now may the blessings that are on the head of the just be on your head. Be faithful unto death, and Christ will give you a crown of life; and if I never meet you again in this world, may I meet you as pillars in the house of my God, where you "shall go no more out." Pray for me when you have access to the throne, when you have a heart for it. I will try to pray for you, that ye may endure to the end. I have a word more for those of you that are still unconverted, whom I may never see again in the flesh. My heart bleeds to think of parting with you; but I must defer this to my next letter, for I expect to write you again before I go. Farewell for the present, and may the grace of the Lord Jesus Christ be with you.

Eighth Pastoral Letter

Warnings to the unsaved. Why so many among us are unsaved.

Edinburgh, March 20, 1839.

TO all of you my dear flock, who are dearly beloved and longed for, my joy and crown, your pastor wishes grace, mercy, and peace, from God our Father, and from our Lord Jesus Christ.

In my last letter I showed you that, in all human probability, there are many of you to whom I have preached the gospel of salvation, to whom I shall never preach it again face to face. I cannot be blind to the many dangers that accompany foreign travel—the diseases and accidents to which we shall be exposed; but if, through your prayers, I be given to you again, how many blanks shall I find in my flock! How many dear children of God gone to be "where the weary are at rest," where the imperfect "are made perfect!" How many of you that have stood out against all the invitations of Christ, and all the warnings of God, shall I find departed, to give in your account before the throne! It is to these last I wish now to speak.

For two years I have testified to you the gospel of the grace of God. I came to you in "weakness, and in fear, and in much trembling"; and if the case of the children of God and of backsliding souls has often lain heavy at my heart, I can truly say that your dreadful condition—"settled like wine upon her lees," when you are about to be "turned upside down, as a man turneth a dish and wipeth it"—has been a continued anxiety to me; and sometimes, when I have had glimpses of the reality of eternal things, it has been an unsupportable agony to my spirit. I know well that this is a jest to you, that you care not whether ministers go or stay; and if you get a short sermon on the Sabbath day that will soothe and not prick

your conscience, that is all you care for. Still, it may be the
Lord who opened Manasseh's heart will open yours, while I
go over solemnly, in the sight of God, what appear to be the
chief reasons that, after my two years' ministry among you,
there are still so many unconverted, perishing souls.

One cause is to be sought in *your minister.* In Malachi 2:6
you will find a sweet description of a faithful and successful
minister: "The law of truth was in his mouth, and iniquity was
not found in his lips: he walked with me in peace and equity,
and did turn many away from iniquity." This is what *we should*
have done; but the furnace brings out the dross, and afflictions
discover defects unknown before. Oh, that I could say with
Paul: "That I have been with you at all seasons serving the
Lord with all humility of mind, and with many tears!" Ye
are witnesses, and God also, "how holily, and justly, and un-
blameably, we behaved ourselves among you that believe." I
am indeed amazed that the ministry of such a worm as I am
should ever have been blessed among you at all; and I do this
day bewail before God every sin in my heart and life that
has kept back the light from your poor dark souls. Oh, you
that can pray, pray that I may come back a holy minister—a
shepherd not to lead the flock by the voice only, but to *walk*
before them in the way of life.

Looking back over my pulpit work, alas! I see innumerable
deficiencies. I always prayed that I might "not keep back anything that was *profitable,*" that I might not shun to declare
the whole counsel of God, "that I might decrease, and Christ
increase." Still, alas! alas! how dimly I have seen and set before you "the truth as it is in Jesus!" How coldly have I
pleaded with you to "save yourselves from this untoward generation!" How many things I have known among you "besides
Christ and Him crucified!" How often have I preached myself, and not the Saviour! How little I have "expounded to
you in all the scriptures the things concerning Jesus!"

One error more has been in my private labors among you. How much fruitless intercourse have I had with you! I have not been like a *shepherd* crying after the lost sheep, nor like a *physician* among dying men, nor like a servant bidding you to the marriage, nor like one plucking brands from the burning! How often have I gone to your houses to try and win your souls, and you have put me off with a little worldly talk, and the words of salvation have died upon my lips! I dared not tell you, you were perishing, I dared not to show you plainly of the Saviour. How often I have sat at some of your tables, and my heart yearned for your souls, yet a false shame kept me silent! How often I have gone home crying bitterly, "Free me from *blood-guiltiness*, O God, thou God of my salvation!"

I turn now to the causes in you, dear children of God. You also have hindered in great measure God's work in the parish. *First*, by your want of *holiness*. "Ye are the light of the world." I have often told you that a work of revival in any place almost always begins with the children of God. God pours water first on "him that is thirsty," and then on the dry ground. But how little has "the word of the Lord sounded out from you!" I do not mean that you should have been loud talkers about religious things. "In the multitude of words there wanteth not sin, and the talk of the lips leadeth to penury." But you should have been "living epistles, known and read of all men."

You know that a lighted lamp is a very small thing, and it burns calmly and without noise; yet "it giveth light to all that are within the house." So, if you had day by day the blood of Christ upon your conscience, walking a forgiven and adopted child of God, having a calm peace in your bosom and a heavenly hope in your eye, having the Holy Spirit filling you with a sweet, tender, chaste, compassionate, forgiving love to all the world—oh! had you shone thus for two years back, how many of your friends and neighbors that are going down to hell might have been saying this day, "Thy people shall be my people, and thy God my God!" Think, my beloved friends, that every act of unholiness, of conformity to the world, of selfishness, of whispering and backbiting, is hindering the work of God in the parish and ruining souls eternally.

And what shall I say to those of you who, instead of emitting the sweet winning light of holiness, have given out only rays of darkness? "I have this against thee, that thou hast left thy first love. Remember, therefore, from whence thou art fallen, and repent, and do thy first works, or else I will come unto thee quickly, and will remove thy candlestick out of his place, except thou repent."

Second, you have hindered God's work by your want of prayer. When God gives grace to souls, it is in answer to the prayers of His children. You will see this on the day of Pentecost (Acts 2); Ezekiel 37:9 shows, that in answer to the prayer of a single child of God, God will give grace to a whole valley full of dry and prayerless bones. Where God puts it into the heart of His children to pray, it is certain that He is going to pour down His Spirit in abundance. Now, where have been your prayers, O children of God? The salvation of those around you depends on your asking, and yet "hitherto ye have asked nothing in Christ's name." Ye that are the Lord's remembrancers, keep not silence, and give Him no rest. Alas! you have given God much rest—you have allowed His hand to remain unplucked out of His bosom.

It is said of John Welsh, minister of Ayr, that he used always to sleep with a plaid upon his bed, that he might wrap it around him when he arose in the night to pray. He used to spend whole nights in wrestling with God for Zion, and for the purity of the Church of Scotland; and he wondered how Christians could lie all night in bed without rising to pray. Oh! we have few Welshes now; therefore our church is so dim, and our land a barren wilderness. Dear Christians, I often think it strange that ever we should be in heaven, and so many in hell through our soul-destroying carelessness. The good Lord pardon the past, and stir you up for the future. I learn that you are more stirred up to pray since I left, both in secret and unitedly. God grant it be so. Continue in it, dear children. Do not let it slip again. Plead and wrestle with God, showing Him that *the cause is His own,* and that it is all for *His own glory* to arise and have mercy upon Zion.

Last of all, think of the causes in yourselves, O unconverted souls! Be sure of this, that you will only have yourselves to blame if ye awake in hell. You will not be able to plead God's secret decrees, nor the sins of your minister, nor the carelessness of your godly neighbors—you will be speechless. If you die, it is because you *will* die; and if you *will* die, then you must die.

Think, first, on your carelessness about ordinances. They are the channels through which God pours His Spirit. The Bible, prayer, the house of God—these are the golden pipes through which the golden oil is poured. How many of you utterly neglect the Bible! You know not the blessedness of the man spoken of in the First Psalm. How many of you restrain prayer before God! How many of you have dead, useless prayers, learned by rote! And oh, how you despise the house of God! Alas, that church shall rise against you in judgment. It was a door of the ark brought near to you. Two years and more, its gates have been wide open to you, and yet how you have slighted it! Already I seem to hear your loud wailing when you mourn at the last, and say, "How have I hated instruction, and my heart despised reproof, and have not obeyed the voice of my teachers!"

Think, second, how you have been mockers. It has been too common for you to make a mock of eternal things and of godly people. When there have been anxious souls seeking the way to be saved, and they could not conceal their tears, you have called them hypocrites! When some have got a new heart, and have changed their way of life, you have spoken scoffingly of them, and tried to bring them into contempt. Alas! poor soul, look within. You have hardened your hearts into an adamant stone. Look at Proverbs 17:5: "He that mocketh the poor reproacheth his maker." And again, Isaiah 28:22: "Now, therefore, be ye not *mockers,* lest your bands be made strong."

To sum up all. The great cause that I leave you hardened is, that you "despise the Son of God." You see no beauty in Him that you should desire Him. You lightly esteem the Rock of your salvation. You have not had a soul-piercing look at a pierced Saviour. You have not seen the infinite load of sins that weighed down His blessed head. You have not seen how open His arms are to receive, how often He would have gathered you. You have not heard that sweet word whispered of the Spirit, "Behold me, behold me," which, when a man once hears, he leaves all and follows. You have trampled under foot the blood of the Son of God. Farewell, dear, dear souls. God knows that my whole heart prays that you may be saved.

Perhaps there are some of you that never would bend under my ministry, that will melt like wax before the fire under the word of the dear young minister who is to speak to you in my absence. May the Lord give him hundreds for my tens! I will often pray for you, and sometimes write to you, when I am far away. If I reach Immanuel's land, I will say, "The Lord bless you out of Zion." And if you will not turn, remember I take God for a record that I am pure from the bood of you all.

Dear children of God, I now cast you on Him who cast you on me when I was ordained over you. He said to me, "Feed my sheep . . . feed my lambs . . . feed my sheep." Now, when He sends me away, I would humbly return His own words to Him, saying, "O Shepherd of Israel, feed my sheep, feed my lambs, feed my sheep." Little children, love one another. Keep yourselves from idols. Bear me ever on your hearts. Pray that when I have preached to others, I may not be a castaway. Pray that I may save some.

"Now the God of peace, that brought again from the dead our Lord Jesus Christ, that great Shepherd of the sheep, through the blood of the everlasting covenant, make you perfect in every good work to do His will, working in you that which is well pleasing in His sight, through Jesus Christ; to whom be glory for ever and ever. Amen."

My next, if God will, may be from England.

NINTH PASTORAL LETTER

Incidents of the way as far as Leghorn. Exhortations.

Leghorn, May 2, 1839.

TO all of you, my beloved flock, who have received Christ, and walk in Him, your pastor wishes grace, and mercy, and peace, from God our Father, and from our Lord Jesus Christ.

My heart's desire and prayer for you every day is that you may be saved. I am now far from you in the flesh, yet am I with you in the spirit. I thank my God without ceasing, for as many of you as have been awakened to flee from the wrath to come, have rested your souls upon the good word of God concerning Jesus, and have tasted the love of God. In every prayer of mine for you all, I ask that ye may continue in the faith, grounded and settled—that ye may be like trees, rooted in Christ Jesus, or like a holy temple built up in Him who is the only foundation stone.

I expected to have written you from London, and again before leaving France; but we have traveled so rapidly, often day and night, and the fatigue was so great to my weak frame, that I was disappointed in this; but I did not forget you night or day, and I know well I am not forgotten by you. Since I wrote you last I have passed through many cities and countries, and seen many faces and things strange to me. Many lessons for my own soul, and for yours, I have learned. At present I must write you shortly.

We left London on April 11, and next morning crossed the British Channel from Dover to Boulogne, and found ourselves on the shores of France. The very first night we spent in France, we were visited by a most interesting Jew, evidently anxious about his soul. He spoke with us for many hours, accepted the New Testament in Hebrew, and bade goodby with much emotion. We thanked God for this token for good. Pray for us, that God may give us good success, that we may have the souls of Israel for our hire.

From Boulogne we traveled to Paris, by day and by night, and spent a Sabbath there. Alas! poor Paris knows no Sabbath; all the shops are open, and all the inhabitants are on the wing in search of pleasures—pleasures that perish in the using. I thought of Babylon and of Sodom as I passed through the crowd. I cannot tell how I longed for the peace of a Scottish Sabbath.

There is a place in Paris called the *Champs Elysées,* or Plains of Heaven, a beautiful public walk, with trees and gardens; we had to cross it on passing to the Protestant church. It is the chief scene of their Sabbath desecration, and an awful scene it is. Oh, thought I, if this is the heaven a Parisian loves, he will never enjoy the pure heaven that is above. Try yourselves by that text, Isaiah 58:13, 14. I remember of once preaching to you from it. Do you really delight in the Sabbath day? If not, you are no child of God. I remember with grief that there are many among you that despise the Sabbath, some who buy and sell on that holy day, some who spend its blessed hours in worldly pleasures, in folly and sin. Oh! you would make Dundee another Paris if you could. Dear believers, oppose these ungodly practices with all your might. The more others dishonor God's holy day, the more do you honor it, and show that you love it of all the seven the best. Even in Paris, as in Sardis, we found a little flock of believers. We heard a sweet sermon in English, and another in French. There are only two thousand Protestant hearers out of the half million that inhabit Paris, and there are fourteen faithful sermons preached every Sabbath.

We left the French capital on April 16, a lovely evening, with a deep blue sky above, and a lovely country before us, on the banks of the Seine. This would be a delightsome land, if it only had the light of God's countenance upon it. We traveled three days and three nights, by Troyes, Dijon, and Chalons, till we came to Lyons, upon the rapid river Rhone, in the south of France. The Lord stirred up kind friends to meet us. Lyons is famous as being the place where many Christians were martyred in the first ages, and where many were burned at the time of the Reformation because they loved and confessed the Lord Jesus. God loves the place still. There is a small body of three hundred believers, who live here under a faithful pastor, Mr. Cordées. He cheered our hearts much, and sent us away with affectionate prayers.

That day we sailed down the Rhone more than 100 miles, through a most wonderful country. We hoped to have spent the Sabbath at Marseilles; but just as we entered the Mediterranean Sea, a storm of wind arose, and drove the vessel on a barren island at the mouth of the Rhone. We all landed and spent our Sabbath quietly on the desert island. It was your communion Sabbath, and I thought that perhaps this providence was given me that I might have a quiet day to pray for you. There were about twelve fishermen's huts on the island, made of reeds, with a vine growing before the door, and a fig tree in their garden. We gave tracts and books in French to all our fellow passengers, and to the inhabitants, and tried to hallow the Sabbath.

My heart went up to God the whole day for you all, and

for my dear friends who would be ministering to you. I tried
to go over you one by one, as many as I could call to mind.
My longing desire for you was, that Jesus might reveal Himself to you in the breaking of bread, that you might have
heart-filling views of the lovely person of Immanuel, and
might draw from *Him* rivers of comfort, life, and holiness.
I trust your fellowship was with the Father, and with His
Son, Jesus Christ. Many I know are ignorant of Jesus. I
trembled when I thought of their taking the bread and wine.
You all know my mind upon this.

The next morning the storm abated, and we sailed over
the tideless sea, and reached the beautiful harbor of Marseilles
by eight o'clock. We had conference with a faithful young
minister, and with the rabbi of the Jews. We also attended
the synagogue the same evening. The Jews of France are
fast falling into infidelity, especially the younger Jews. They
do not love the law and the prophets as their fathers did.
They are, indeed, the dry bones in Ezekiel 37. Still God can
make them live. It is our part to speak to them the Word of
the Lord, and to pray for the quickening Spirit.

True Christians in France are increasing. There are four hundred Protestant ministers, and nearly one-half of these are faithful men, who know nothing among their flocks but Christ and
Him crucified. In some places Christians seem more bold and
devoted than in Scotland. It is very pleasant to hear them
singing the French psalms: they sing with all their heart,
and are much given to prayer. Oh, my dear Christians, be like
them in these things! May the same Holy Spirit, who has
often visited you in times gone by, fill your hearts more than
ever with praise and prayer!

Catholicism in France is waxing bolder. The first day we
landed on the shore, it was evident we were in a land of darkness. On the height above Boulogne, a tall white cross attracted our eyes. We found on it an image of our Saviour

nailed to the tree, larger than life; the spear, the hammer, the nails, the sponge, were all there. It was raised by some shipwrecked fishermen; and sailors' wives go there in a storm to pray for their absent husbands. The Catholic priests meet us in every street: they wear a three-cornered hat, black bands, a black mantle with a sash, and large buckles on their shoes; they have all a dark, suspicious look about them. At the entrance of every village there is a cross, and the churches are full of pictures and images. I went into one church in Paris, the finest in France, where the crosses were all of pure silver, and there was a large white image of the Virgin Mary, holding the infant Jesus in her arms. Many rich and poor were kneeling on the pavement before the image, silently praying. Gross darkness covers the people.

A priest traveled one whole night with us in the coach. We argued with him first in French and then in Latin, trying to convince him of his errors, showing him his need of peace with God, and a new heart. In Psalm 137 you will see that Babylon, or Catholicism, is "doomed to destruction"; and in Revelation 18 you will see that her destruction will be very sudden and very terrible. Oh, that it may come soon, for thousands are perishing under its soul-destroying errors! And yet remember what I used to read to you out of Martin Boos, and remember the saying of the Lord to Elijah, I Kings 19. There may be many hidden ones even in Babylon. The whole way through France we distributed French tracts. Many hundreds in this way received a message of life. In every village they came crowding around us to receive them. Pray that the dew of the Spirit may make the seed sown by the wayside spring up.

We were too late for the first vessel to Malta, and therefore resolved to sail into Italy. We left Marseilles on April twenty-third, and landed at Genoa on the twenty-fourth. Genoa is one of the most beautiful towns in the world: the most of the houses and churches are of pûre white marble, and from the sea look like palaces. But Satan's seat is there: we dared not distribute a single tract or book in Genoa—we would have been imprisoned immediately. The Catholic priests, in their black, dismal cloaks, and the monks with their coarse, brown dress, tied with a cord, a crucifix and beads hanging round their neck, bare feet, and cowl, swarm in every street. I counted that we met twenty of them in a ten minutes' walk. Catholicism reigns here triumphant, yet the people "are sitting still, and at ease," living for this world only. Oh! it is an awful thing to be at ease when under the wrath of God. Every place I see in Italy makes me praise God that you have the gospel so freely preached unto you. Prize it highly; do not neglect the wells of salvation that flow so freely for you.

The next day we sailed for Leghorn, where we have been ever since. We are living in the house where the excellent Mr. Martin, once minister of St. George's, Edinburgh, died in 1834. We visited his grave. I prayed that, like him, we might be faithful unto the end.

There are from ten to twenty thousand Jews here. We went to the synagogue the night we arrived, and twice since; it is a beautiful building inside, capable of holding two thousand persons. The place where they keep the law, written on a parchment roll, is finely ornamented with marble; so is the desk kept where they read the prayers. Lamps are continually burning. One rabbi was chanting the prayers when we entered. Beside the ark there stood three rabbis, in the Eastern dress, with turbans and flowing robes, and long beards. They were much reverenced, and many came to kiss their hand and receive their blessing. One of them is from Jerusalem; we have had many interesting conversations with him. Every day we have met with several Jews; they are very friendly to us, and we try to convince them out of the Scriptures that Jesus is the Christ. There are about 250 Protestants here; and we have tried to stir them up also to care for their souls. Dr. Black preached to them in our hotel last Sabbath evening.

Hitherto the Lord hath helped us. Tomorrow we sail from Italy to Malta, then for Egypt, and then for the Holy Land. Dear believers, it is a sweet consolation to me that your prayers go with me wherever I go. Often, perhaps, they close the mouth of the adversary, often keep back the storms from our vessels, often open a way to the hearts of those we meet, often bring down a sweet stream of the Spirit to water my thirsty soul. May I be enabled to make a sweet exchange with you, praying my heavenly Father to render double unto each of your bosoms what you pray for me! May my dear brother, who, I trust, fills my place among you, be made a blessing to you all! May his own soul be watered while he waters yours! Join him with me in your supplications. May he win many souls among you that I could never win.

This is Thursday evening. I trust you are at this moment met together in the prayer meeting. Oh! do not forsake the assembling of yourselves together. My heart is with you all. May the Spirit fill the whole church and every heart with His presence and power. My body is still far from being strong. I am more and more convinced that I did right in leaving you. I trust to be restored to you again in the fullness of the blessing of the gospel of Christ. "The will of the Lord be done."

My dear brother who is with me, whom you know well, and who daily joins me in fervent prayers for you, sends his salutations. Remember me to all who are sick and afflicted. Alas! how many of you may be laboring and heavy laden, that I know not of; but Jesus knows your sorrows. I commend you to the good Physician.

My dear classes, I do not, and cannot forget. I pray Psalm 119:9 may be written in your hearts.

My dear children in the Sabbath schools I always think upon on the Sabbath evenings, *and on those* who patiently labor

among them. The Lord Himself give you encouragement, and
a full reward.

To all I say, keep close to Christ, dear friends. Do not be
enticed away from Him; He is all your righteousness, and
all mine; out of *Him* you have all your strength, and I mine.
It pleased the Father that in *Him* should all fullness dwell.

The grace of the Lord Jesus Christ be with your spirits.
Farewell.

TENTH PASTORAL LETTER

Incidents of the way in Palestine and other lands—Request.

Breslau, in Prussia, October 16, 1839.

TO my dear flock, whom I love in the Lord Jesus, grace,
mercy, and peace, be multiplied from God the Father,
and from His Son, Jesus Christ.

I fear that many of you will be thinking hardly of your
distant pastor, because of his long silence; and, indeed, I
cannot but think hardly of myself. I little thought, when
leaving Italy, that I would be in Europe again before writing
to you. I did not know how difficult it is to write at any
length when traveling in the East.

From the day we left Egypt till we came to Mount Lebanon,
for more than two months, we were constantly journeying
from place to place, living in tents, without the luxury of a
chair or a bed. In these circumstances, with my weak body,
and under a burning sun, you must not wonder at my silence.
At the foot of Mount Carmel I began one letter to you, and
again in sight of the Sea of Galilee I began another, but
neither did I get finished. Last of all, before leaving the
Holy Land, I set apart a day for writing to you; but God
had another lesson for me to learn. He laid me down under

a burning fever, bringing me to the very gates of death. Indeed, my dear people, I feel like Lazarus, whom the Lord Jesus raised from the tomb. I feel like one sent a second time with the message of salvation, to speak it more feelingly and more faithfully to your hearts, as one whose eye had looked into the eternal world.

In all our wanderings, you have been with me by night and by day. Every scene of Immanuel's land brought you to my remembrance, because every scene tells of Jesus Christ and Him crucified. In the wilderness, in Jerusalem, beside the Sea of Galilee, at Smyrna, on the Black Sea, on the Danube, you have all been with me. I have, day and night, unceasingly laid your case before God. It has been one of my chief comforts, that, though I could not preach to you, nor come to you, I could yet pray for you. Perhaps I may obtain more for you in this way, than I could have done by my personal services among you.

Another joy to me has been, that I know all of you who pray, pray for me. This has been a lamp to me in many a dark hour. God has wonderfully preserved us through your prayers. In the south of the Holy Land, we were daily exposed to the plague. Every night we heard the wail of the mourners going about the streets of Jerusalem; yet no plague came near our dwelling. Near the Sea of Galilee we were often in danger of being robbed and murdered by the wild Arabs; yet we passed unhurt through the midst of them. Sailing to Smyrna, your pastor was brought low indeed, insomuch that I never thought to see you again; yet He sent His word and healed me. In Poland, the Sabbath before last, I was actually in the hands of robbers; but through God's wonderful mercy, I escaped safe. In every step of our journey, I am persuaded we have been watched over by our all-loving Father, who is the hearer of prayer! And the Lord shall deliver us from every evil work, and will preserve us unto His heavenly king-

dom. I speak of these things only that you may give Him
the glory, and trust in Him to your dying day. Sing Psalm 116
in all your families.

Another joy to me has been, that God has given you the
dear brother who watches over you so tenderly. You know
not what joy it gave me to hear of you all through him. The
letter reached me at Smyrna, when I was so weak that I
could not walk alone. It was like health and marrow to my
bones, to hear that the Lord's work is not yet done in the
midst of you, and that so many of you stand fast in the Lord,
having your conversation in heaven. I have no greater joy
than to hear that my children walk in the truth. It is not like
common joy. All joys of this world are short and fading,
they reach not beyond the dark boundary of the grave; but to
rejoice over those whom the Lord has given me out of a perishing world—this is joy which God Himself shares, and which
reaches into the light of eternity. Ye are my joy and crown.

In like manner, there is no sorrow like the sorrow of the
pastor, who has to weep over a backsliding people. I do
tremble to return to you, for I know well I shall have deep
sorrow from some of whom I expected joy. I fear lest I have
to mourn over some branches that are without fruit, on the
good vine tree; over some, who once gave their hand to the
Saviour, but are now saying, "I will go after my lovers." Are
there none of you who have left your first love, and broken
the bands that bound you to follow Jesus? Shall I find none of
whom I must needs say, "They went out from us, but they
were not of us"? Oh, there is no sorrow like unto this sorrow.
Had I been able, as I hoped, to have written you from all
the chief places in our journeyings, I would have attempted
to describe to you all I saw; but now there are so many countries to look back upon, that it would be vain to attempt it.
I do hope, that if the Lord bring us together again, I may
be able to tell you many things of our wanderings, and es-

pecially of Immanuel's land, which may both refresh and improve you. Nothing that I have heard I keep back from you, if only it be for your soul's good and God's glory.

Of the Holy Land, I can only say, like the Queen of Sheba, "that the half was not told me." It is far more wonderful than I could have believed. I shall always reckon it one of the greatest temporal blessings of my lot, that I have been led to wander over its mountains with the Bible in my hand, to sit by its wells, and to meditate among its ruined cities. Not a single day did we spend there without reading, in the land itself, the most wonderful traces of God's anger and of His love. Several times we went to the Mount of Olives, to the Garden of Gethsemane, to the Pool of Siloam, and to the village of Bethany, and every stone seemed to speak of the love of God to sinners. These places are probably very little altered from what they were in the days when Jesus tabernacled among men, and they all seemed to say, "Hereby perceive we the love of God, because He laid down His life for us."

We were four days in sight of the Sea of Galilee. I could not help thinking of you, my dear young people, for we used to go over the Sea of Galilee so often on the Monday evenings, and all the scenes of divine love it has been witness to. One day we rode through the plain of Gennesaret, and passed the moldering ruins of Capernaum, the Saviour's city, where His voice of mercy was so often heard, and where His hand was so often stretched out to heal. We asked in vain for Chorazin and Bethsaida. The woe which Jesus pronounced has fallen upon them.

Oh, my dear flock, "how shall you escape if you neglect so great salvation?" See how desolate they are left, that refuse Him that speaketh from heaven. The free offer of a divine Surety rings through your churches, now that God continues faithful teachers among you. Every Sabbath, and oftener, the fountain for sin is publicly opened for you, and souls, all defiled with sin, are invited to come and wash. But these mercies will not always last.

If you tread the glorious gospel of the grace of God under your feet, your souls will perish; and I fear Dundee will one day be a howling wilderness like Capernaum. I spent nearly the whole of August, during my illness in Bouja, a village near Smyrna, under the care of tenderest friends, whom the Lord wonderfully provided for me in a strange land. You remember Smyrna is one of the Seven Churches in Asia to which the Saviour sent those quickening messages in the Revelation of St. John. I thought again and again of the happy Thursday evenings which I once spent with you in meditating on these seven epistles to the churches. You know it is said of Samuel, even when he was a child, that God did not let one of his words fall to the ground; and the same is true to this hour of the very weakest of God's faithful ministers. What we have spoken to you is not like the passing wind, which hurries on and leaves no trace behind. It is like the rain and snow—it will not return to God without accomplishing some end in your hearts, either melting or hardening. Smyrna is the only one of these churches where a pure golden candlestick is now to be found with the light burning. There is a small company who believe in Jesus. It was pleasant indeed to hear the gospel preached there in all its purity and power. Be you also faithful to death, and you shall receive a crown of life.

Leaving Smyrna, we sailed past Troas and Bithynia, and visited Istanbul, the most beautiful city in the world, and yet the most miserable. Looking round from the deck of the vessel, I could count above ninety minarets, many of them pure marble, carved and gilded in the richest manner. These all form part of mosques, or temples of the false prophet Mohammed. This religion is a singular invention of Satan;

their Koran, or Bible, is a book filled with nonsense, and with much wickedness. All their belief is comprehended in the short saying, "Lo Ullah il Allah, a Mahomed Rasal Allah"— "There is no God but God, and Mohammed is His prophet." They expect to be saved chiefly by making pilgrimages to Mecca, by abstaining from wine and pork, and by praying five times a day. Every day, at sunrise or sunset, we saw them at prayer; wherever they are, in the open street, on the top of the house, or on the deck of a ship, they take off their shoes, wash hands, face, and feet, spread their garment before them, and turning their face towards Mecca, pray, bending and kissing the ground, often fifteen and twenty times. They are rather pleased if you look at them. They are very proud of their own faith, and will not listen for a moment to the gospel of Jesus. It would be instant banishment or death if any missionary were to attempt their conversion.

Ah! my dear flock, how differently you are situated! How freely salvation is offered to you—a faith that really saves you from your sins—that makes you love one another! For love is of God, and every one that loveth is born of God. If you are not growing humble and loving, be sure your faith is no better than a Mohammedan's. You are not of God, but of the world. The next countries we visited were Walachia and Moldavia. We sailed to them from Istanbul, across the raging waves of the Black Sea, and up the mighty river Danube. These are two singular countries, seldom visited by travelers; they are governed by two princes, and the established religion is of the Greek Church. I wish I could show you all that I have seen of the superstitions and wickedness practiced among them, that you might give more earnest heed to the pure gospel that flows as freely as air and water through our beloved land.

One day, in Bucharest, the capital city of Walachia, I was present at a festival on the prince's birthday. An immense

crowd was present in their finest church, and all the nobles
of the land. The service consisted of prayers and chanting by
a number of priests, dressed in the most splendid manner.
When all was over, I stayed behind to see a curious superstition. At one side of the altar lay an open coffin, highly ornamented; within I observed a dead body wrapped in cloth of
gold; a dead withered hand alone was left out. This is said
to be the body of St. Demetrius, lately found in a river, by
the water parting asunder miraculously. Such is the tale we
are told.

I stood beside it when the worshipers approached the coffin
in great numbers, men and women, rich and poor. First
they crossed themselves and kneeled, kissing the floor three
times. Then they approached reverently, and kissed the withered hand of the dead body, and a cross that lay beside it.
Then they gently dropped a small coin into a little plate at
the dead man's feet, and after receiving a blessing from the
priest, with three prostrations more to the ground, they retired.

This is one specimen of their abominable worship of dead
men. Do I tell you these things that you may be proud of your
superior light? Ah! no. I write these things, that those of you
who live no better lives than they do, may be convinced of
your danger. What can you expect of these poor idolaters, but
that they will live after the flesh, in rioting and drunkenness,
in chambering and wantonness, in strife and envying? But
are there none of you, my dear flock, for whom night and
day my prayers ascend—are there none of you who do
the same things, though you have the holy Bible, and a freely
preached gospel, and no superstition? Yet how many of you
live an unholy life! Ah! remember Sardis: "I know thy
works, that thou hast a name that thou livest, and art dead.
Be watchful, and strengthen the things which remain, that
are ready to die; for I have not found thy works perfect
before God."

The next kingdom we came through was Austrian Poland
—the land of graven images. We came through its chief
towns, Tarnopol, Brody, Lemburg, and from thence to Krakow,
traveling many hundred miles. You would be amazed, as I
have been, if you saw the abominable idolatry of this land.
The Roman Catholic is the established faith; and the govern-
ment is a bitter persecutor of any who change. At every
village there are numbers of crosses, of immense size, with
the image of the Saviour. There are also statues of the Virgin
Mary, and of other saints as large as life, all along the roads.
Often there are wooden boxes set up full of images; often
in the middle of a square there is a small covered chamber
full of these idols, of wood and stone, whom the poor people
worship every day.

The Bible is an unlawful book in this country. All our
Bibles were taken away from us, even our Hebrew ones,
that we might not preach to the Jews the glad tidings of a
Saviour. Blessed be God, they could not take them from our
memories and hearts. Should not this make you all pray for
the coming of the day when the towers of Catholicism shall
fall—the day when God shall avenge us on her? For the
Bible which she hates so much says, "Her plagues shall come
in one day, death, and mourning, and famine; and she shall
be utterly burned with fire; for strong is the Lord God who
judgeth her." Pray for that day, for it will be the same day
when God will bind up the breach of His people Israel, and
shall heal the stroke of their wound. It will be the day when
the Lamb's wife shall come forth in all her loveliness and
when the Lord Jesus shall wear the crown of His espousals.

I began this letter to you in Krakow, the ancient capital of
Poland, but now an independent state. We spent three days
there inquiring after the poor despised Jews. We had much
intercourse with a faithful, prayerful missionary, who labors
among them there; and on the Sabbath we celebrated the

Lord's Supper. During the four years he has been in Krakow, the missionary had never once enjoyed the ordinance, for all around are sunk in Catholicism or infidelity. We were but five souls in all, and yet we felt it very pleasant, when surrounded with them that hated us, and far from our homes, with the door of the chamber shut, to remember Jesus.

My thoughts and desires were much toward you. I had greatly hoped to be present at your next Lord's Supper, but now I see it cannot be. My only comfort is, I have committed you to those who are beloved of the Lord, workmen that need not to be ashamed, whose names are in the Book of Life; and the Chief Shepherd, I feel persuaded, will not leave you orphans, but will come to you, and breathe upon you. May the Lord keep back from the table all who are not united to Christ; and may you, who are His own children, have communion with the Father, and with His Son, Jesus Christ.

Since yesterday morning we have traveled 180 miles nearer home. We are now in Breslau, and we breathe more freely, for this is the Protestant kingdom of Prussia. It makes my heart light to think that I am really on my way to you. It has been a sweet work indeed to me to carry, with poor stammering lips, the word of salvation to the scattered sheep of the house of Israel; still, I do long, if it be the Lord's will, to feed once more the flock that was given me in the dew of my youth. Whether I shall be permitted, and how long, to take up so great a work again, my Master only knows; but if you wish for it as fervently as I do, solemnly agree, in the presence of God, on the night on which this letter is read to you, to these two things:

First, strive together with me in your prayers to God for me, that it would please Him to forgive and forget our past sins and shortcomings—mine in carrying the message, yours in receiving it; and that He would really heal my body, and strengthen my soul, for again taking up the blessed work of the gospel ministry among you, and that He would grant us a prosperous journey to come unto you.

Second, solemnly agree, in the strength of the Lord Jesus, to break off your sins by righteousness, and your iniquities by showing mercy to the poor. The sin of one Achan troubled the whole camp of Israel. If any one of you who are God's children willfully continue in some old sin, then it may be God's will, for your sake, to trouble our camp, and continue His chastening. See that no fleshly lust, no covetousness which is idolatry, no hankering after the world and its unholy pleasures, no unlawful affection, be reigning in you. Clean out the old leaven from all your houses, so that we may meet again in peace, and be refreshed together by days of the Lord's presence and of the Spirit's power, such as we have never seen before. This is the hearty desire and prayer of your affectionate pastor.

To Rev. John Roxburgh, of St. John's, Dundee

The Holy Land.

Jerusalem, June 17, 1839.

I AM SURE you will be glad to hear from your brother in the ministry, in this land trodden by the feet of "God manifest in the flesh." My thoughts wander continually to the spot where God first counted me faithful, putting me into the ministry; where, for two years, He made me a happy minister of the gospel, and where I believe I have many praying friends who will not forget me so long as I live. In these sweet remembrances—whether in the vales of Italy, or on the mighty waters, or in the waste howling wilderness, or in this land of promise—you and your family have their constant place. I doubt not also that you often think and talk of me.

When some Church Extension expedition has turned out well, you will say, "What would our traveling friend say to this?" Or when the liberties of our church are infringed, and the arm of unhallowed power is raised against her, you perhaps think a moment, "How will our traveler bear this?" I am thankful to Him who dwelt in the bush that we are all here in safety, and I myself in moderate health, quite able to endure the fatigues of traveling, although these have been very great.

You would hear of our swift journey through France, and our pleasant stay in Italy. Malta was the next place of interest we came to. It is a very lovely island, having customs from almost every nation under heaven. It is highly important as a center of missionary operations, having a printing press, and some useful, excellent men employed. In riding round its rocky shore, we looked on every creek with interest, remembering Paul's shipwreck here, and his three months' stay in the island. The atmosphere is truly pleasant, and the sky has a peculiarly fine tinge of yellowish red.

We had a pleasant sail past Greece, and among the wonderful islands of the Aegean Sea. We landed on one called Syra, and saw the mission actively engaged, six hundred Greek children reading God's Word in Greek. The same evening we sailed between Naxos and Paros, where the beautiful marble was found, and stretched our eyes to see Patmos, where the beloved John wrote the Revelation. We could only see the waves that washed its shore.

We passed Crete, and read the Epistle to Titus with a new interest; and the next day at four (May 13th) sailed into the harbor of Alexandria. The costumes of the East are very striking to the eye at first. The turban, the beard, the hyke or immense plaid, the wide Arab trousers, the black visages and legs of the men, quite arrest the attention. The close veil, the forehead ornaments, the earrings, the anklets, the burden carried on the head, the children carried on the shoulder, or on the side—all these in the women are striking, especially at first. They will recall to you many of the words of the prophets. The plague having broken out at Alexandria the day we arrived, we were prevented from going up to Cairo; and after having visited the Jews in the synagogues, we determined on proceeding through the desert for the Holy Land, that we might escape quarantine. We left Alexandria on the fourteenth of May, and reached Jerusalem on the seventh of June. We were about twenty-two days living after the manner of Bedouins in the wilderness.

Mount Carmel, June 24th, 1839.—I thought to have got this letter finished in Jerusalem; but we were hurried away so unexpectedly in consequence of a considerable increase of the plague in the Holy City then, that I had to leave this and many others things undone. You will see by the heading that we are now beside that mountain where God did such wonders in the days of Elijah. We are encamped in our tents within a few yards of the sea. I am now writing upon a mat on the sand. The thermometer is somewhere about 80°, and I am writing with my desk on my knee. For the sake of distinctness, I will take up the thread of our story where I last left it off.

Our journey through the desert was a very trying one in many ways. I *now* understand the meaning of the text which says, "God led the Israelites through the wilderness to try them, and prove them, and make them know what was in their hearts." The loneliness is very great. The utter silence of all the world to you, the want of every necessary except what you carry along with you—all these try the soul in a way you can hardly imagine, whether we will cast all our care upon God or no. The first part of the desert journey we went upon asses; but the second and longest part upon camels—a mode of journeying of all others the most fatiguing.

I have thought a hundred times what a singular picture it would make, to draw our company riding through the desert,

Lincoln Christian College

exalted to the giddy height of the hunch of the camel. I
have often thought also, more seriously and properly, how
plainly God heard the prayers of all our dear friends in pre-
serving us from many dangers. It is quite a miracle that I
was enabled to bear the fatigue of being up before sunrise,
and sailing over that burning wilderness, often twelve hours
a day.

We came the nearest way from Egypt, alluded to in Exodus
13:17, and had opportunity of seeing Rosetta and Damietta,
two curious Egyptian towns. We sailed across a lake called
Menzaleh, and encamped one night beside the ruins of the
ancient Zoan. Amid these we could plainly trace the finger
of God in the fulfillment of the words in Ezekiel 30:14: "I
will set fire in Zoan." At El Arish, the last town of Egypt,
we clearly traced what we believed to be the river of Egypt,
so often spoken of as the boundary of Judah. Like all the
streams in the South, it is perfectly dry; but the watercourse
was very evident. By the way, this suggests the meaning of
a text which I never understood before, Psalm 126: "Turn our
captivity as the streams in the south." In the whole of the
south part of Canaan the streams dry up in the summer. I
think we only came upon *one* flowing stream between the Nile
and Jerusalem. In the winter God restores these streams, supplying them with abundance of water. Now this is the very
prayer of the Psalmist: "Do for our brethren in captivity
what thou doest for the streams in the south. Restore them
in all their life, and fullness, and beauty." So may it be in
all our parishes in all our beloved Scotland, never so lovely
or desirable as when we are far from it and from its pleasant
Sabbaths.

I must tell you now about Jerusalem. It is indeed the most
wonderful place I was ever in. We reached it about twelve
o'clock, under a burning sun. The bleak, rocky hills over
which we crossed were like a heated oven; but all was forgotten

when the city of the great King came in sight. "Your house is left unto you desolate." That word was upon every tongue. Almost every approach to Jerusalem gives you this desolate feeling; but when you stay there, and wander down into its deep valleys, or climb its terraced hills, or sit beside shady Siloam, whose waters flow softly, or meditate on Mount Zion, ploughed like a field, the whole current of your feelings is made to flow, and Jerusalem presents the remains of departed beauty such as you seek for in vain in any other land.

The scene which might seem of greatest interest in Jerusalem is Calvary, where the Son of God died. But God has so willed it that nothing but pain and disappointment follow the inquirer after the spot where the blood flowed which cleanses from all sin. You know there is a great church built over the place. The hole made by the cross is enclosed in a star of gold; and a marble slab covers what *they call* the sepulchre. They tell you so many heinous falsehoods, that we were all inclined to doubt the whole matter. The place in Jerusalem is now within the walls, instead of "without the gate." There is no mount, no garden—nothing to remind you of that day of awful interest.

Gethsemane makes up in interest all that we want in Calvary. The very place remains, and by its simplicity convinces the mind that it was the spot that Jesus loved. Above you, on the opposite side of Kedron, the high steep brow of Moriah rises; then the wall of the city, and above it the Mosque of Omar, which stands on the site of God's holy Temple. The road to Bethany passes in front of the garden. The path up the Mount of Olives forms another boundary. It is enclosed with old stone walls like all the walls of Judea, of rude stones, without any cement. Eight very old olives, of a thousand years at least, stand as monuments in the place. It is a sweet and sacred spot; and you will not wonder that we were often drawn to visit it, and to pray on the spot where Jesus sweat drops of blood.

The Mount of Olives is a hill of which you never weary. As you ascend it from Gethsemane, every step gives you a new prospect. We turned round again and again to look upon Jerusalem. Jeremiah says, "From the daughter of Zion all beauty is departed." And I believe, if we had seen "the perfection of beauty" in the day of its glory, we would say the same. Still from the Mount of Olives it is most beautiful. You see "the mountains all standing round about Jerusalem." The whiteness of the buildings gives it a dazzling appearance. The deep valleys on every side are very remarkable. On the north, a rising tower marks Ramah, where Samuel was born; and on the south, the eye fixes on Herodion, a conical hill beside Bethlehem.

When you come to the top of Olivet, you look to the east, and the Dead Sea seems to be stretched at your feet. The mountains of Moab look quite near; and you try to find out Pisgah, where Moses enjoyed his view of the good land. Bethany appears upon the east side of a declivity near you—a pleasant village. Twice we wandered out as far as Bethany. It was pleasant indeed to sit under its spreading fig trees, and to read over John 11.

Returning by the Jericho road, we stopped at the spot where Jesus wept over the city. It is the place where you "come near and behold the city," at the descent of the Mount of Olives. After full consideration, I believe it to be the very spot. *Zion* is literally ploughed like a field. I have brought with me some barley that I found growing on its summit. Jerusalem is become heaps. The heaps of ruins within the city are amazing; in some parts they are higher than the walls. "The mountain of the house is like the high places of the forest." Mount Moriah has now two Turkish mosques upon it.

Aceldama is a peaceful spot, overhanging the pleasant valley of Hinnom, once the scene of hideous rites. The plague was very severe in the city during our stay there, which prevented us from having that close intercourse with the inhabitants, and especially with the Jews, which was so desirable. Mr. Nicolayson, the English missionary, acted towards us like a brother. He lodged us in one of the mission houses upon Mount Zion, and gave us opportunity of preaching and of receiving the Lord's Supper. It was truly pleasant to eat of that bread and drink of that cup in an upper room in Jerusalem.

There are about five thousand Jews in Jerusalem, very poor and very divided among themselves, looked down upon as dogs by the Moslems; still they bear in their faces and manners the proof that the land is their own. They are entirely supported by contributions from Europe. They devote themselves to the study of the Law and the Talmud. I had an interesting meeting with one Jew at the large stones, the only remains of God's Temple. He was sitting praying, and looking very sad. I asked him what he was reading. He showed me; it was Psalm 22 in Hebrew. I took it up and read it over to him. He said he understood it, and that it applied to David. I showed him that could *not* be, for David was never pierced in hands and feet. I shortly explained to him the gospel, and showed him the only way of forgiveness. He looked very sad sitting on the ground.

I must hurry on. We visited Hebron, and had an interesting meeting with the Jews there. It is a delightful place. We visited Bethlehem on our return. It is curious that almost all the inhabitants of Bethlehem are Christians, that is, Greeks and Catholics. We left Jerusalem on the eighteenth and proceeded north by Ramah, Gibeon, Bethel, Sychar and Samaria to Carmel. I cannot tell you the delightful and solemn feelings with which we traverse this Land of Promise. The fulfillment of prophecy is everywhere remarkable. At Sychar we tried to find out the well where Jesus sat wearied. Mr. Bonar found it, and let his Bible fall into it. He could not get it

again, "for the well is deep." Ebal on the north, is a frowning
rocky hill. Gerizzim is also precipitous, but smiles with verdant
gardens. Sychar is a beautiful place. We spent a most interesting morning among the Jews and Samaritans, saw both their
synagogues, and reasoned with them out of the Scriptures, prov-
ing that Jesus is the Christ. Oh, that the Saviour would do
as He did before in this place—say plainly, "I that speak unto
thee am *He!*"

When we meet, if that be the will of God, I shall have
many descriptions to give you of the scenes of this land. It
has far surpassed all my expectations. We arrived at Carmel
on Saturday, and are now in quarantine. We and all our
clothes were yesterday bathed in the sea. In consequence of
undergoing this process our quarantine is seven days shorter;
and on Monday next we hope to proceed to Tiberias and
Saphet, the only places of importance for Jews, except Tyre
and Sidon, which we shall visit on our way to Beirut. We are
sorry that so much of our time is taken up, but we have gone
as quickly as possible in the circumstances.

We are all in good health. I suffer occasionally from my
heart, but much less than I did. I do hope, if it be the will
of my Master, that I may yet again serve Him in the gospel
of His Son. This is a delicious climate. I have heard once
from home. I am thankful to hear of the peace and grace
given to my people on our communion day. Dear people, may
the Great Shepherd feed them! I was happy to hear of Dr.
Chalmers' success. Dismayed at the decision of the Lord
Chancellor; but "Jehovah nissi," the Lord is our banner. My
kindest regards to Mrs. R., and to the brethren that ask for
me. I often pray most humbly for *all,* even my enemies.

To Rev. R. Macdonald of Blairgowrie

The Holy Land.

Mount Carmel, June 26, 1839.

I WROTE to you from the land of Egypt, and now from the Land of Promise. I would have written from Jerusalem; but our departure was so hurried, owing to an increase of the awful disease of plague, that I could not accomplish it. Indeed, I thought it would be more for the pleasure and advantage of all my friends if I spent my time in fully seeing the wonders of the city of the great King. It is all deeply graven on my memory and my heart.

The first sight of Jerusalem made my heart sink within me, it was so desolate; the walls appeared so low, so dark, so poor. But better acquaintance with its deep valleys and singular hills, its trees and fountains, has made it appear one of the loveliest spots Jesus visited. There is a holy beauty about Jerusalem, for you cannot walk a step without remembering the scenes that have passed there, and without looking forward to a time when it will again become the joy of the whole earth.

You will be glad to know that I have stood all our great fatigues wonderfully, and even without being the worse of them, but rather the better. I may almost say I feel that God has been answering the continued prayer of those that love me; still I am not yet what I was, though I hope to be. All my companions had the privilege of preaching in Jerusalem. I felt that it was kept from me; but that it was overflowing goodness that gave us to receive the broken bread and poured-out wine in an upper chamber, where Jesus first instituted it. I wish I could recount to you all that we have seen with our eyes, so as to make you almost see it all over again. Joy is increased by spreading it to others. Thus Christ's joy and glory are increased by making us partakers of it.

Our life in the wilderness was a singular one. Since the day I wrote you we have never known the luxury of a bed. We spread our mats upon the sand, and God watches over us, when we are under the cover of our frail tent, as much as if we were within brazen gates and bars. We often hear the cry of the wolves at night, and there are many lynxes and hyenas in this very mountain; but God keeps us safely. The burning heat of the desert, the long fatiguing journeys—sometimes twelve hours or fourteen in the day upon a camel—the insatiable thirst and our weakness, were very trying to our faith and to our temper; it proved us and made us know what was in our heart. Ah! dear friend, wherever we journey, union to Jesus and holiness from His Spirit flowing into us, is our chief and only happiness. Never cease to show your people that to be holy is to be happy; and that to bring us to perfect holiness and likeness to God was the very end for which Christ died.

We entered the land of the Philistines the first of June. You know the prophets say that the seacoast there is to be "cottages for shepherds and folds for flocks" (Zeph. 2:6). It is really so. You cannot imagine a country more completely covered with flocks and herds—camels and asses, and oxen and sheep and goats. The inhabitants are Arabs, a poor and ignorant race of men. How often we have wished for the Arabian tongue, to preach to them the unsearchable riches of Christ! We passed like the spies through the valley of Eshcol. We came to a small Arab town, Bet-hanoon. In all Arab towns, every roof is flat, so that the people sit there, pray there, dry their corn and sift it there.

There are no vines in Eshcol now, but immense bunches of grapes are still produced in some places of the Holy Land. The trees around the village are figs, beautiful, dark green trees. We are now tasting the first ripe figs, which are, like Jeremiah's, very good. We crossed the brook Sorek—quite dry; indeed, I think we met with only one flowing stream between the desert and Jerusalem. The streams in the South are all dry in the summer (see Psaim 126). We slept that night beside a small town, which we take to be Eshtaol, near which Samson was born. We saw there the brown tents of some Bedouin Arabs, illustrating Song of Solomon 1—the brown tents of Kedar. This was in the tribe of Dan.

Next day we went due east, across the vast plain Sephela, where Asa fought his battle (II Chron. 14), till we entered among the lovely hills of Judah. A wonderful fulfillment of God's Word was pressed on our attention all that day. The quantities of weeds in the plains are quite remarkable, and all of them are of a briery, prickly nature. I counted eleven different kinds of thistle, some of them of gigantic size. In a field where barley had been sown, there were more of these thorns and briers than of the barley. Now turn to Isaiah 32:13: "Upon the land of my people shall come up thorns and briers"; and see how long (v. 15), "Until the Spirit be poured upon us from on high." Indeed, every mountain and valley of this land is a witness for God, speaking silently but mightily, declaring that God's Word abideth for ever.

We arrived at Jerusalem on June seventh, and lighted off our camels within the Jaffa gate. The first thing that struck me was the quantity of various heaps. (See Micah 3:12.) It was two or three days before we recovered from fatigue. The first time we went out was to the two pools of Gihon; the upper pool still contains water.

Again we went to Mount Olivet. Winding round the noble walls at Jerusalem, Mount Olivet appears with its softly rounded, triple point. It is a beautiful hill of very great extent. It is composed of a pure white limestone, which appears in many places, and gives the whole a whitish appearance. Fine old olives adorn it on every side; fig trees here and there, and pomegranates, with their beautiful deep red flowers. A monas tery and a mosque are on the top, and three or four small towers, on different points of it. Crops of barley may be discerned here and there. It is altogether a pleasant hill. Between you and it lies the deep valley of Jehosaphat. The bed of the Kedron, quite dry, forms the lowest part.

Going along by the east wall of Jerusalem till you are nearly opposite the place where the Temple stood (now the Mosque of Omar), you then descend the steep bank of Moriah to the Kedron. A small bridge now helps you to cross. Here David went flying from Absalom. Here Jesus used to cross going to Gethsemane or to Bethany. The path before you leads right up the steepest part of Mount Olivet. It is a pleasant path. Turning every now and then, you see Jerusalem in all its faded glory, minarets and cupolas lying beneath you.

Another path winds upwards round the hill to Bethany, the sweet village of Martha and Mary, two miles off. The little nook between these two paths forms all that remains of Gethsemane. It is a pleasant spot. No one that knows the Saviour can visit it and look upon its eight old olive trees without feeling drawn to it. We tried to pray there, where Jesus sweat blood for us. It was sweet to intercede for you and all we love in that sacred spot.

Another favorite spot was the fountain of Siloam, farther down the valley of Jehoshaphat. It flows so softly from under the Temple that you cannot hear the ripple of its waters. You descend a great many steps in the rock, and drink its delightful waters. I send you a small hymn on the other side, which will imprint it on your memory. The valley of Hinnom is a deep gorge or vale to the south of Jerusalem. Mount Zion is actually ploughed like a field. It descends steeply into Hinnom, which again has a rocky barrier on the opposite side. Aceldama is a fearful spot above.

We left Jerusalem on June eighteenth and arrived here on the twenty-first. Many a pleasant scene we saw between. It is a delightsome land. One only I can mention—Sychar. It was a sweet evening when we entered the valley made by Ebal, a gloomy barren hill, and Gerizim, a rocky hill, but garnished with gardens. The town lies beautiful between, keeping nearer to Gerizim. The next morning we visited the synagogue. Andrew Bonar was in time for the service at six o'clock. He had very interesting discussions with several of the Jews, all carried on in Hebrew. You may believe we are not very fluent in the holy tongue, and yet it is wonderful how we get on. We visited the Samaritans also, and, after taking off our shoes, we were admitted into their synagogue to see the manuscript of the Pentateuch, 3,600 years old. Andrew alone found out the well where Jesus sat, and dropped his Bible in by accident.

The Jews here are far kinder and pleasanter than in Europe. They wear a beautiful dress. They are much fairer in color than the Arabs, and every way a more noble people; and then, when you look at your Bible, and see the promises that are waiting to be fulfilled to them, how does the heart fill towards them! God will yet gather them one by one. Pray still for their inbringing. It is not easy to pray really for Israel; it needs you to have much of the peculiar mind of God.

The same evening we visited Samaria, about six or eight miles north of Sychar. It is now a poor Arab village, but the finger of God is there. It is a hill surrounded by hills on all sides. Micah 1:6 is the clearest description of it. It is like an heap of the field. Just as you have seen the stones gathered out of a field into heaps, such is Samaria. The vast ruins are all thrown down, and form just heaps in the field. It is as the plantings of a vineyard. There is but one vine on the whole hill, but it is all terraced and cleared, just as if it were to be planted with vines. "And I will pour down the stones thereof into the valley, and I will discover the foundations thereof." This is wonderfully fulfilled. It filled me with holy awe to look at the heaps of stones—fragments of pillars all rolling down into the valley. The foundations are actually discovered. What a monument of the truth of God! I have only time to commend you to God, and to say, Brother, pray for us.

P.S.—Commend me to your true yokefellow, Mr. Smith, and to Mr. Gillies, and to Mr. Baxter. I cease not to mention all in my prayers, and hope that they do not forget me. "We are made partakers of Christ if we hold the beginning of our confidence firm unto the end."

To Rev. William C. Burns, Dundee

Inquiries about the revival on first coming home.

20 Hill Street, Edinburgh, November 15, 1839.

I ARRIVED last night once more in my beloved home, conducted through every danger by the unseen hand of our Father in heaven. I cannot lose a moment in writing you a few lines. It was not till we arrived in Hamburg that we heard anything of what has been doing in our beloved land for the last five months. There we heard only a rumor that God had visited His people in love, and those also that were Lo-Ammi. You may believe that it was with a thankful, joyful spirit that we read of these things.

I cannot rest till I hear from you what has been done among my own dear flock. I do not like to impose a task on you; but if you have an hour's leisure, it would be truly gratifying to me to hear from you, before I come over, a minute account of all that God seems to have wrought in Dundee during my absence. You remember it was the prayer of my heart when we parted, that you might be a thousandfold more blessed to the people than ever my ministry had been. How it will gladden my heart, if you can really tell me that it has been so! My poor, dear flock, hardhearted and stiff-necked as they were, if the Lord has really opened their hearts, and brought them to a saving knowledge of Christ, and if their hearts and lives are together changed, I will bless God while I have any being!

The work at Kilsyth seems to be owned by all God's true servants as not the work of man, but indeed divine. What a great joy to you and to your excellent father, to have your labor thus honored of God! The Lord preserve you both from all the personal danger to your own souls which such success exposes you to!

I must not write much, having agreed to preach on Sabbath. I would often have written you when away; but you know my weakness, and I was always uncertain as to your movements. Do write me if you have time. Tell me all the good and all the bad. I know well that when Christ is nearest, Satan also is busiest. What of my elders? of my dear, established Christians? What of those who were but lambs? And what of those whom I left in darkness and in the shadow of death?

The Lord send me good news.

I shall try to be over on Thursday evening next, if I am well, and trust to join you in praising God together for all His mercy and grace and faithfulness since we parted. Whether I shall be able to resume the full work of the ministry again or no, I cannot tell. My heart still beats too much. But I shall try; and if the Lord shows me that my work in that way is done, I shall pray for submission.

Do write me speedily, for I weary to hear.

With regard to temporal things, remember I shall expect you honestly to tell how far your small salary has gone to cover your expenses. And if it has not covered them, remember I insist on your demanding as much more as will. The workman is worthy of his hire.

And now the Lord keep you humble and prayerful in secret,

and may it not be needful that you be afflicted as I have been;
and may your ministry be blessed still a thousand times more!
With kindest love to all my people.

To Miss Collier, Dundee

Riches of Christ—resemblance to Him.

Edinburgh, February 26, 1840.

I AM sorry to leave town without seeing you, but I find
myself obliged to do so. A long and interesting meeting
of presbytery took up the greater part of my time. I am
delighted to hear that you are still keeping a little better,
and fondly hope the Lord may restore you to us once more, to
help us by your prayers in these trying but glorious times. I
would like to have seen you once again before going back;
but I must just content myself with casting you on the Lord
on whom you believe. Precious friend and unchangeable
priest is Christ—sweeter to you than honey and the honeycomb.
How great is the goodness He hath *laid up* for them that fear
Him! Just as the miser lays up money that he may feast his
eyes upon it, so Christ has laid up unsearchable riches that
He may supply all our need out of them. Unfathomable oceans
of grace are in Christ for you. Dive and dive again, you will
never come to the bottom of these depths. How many millions
of dazzling pearls and gems are at this moment hid in the
deep recesses of the ocean caves! But there are unsearchable
riches in Christ. Seek more of them. The Lord enrich you
with them. I have always thought it a very pitiful show
when great people ornament themselves with brilliants and
diamonds; but it is truest wisdom to adorn the soul with
Christ and His graces. "Can a maid forget her ornaments,
or a bride her attire? yet my people have forgotten me, days
without number."

You see my pen runs on, though I fear you will hardly be able to read what I write. The Lord Jesus give you out of His fullness, and grace for grace. In a mirror you will observe that every feature of the face is reflected—both the large and small features. Now our soul should be a mirror of Christ; we should reflect every feature; for every grace in Christ there should be a counterpart grace in us. The Lord give you this; then I can ask no more for you. Your times are in His hand—Psalm 31. May you have the blessing of Asher: "As thy days, so shall thy strength be."

Farewell till we meet. Kindest regards to Miss N. and Mrs. Coutts, and believe me ever yours in lasting bonds.

————

TO MR. J. T. JUST

How to conduct prayer meetings.

March 27, 1840

I WAS GLAD to receive your letter, and am happy to answer you on the matter in which you apply to me. No person can be a child of God without living in secret prayer; and no community of Christians can be in a lively condition without unity in prayer. In Daniel's time you see how it was (Dan. 2:17, 18). You see what Jesus said to His disciples on it (Matt. 18:19), and what a sweet promise of His presence and a gracious answer He connects with meeting for prayer. You see how it will be in the latter day (Zech. 8:21), when meetings for prayer, or at least concerts for prayer, shall be held by different towns.

One great rule in holding them is, that they be really meetings of disciples. If four or five of you that know the Lord would meet together regularly, you will find that far more profitable than a meeting open to all. In an open meeting you are apt to become teachers, and to be proud. In a secret meeting you feel all on a level, poor and needy, seeking water. If a young man, acquainted with any of you, becomes concerned about his soul, or a lively Christian is visiting any of you, these may be admitted; but do not make your meeting more open.

The prayer meeting I like best is where there is only praise and prayer, and the reading of God's Word. There is then least room for frail human nature to pervert the meeting to an improper end. It is well to read regularly through a book of Scripture, or at least to fix the chapter the evening before, that it may be prayed over in secret, before coming to the meeting. If you *only read,* then two chapters may be read, and then two members pray at a meeting. Each member would take his turn. Let there be no presiding of one over another, for all are brethren. When a godly minister or elder or experienced Christian is visiting you, he should be invited to take the whole service.

Many meetings are not contented with merely reading God's Word; they fix upon some verse or two as matter of conversation, and each one gives his opinion round. Some take a question of the Shorter Catechism each evening, and speak on it in the same manner. Some propose cases of conscience, and how Christians ought to act in different cases. Now, I never forbid any of these where the members prefer this; still, I must confess I feel the danger to which they are exposed. You require more grace to be kept humble and meek and loving, if you engage in this service. You are exposed to the danger of differing from one another—disputing, seeking admiration and pre-eminence, to all which you know, dear John, your hearts are naturally most prone. If you choose any of these, the first appears the best, that of fixing on a verse or two of the chapter read. But do seek meekness in speaking together upon it.

Meet weekly, at a convenient hour. Be regular in attendance.

Let nothing keep you away from your meeting. Pray in secret
before going. Let your prayers in the meeting be formed as
much as possible upon what you have read in the Bible. You
will thus learn variety of petition, and a Scripture style. Pray
that you may pray to God, and not for the ears of man. Feel
His presence more than man's. Pray for the outpouring of the
Spirit on the Church of Christ and for the world; for the purity
and unity of God's children; for the raising up of godly ministers, and the blessing of those that are so already. Pray for the
conversion of your friends, of your neighbors, of the whole
town. Pray for the sending of the gospel to the Jews, and to
the Gentile nations.

Pride is Satan's wedge for splitting prayer meetings to
pieces: watch and pray against it. If you have not the Spirit of
God among you, you will have the spirit of the devil. Watch
against seeking to be greater than one another; watch against
lip-religion. Above all, abide in Christ, and He will abide in
you. He is able to keep you from falling, and to make you
happy, holy young men. There is no joy like that of holiness.
May Enoch's Companion be yours.

Write me how you come on.

To a Parishioner on a Sickbed

How cares and troubles sanctify.

March 31, 1840

I MAY not see you for a little, as I am not strong; and therefore I send you a line in answer to your letter. I like to
hear from you, and especially when God is revealing Himself
to your soul. All His doings are wonderful. It is, indeed,
amazing how He makes use of affliction to make us feel His
love more. Your house is, I trust, in some measure like that
house in Bethany of which it is said, "Now Jesus loved Martha,

and her sister, and Lazarus." They had different degrees of
grace. One had more faith, and another more love, still Jesus
loved them all. Martha was more inclined to be worldly than
Mary, yet Jesus loved them both. It is a happy house when
Jesus loves all that dwell in it. Surely it is next door to heaven.

The message of Martha and Mary to Christ (John 11:3)
teaches you to carry all your temporal as well as your spiritual
troubles to His feet. Leave them there. Carry one another's
case to Jesus. Is it not a wonderful grace in God to have given
you *peace in Christ,* before laying you down on your long
sickbed? It would have been a wearisome time if you had been
an enemy to God, and then it would have been over in hell.

Do you feel Romans 5:3 to be true in your experience?
You cannot love trouble for its own sake; bitter must always
be bitter, and pain must always be pain. God knows you cannot love trouble. Yet for the blessings that it brings, He can
make you pray for it. Does trouble work patience in you?
Does it lead you to cling closer to the Lord Jesus—to hide
deeper in the Rock? Does it make you be still and know that
He is God? Does it make you lie passive in His hand, and
know no will but His? Thus does patience work experience—
an experimental acquaintance with Jesus. Does it bring you a
fuller taste of His sweetness, so that you know whom you have
believed?

And does this experience give you a further hope of glory—
another anchor cast within the veil? And does this hope give
you a heart that cannot be ashamed, because convinced that
God has loved you, and will love you to the end? Ah! then
you have got the improvement of trouble, if it has led you thus.
Pray for me still, that I may get the good of all God's dealings
with me. Lean all on Jesus. Pray for a time of the pouring-out
of God's Spirit, that many more may be saved. I hope the Lord's
work is not done in this place yet.

To a Soul Whom He Had Never Seen, But Whose Case Was Laid Before Him by a Friend

Colossians 2:1, 2.

Looking unto Jesus.

March 20, 1840

I DO NOT EVEN KNOW YOUR NAME, but I think I know something of the state of your soul. Your friend has been with me, and told me a little of your mind; and I write a few lines just to bid you to look to Jesus and live. Look at Numbers 21:9, and you will see your disease and your remedy. You have been bitten by the great serpent. The poison of sin is through and through your whole heart, but Christ has been lifted up on the cross that you may look and live. Now, do not look so long and so harassingly at your own heart and feelings. What will you find there but the bite of the serpent? You were shapen in iniquity, and the whole of your natural life has been spent in sin. The more God opens your eyes, the more you will feel that you are *lost in yourself.* This is your disease.

Now for the remedy. Look to Christ; for the glorious Son of God so loved lost souls, that He took on Him a body and died for us—bore our curse, and obeyed the law in our place. Look to Him and live. You need no preparation, you need no endeavors, you need no duties, you need no strivings, you only need to look and live. Look at John 17:3. The way to be saved is to know God's heart and the heart of Jesus. *To be awakened,* you need to know your own heart. Look in at your own heart, if you wish to know your lost condition. See the pollution that is there—forgetfulness of God, deadness, insensibility to His love. If you are judged as you are in yourself, you will be lost. *To be saved,* you need to know the heart of God and of Christ. The four Gospels are a narrative of the heart of Christ. They show His compassion to sinners, and

His glorious work in their stead. If you only knew that heart as it is, you would lay your weary head with John on His bosom. Do not take up your time so much with studying your own heart as with studying *Christ's heart*. "For one look at yourself, take ten looks at Christ!"

Look at Romans 15:13. That is my prayer for you. You are looking for peace in *striving*, or peace in *duties*, or peace in *reforming* your mind; but ah! look at His Word. "The God of hope fill you with all joy and *peace in believing*." All your peace is to be found in believing *God's Word* about His Son. If for a moment you forget your own case altogether, and meditate on the glorious way of salvation by *Christ for us*, does your bosom never glow with a ray of peace? Keep that peace; it is joy in believing. Look as straight to Christ as you sometimes do at the rising or setting sun. Look direct to Christ.

You fear that your convictions of sin have not been deep enough. This is no reason for keeping away from Christ. You will never get a truly broken heart till you are really *in Christ*. (See Ezek. 36:25-31.) Observe the order: *First*, God sprinkles clean water on the soul. This represents our being washed in the blood of Christ. *Then* He gives "a new heart also." *Third*, He gives a piercing remembrance of past sins. Now, may the Lord give you all these! May you be brought as you are to the blood of the Lamb! Washed and justified, may He change your heart—give you a tender heart, and His Holy Spirit within your heart; and thus may He give you a broken heart for your past sins.

Look at Romans 5:19. By the sin of Adam, many were made sinners. We had no hand in Adam's sin, and yet the guilt of it comes upon us. We did not put out our hand to the apple, and yet the sin and misery have been laid at our door. In the same way, "by the obedience of Christ, many are made righteous." Christ is the glorious One who stood for many. His perfect garment is sufficient to cover you. You had no hand in His obedience. You were not alive when He came into the world and lived and died; and yet, in the perfect obedience, you may stand before God righteous. This is all my covering in the sight of a holy God. I feel infinitely ungodly *in myself:* in God's eye, like a serpent or a toad; and yet, when I stand *in Christ alone,* I feel that God sees no sin in me, and loves me freely. The same righteousness is free to you. It will be as white and clean on your soul as on mine. Oh, do not sleep another night without it! Only consent to stand in Christ, not in your poor self.

I must not weary you. One word more. Look at Revelation 22:17. Sweet, sweet words! "Whosoever will, let him take of the water of life freely." The last invitation in the Bible, and the freest—Christ's parting word to a world of sinners! Anyone that pleases may take this glorious way of salvation. Can you refuse it? I am sure you cannot. Dear friend, be persuaded by a fellow worm not to put off another moment. Behold the Lamb of God that taketh away the sins of the world.

You are sitting, like Hagar, within reach of the well. May the Lord open your eyes, and show you all that is in Christ! I pray for you, that you may spiritually see Jesus and be glad— that you may go to Him and find rest.

———

Rev. W. C. Burns

A minister's afflictions to be improved.

June 10, 1840

I AM TRULY THANKFUL that you have been raised up again—renewed, I trust, both in the inner and outer man. "I will cause you to pass under the rod, and I will bring you into the bond of the covenant." Sweet rod that drives the soul into such a precious restingplace! "I will visit their iniquity with stripes; nevertheless, my loving-kindness I will not take from him." This has been the experience of the greater part of my life, at least of my spiritual life. Remember Edwards' magnificent resolution: "Resolved to improve afflictions to the uttermost." Spread the sail when the breeze of adversity blows, and let it drive your vessel onwards on its course.

When I was laid aside from the ministry, I felt it was to teach me the need of prayer for my people. I used often to say, Now God is teaching me the use of prayer. I thought I would never forget the lesson, yet I fear I am grown slack again when in the midst of my work.

All these remarks I have transferred to myself, that you may learn in me the same things. Exhort one another daily. My object in writing now is to say that I have engaged to be at Collessie next Wednesday, at Alloa on Thursday, and at Errol on Sabbath week. Now the people here were disappointed by your not appearing lately; and it would be very gratifying, if you are not better engaged, if the Lord would direct your steps towards us. If you would take both Thursday and the Sabbath, it would be pleasant to me. I have been weakened a little by the hard labors of the Assembly, but I trust to recruit shortly for our glorious warfare. I feel there are two things it is impossible to desire with sufficient ardor—personal holiness, and the honor of Christ in the salvation of souls.

The Lord give you both more than He has given me, and may He send you to us, if it be His will. Send me a line quickly, and believe me, ever yours in sweet bonds.

To Rev. Dan Edwards

Before his ordination as missionary to the Jews. What he must seek.

Dundee, June 15, 1840

THE GRAND MATTER of study, however, must still be divinity,—a knowledge of divine things, a spiritual discernment of the way of pardon for the chief of sinners. I feel that the best of ministers are but babes in this. Pray for more knowledge of your own heart—of the total depravity of it, of the awful depths of corruption that are there. Pray for glorious discoveries of Christ, His person, beauty, work, and peace. But I need not tell you these things; only I feel persuaded that God will put all natural and literary qualifications in the dust, if there be not the simple exhibition of Christ for us in the preaching of our missionaries.

———

To Rev. Dan Edwards

Holiness and success.

Dundee, October 2, 1840

I TRUST you will have a pleasant and profitable time in Germany. I know you will apply hard to German; but do not forget the culture of the inner man—I mean of the heart. How diligently the cavalry officer keeps his sabre clean and sharp; every stain he rubs off with the greatest care. Remember you are God's sword, His instrument—I trust a chosen vessel unto Him to bear His name. In great measure, according to the purity and perfections of the instrument, will be the success. It is not great talents God blesses so much as great likeness to Jesus. A holy minister is an awful weapon in the hand of God.

I am now almost well, but have not yet got my full strength.

We had a sweet night last night, though there was no external movement. Some waited after; one from St. Andrews, awakened deeply, she knows not how. God is still working here, and I look for far greater things. I am very anxious to know how I could do more good to many people and to the whole world; and not to know only, but to do it. It is our truest happiness to live entirely for the glory of Christ—to separate between "I" and "the glory of Christ." We are always saying, What have *I* done?—was it *my* preaching—*my* sermon—*my* influence? whereas we should be asking, What hath God wrought? Strange mixed beings we are! How sweet it will be to drop our old man, and be pure as Christ is pure! I hope you will come and see us again before your departure for your mission station. The Lord direct all your steps, comfort your heart, and stablish you in every good word and work to do His will.

TO MRS. THAIN, HEATH PARK

When invited to rest a while.

Dundee, June 1840

YOU KNOW how glad I would be of some such retreat as Elijah had by the brook of Cherith, where I might learn more of my own heart, and of my Bible, and of my God, where I might while away the summer hours in quiet meditation, or talking of His righteousness all the day long. But it is only said of *the dead* in the Lord that they rest from their labors; and I fear I must not think of resting till then. Time is short, my time especially, and souls are precious; and I fear many are slumbering because I watch not with sufficient diligence, nor blow the trumpet with sufficient clearness.

I have to be away so much on business, that I feel I dare not be away on pleasure only—at least at present. I rather think I must be in Ireland next week, at the Synod of Ulster, which prevents me coming to Mr. Macdonald's communion.

There is some request as to another communion in St. Peter's also, which I shall be glad to see carried into effect, provided it be done with all the heart of the Lord's children. In these circumstances, you must not think me neglectful of your kindness, if I put off my visit to you a little longer.

I trust that you are keeping strong, and able to enjoy the open air, and that your souls all prosper, that you have often such times as Jacob had at Mahanaim, when the angels of God met him, or such times as that at Peniel, when God had to cry out, "Let me go, for the day breaketh." Alas, we do not weary God now with our wrestlings, but with our sins. The dark clouds gather, and the Church and we should all be entering into our chambers, and shutting our doors upon us. "In that day sing ye unto her, A vineyard of red wine." His song will be with us in the dark night. May you and yours be hid in the day of the Lord's anger! A smile of His can lighten up a thundercloud.

Read Psalm 29 and meditate on the last verse. Live near to God, and so all things will appear to you little in comparison with eternal realities.

To a Stranger

Intended to lead on one whose face was Zionward, but who was not fully decided.

Dundee, July, 1840

I DO NOT even know your name; but your cousin has been telling me about your case, and wishes me to write you a line inviting you to lay hold on Jesus Christ, the only refuge for a perishing soul. You seem to have been thinking seriously of your soul for some time. Do remember the words of Peter (II Pet. 1:10), "Give diligence to make your calling and election sure." Never rest till you can say what John says (I John 5:19), "*We know* that we are of God." The world always loves to believe that it is impossible to know that we are converted. If you ask them, they will say, "I am not sure—I cannot tell"; but the whole Bible declares we may receive, and know we have received, the forgiveness of sins. (See Ps. 32:1; I John 2:12.) Seek this blessedness—the joy of having forgiveness; it is sweeter than honey and the honeycomb.

But where shall I seek it? In Jesus Christ. "God hath given to us eternal life, and this life is in his Son." "He that hath the Son hath life, and he that hath not the Son hath not life" (I John 5:12). Get deeply acquainted with yourself, your sins and misery. Most people are like the Laodiceans (Rev. 3:17). Even those that are most deeply concerned about their souls do not see the millionth part of the blackness of their hearts and lives. Oh! if we could but put our sins where God puts them (Ps. 90:8), how we would cry out, Unclean, unclean! Woe is me, for I am undone! Have you ever discovered your lost condition? Many know that they are great sinners; but where God is teaching, He will make you feel as an *undone* sinner. Have you felt this? What things were gain to you, those do you count loss for Christ? Do you know that no human righteousness can cover you? In His holy, pure sight, all our righteousnesses are as filthy rags (Isa. 64:6).

If you have been convinced of sin, have you been convinced of righteousness (John 16:8)? Have you heard the voice of Jesus knocking at the door of your heart? Have you opened the door and let Him in? Awfully momentous question! Your eternity depends upon the answer. "He that hath the Son hath life, and he that hath not the Son hath not life." Oh, what a simple thing the gospel is! How fearful to think it is hid from so many (II Cor. 4:3, 4)!

Jesus stands at your door willing to be your shield (Ps. 84:9, 11); your righteousness (Jer. 33:6); your all in all. Now, then, throw open the door and let Him in. Accept His white raiment, that you may be clothed. And oh! remember, if Christ justifies you, He will sanctify you. He will not save you and leave you in your sins. Why did He get the name Jesus? (Matt. 1:21). Here is a prayer for everyone that has been found of Christ: "Order my steps in thy word, and let not any inquity have dominion over me" (Ps. 119:133). If you are redeemed, you are not your own—not the world's—not Satan's. Think of this when you are tempted to sin.

Now, did I not say well that you should make your calling and election sure? Oh, beware of being a hypocrite, a mere professor, with an unholy heart and life. That your sister is on the road to Zion, I am glad, and pray that you may go hand in hand. Be diligent; the time is short. Try and persuade your friends to go with you. It is an awful thing to separate at the throne of Christ, for that will be for eternity. Pray much for the Holy Spirit to open your eyes, to soften your heart, to make Christ lovely and precious, to come and dwell in your hearts, and fit you for glory. Come to the Living Stone, and you will be built up as living stones (I Pet. 2:4, 5). Oh, how sweet to be made living stones in that glorious temple!

Pray much in secret. Pray for ministers that we may speak the Word boldly. Christ is doing great things in our day, which should make us wrestle at a throne of grace. Oh, that the Lord, that was pierced with many thorns, might soon be crowned with many crowns!

Praying that you and your sister may both be saved, I am, your friend in the gospel . . .

To Miss A. S. L.

The person and heart of Jesus. Consolation to believers.

August 16, 1840

I MAY NOT be able to see you for a little time, and therefore I am sending you a few lines to minister a little of the peace and grace of the Lord Jesus to you. I hear that you are worse in health than when I saw you; still I have no doubt you can say, "It is well . . . He doeth all things well." You remember Jacob said, when they wanted to take Benjamin away from him, "All these things are against me" (Gen. 42:36). But in a little while he saw that all these things were working together for good to him. In a little while all his lost children were restored to him, and he and his seed preserved from famine.

So will it be with you. If at any time unbelief steals over your heart, if you lose sight of Jesus, our Passover sacrificed for us, if you forget the hand of the all-tender gracious Father of Jesus and of your soul, you will be crying out, All these things are against me. But ah! how soon you will find that everything in your history, except *sin,* has been *for* you. Every wave of trouble has been wafting you to the sunny shores of a sinless eternity. Only believe. Give unlimited credit to our God.

Think on Jesus when your mind wanders in search of peace; think where He came from—from the bosom of His Father. He was *from the beginning.* He is the life—the life of all that truly live. He is that eternal life which was with the Father. Let the beams of the divinity of Jesus shine in upon your soul. Think how He was manifested—God manifest in the flesh—to be a Surety for sinners. Made sin for us, although He knew no sin, made a curse for us. Oh, if I could declare Him unto you, you might have fellowship with apostles, and with the Father, and with His Son, Jesus Christ. These things will we write unto you, that your joy may be full. Other joys do not fill the heart.

But to know the Lord Jesus as our Surety, satisfies the soul; it brings the soul unto rest under the eye of our pardoning God.

I met[1] the other day with a thought which has filled my heart often since. It is intended to explain that wonderful verse, John 14:18, "I will not leave you orphans: I will come to you." Jesus, at the right hand of the Father, is yet present with all His younger brethren and sisters in this vale of weeping. His *human nature* is at the right hand of God upon the throne—a Lamb as it had been slain. But His divine nature is unlimited, fills all worlds, and is present in every dwelling of every disciple in this world. His divine nature thus brings in continual information to His human heart of everything that is going on in the heart and history of His people; so that His human heart beats towards us just as if He were sitting by our side. Hence He cried to Saul, "Why persecutest thou me?"

Dear friend, do you feel that Jesus is your Surety and Elder Brother? Then remember that, by reason of His real divinity, He is now by your bedside, afflicted in all your afflictions, touched with a feeling of your infirmities, and able to save you to the uttermost. He is as really beside you as He was beside Mary when she sat at His feet. Tell Him all your sorrows, all your doubts and anxieties. He has a willing ear. Oh, what a friend is Jesus, the sinner's friend! What an open ear He has for all the wants, doubts, difficulties of His people! He has an especial care for His sick, weakly, and dying disciples. You know how it is with a kind mother, even though a worldly person. In a time of danger she clasps her children to her breast. In a time of health she may often let them wander out of her sight, but in hours of sickness she will *watch* beside their bed. *Much more* will Jesus watch over you.

I trust you feel real desire after complete holiness. This is the truest mark of being born again. It is a mark that He has made us meet for the inheritance of the saints in light. If a

---

[1] It was in a sermon by J. B. Patterson of Falkirk.

nobleman were to adopt a beggar boy, he would not only feed
and clothe him, but educate him, and fit him to move in the
sphere into which he was afterwards to be brought; and if you
saw this boy filled with a noble spirit, you would say he is meet
to be put among the children. So may you be made meet for
glory. The farmer does not cut down his corn till it is ripe. So
does the Lord Jesus: He first ripens the soul, then gathers it
into His barn. It is far better to be with Christ than to be in
Christ. For you to live is Christ, and to die is gain. Nevertheless, I trust God will keep you a little longer for our sake, that
you may pray for us, and encourage us to work on in the service of Jesus till our change come.

I began this letter about two weeks ago, and now send it
away to you. I was called very suddenly to Edinburgh, and
then sent to the north, and am just returned again, so that I did
not get it sent away. I will try to see you this week, if it be the
will of God. However, you must not be disappointed if I am
prevented. I pray for you, that according as your day, so your
strength may be. Keep your eye upon Jesus and the unsearchable riches that are in Him; and may the gentle Comforter fill
your soul, and give you a sweet foretaste of the glory that is to
follow. May He leave His deep eternal impress upon your
soul, not healing you and going away, but abiding within you,
keeping the image of Christ in your heart, ever fresh and full—
Christ in you the hope of glory. The Comforter is able to fill
you with calmness in the stormiest hour. May He fill your
whole soul and transform you into a child of light. Good-by till
we meet, if it be the Lord's will. If not in this world, at least
before the throne, casting our crowns at His feet.

To Rev. W. C. Burns

Awakenings. Personal holiness in ministers.

Dundee, September, 1840

I HAVE HAD a severe illness, or would have answered your kind note long before this. I fear you may have left Breadalbane before this can reach it; still I write in hope. You may be sure I ever follow you with my prayers and earnest longings of heart that God may humble, purify, and make use of you to carry glad tidings of great joy to the inmost hearts of poor, guilty, perishing sinners, wherever you go.

I have been much interested by all that I have heard of the good that has attended you in the north. I long to hear still more. The very name of Moulin stirs up the inmost depths of the heart, when I remember what great things the Lord Jesus did there of old. Do write to me when you have a moment, and stir me up. You know a word to a minister is worth a word to three or four thousand souls sometimes. Nothing stirs me up so much to be instant and faithful as hearing of the triumphs of the Lord Jesus in other places.

I am glad and thankful to say that we are not left quite desolate. There have been evident tokens of the presence of the Spirit of God among my dear people many nights, more, I think, upon the Thursday nights than on the Sabbaths. Some I have met with seemingly awakened without any very direct means. A good number of young mill-girls are still weeping after the Lord Jesus. I have been out of my pulpit only one Sabbath, and I hope to be back to it next Sabbath, if the Lord will.

What Mr. T. mentioned to you was true of some having followed after an enthusiastic kind of man, who in my absence came among them. Doubtless Satan wanted to carry off some of the sheep, and succeeded so far. Still I trust it will end in good. Some have been a good deal humbled in the dust on account of it, and I have been roused up to cry for more knowledge to guide them in the right way. I think, if strength were restored to me, I will try, in the name of the Lord Jesus, to catechize through my parish. I ask your advice and prayers on this. If it could be conducted humbly and with patience and aptness to teach, I am persuaded it would tend to ground them more deeply in divine things. Hypocrites also might be denounced and warned, and the unconverted pointedly dealt with. I feel the immense difficulty of it in a town, and such a neglected, ignorant one as this. Still, if God were with me, who can be against me?

Everything I meet with, and every day I study my Bible, makes me pray more that God would begin and carry on a deep, pure, widespread, and permanent work of God in Scotland. If it be not *deep and pure,* it will only end in confusion, and grieving away the Holy Spirit of God by irregularities and inconsistencies; Christ will not get glory, and the country generally will be hardened, and have their mouths filled with reproaches. If it be not *widespread,* our God will not get a large crown out of this generation. If it be not *permanent,* that will prove its impurity, and will turn all our hopes into shame. I am much more afraid of Satan than I used to be. I learned a good deal by being with Cumming in Strathbogie.

I am also deepened in my conviction, that if we are to be instruments in such a work, we must be purified from all filthiness of the flesh and spirit. Oh, cry for personal holiness, constant nearness to God by the blood of the Lamb! Bask in His beams, lie back in the arms of love, be filled with His Spirit; or all success in the ministry will only be to your own everlasting confusion.

You know how I have always insisted on this with you. It is because I feel the need thereof myself. Take heed, dear friend; do not think any sin trivial; remember it will have everlasting consequences. Oh, to have Brainerd's heart for perfect holiness

—to be holy as God is holy, pure as Christ is pure, perfect as our Father in heaven is perfect! Oh, what a cursed body of sin we bear, that we should be obliged by it to break these sweet gospel rules! How much more useful might we be, if we were only more free from pride, self-conceit, personal vanity, or some secret sin that our heart knows! O hateful sins, that destroy our peace, and ruin souls!

But I must be done. I have not attained the full use of the pen. Go on, dear brother; but an inch of time remains, and then eternal ages roll on forever—but an inch on which we can stand and preach the way of salvation to a perishing world. May He count us faithful, keeping us in the ministry.

To Rev. Patrick L. Miller

Then laboring in Strathbogie, on his being elected minister of Wallacetown.

Dundee, September 18, 1840

I CANNOT TELL YOU how sincerely I thank God for the event of this evening. You are unanimously chosen minister of Wallacetown. I have already been on my knees to praise God for it, and to pray that you may be filled with the Holy Spirit for this glorious work. I hope you will see your way clear in leaving your attached people at Botriphnie. Make good use of your last days among them. Warn every man. Take each aside, and tell him you will be a witness against him at the last day if he do not turn and obey the gospel. The Lord give you a spiritual family in that place; and may you come to us in the fullness of the blessing of the gospel of Christ. I am persuaded the Spirit of God is still remarkably present in this town. You could not become a minister in a more blessed season, or in a more promising field. Oh, pray to be fitted for the arduous work! I was just praying this morning over Matthew

9:36-38, and little thinking that God was about to answer so graciously.

I have had a severe illness of late, and been taught to look more toward the Church above. But I am better, and my heart warms again towards the Lord's work below. Now, farewell! The Lord humble, empty, satisfy, and fill you—make you a Boanerges and a Barnabas all in one. May the Lord arise, and His enemies be scattered; and may poor parched Angus become like the garden of the Lord.

To Mr. George Shaw, Belfast

Prophecies concerning Israel. Revival. Conduct of Studies.

Dundee, September 16, 1840

IT GIVES ME GREAT JOY to be able to answer your kind letter, although I fear you have almost despaired of me. In writing your esteemed pastor, I mentioned to him my intention of writing you very soon; but I have since then been laid down upon a sickbed by a severe, feverish illness, from which I am now only recovering. Like you, my dear friend, God has seen it meet to train me often by the rod, and I have always found that He doeth all things well. Indeed, who would have his own health in his own guidance? Ah! how much better to be in His all-wise, all-powerful hand, who has redeemed us, and is making us vessels to hold His praise, now and in eternal ages! I have been only twice in the open air, and cannot yet manage the pen with facility; but I cannot delay writing to you any longer.

You cannot tell how much real joy your letter gave me when you tell me of the dear brethren who meet along with you on Monday mornings, to read and pray concerning Israel. This is indeed a delightful fruit of my short visit among you, for which I give humble and hearty thanks to Him who has stirred up

your hearts in what I have felt, by experience, to be His own
blessed cause. I feel deeply persuaded from prophecy, that it
will always be difficult to stir up and maintain a warm and holy
interest in outcast Israel. The lovers and pleaders of Zion's
cause will, I believe, be always few. Do you not think this is
hinted at in Jeremiah 30:13: "There is none to plead thy cause,
that thou mayest be bound up"? And again, verse 14: "All
thy lovers have forgotten thee; they seek thee not." And is not
this one of the very reasons why God will at last take up their
cause? See verse 17: "I will restore health unto thee . . . because they called thee an outcast, saying, This is Zion, whom no
man seeketh after."

It is a sweet encouragement also to learn, that though the
friends of Zion will probably be few, so that it may almost be
said, no one seeketh after her, yet there always will be some
who will keep watch over the dust of Jerusalem, and plead the
cause of Israel with God and with man. See Isaiah 62:6, 7. If
any of your company know the Hebrew, you will see at once
the true rendering: "I have set watchmen *over* thy walls, O
Jerusalem, which shall never hold their peace day nor night.
Ye that are the Lord's remembrancers, keep not silence, and
give Him no rest till He establish, and till He make Jerusalem
a praise in the earth." Oh, my dear brethren, into whose hearts
I trust God is pouring a scriptural love for Israel, what an
honor is it for us, worms of the dust, to be made watchmen by
God over the ruined walls of Jerusalem, and to be made the
Lord's remembrancers, to call His own promises to His mind,
that He would fulfill them, and make Jerusalem a blessing to
the whole world! The first verse is supposed to be the language
of our Lord Himself—our glorious Advocate with the Father.
Oh, what an example does He set us of unwearied intercession!
The second verse showeth the great effect which the conversion
of Israel will have on the Gentile world. The third verse shows
how converted Israel will be a glorious diadem in God's hand,

held out to show forth His praise. The fourth verse shows
that it is *literal Israel* that is spoken of, for there is a sweet
promise to *their land*.

I think you must take these two verses, 6, 7, as the motto of
your praying society, not in boasting, but in all humility of
mind, and with much self-upbraiding for the neglect of the
past. Indeed, you will find it a difficult matter to keep your
heart in tune really to desire the salvation of Israel, and the
widely extended glory of the Lord Jesus. You must keep in
close union to Jesus, and much in the love of God, and be much
filled with the infinite, almighty Spirit of God. He will help
your infirmities. It is when you feel the sweetness of the kingdom of God within you, that you will truly fall down on your
knees, and pray, "Thy kingdom come." The possession of
grace fills us with very different feelings from the possession
of anything else. A man who has much money is not very
anxious that all the world should be rich; one who has much
learning does not long that all the world were learned; but if
you have tasted the grace of the gospel, the irresistible longing
of your hearts will be, Oh, that all the world might taste its
regenerating waters! And if it be true, as I think it is, that
God's method of bringing in the kingdom is to be by the salvation of Israel, how can an enlightened, gracious soul but pray,
"Do good in thy good pleasure unto Zion"?

As to the mode of studying prophecy, dear friend, I am far
from being a capable adviser. My advice, however, is that you
begin with the simple and more unquestioned parts, and then
advance to the more difficult ground. Begin with fulfilled
prophecy: you will thus gain an intimate acquaintance with the
language and manner of the prophetic writings. Then advance
to the marks of unfulfilled prophecy, and cautiously and prayer-
fully to those parts that are obviously unfulfilled. This would
be a most interesting course, and, if humbly followed out,
cannot but give you great light and interest in the cause of Is-

rael, and the world's conversion. For fulfilled prophecy, you might follow the guidance of Keith on *Fulfilled Prophecy,* or Bishop Newton, or both.

I am delighted to hear of the thankoffering you mention. It is sweet when thankfulness does not end in mere words, but in gifts to God and devotedness of our all to Him. I am happy to say that the Lord's cause seems still to advance in Scotland. On the very day I arrived from Ireland we had very sweet tokens of the presence of the Spirit of God in the congregation, and many Thursday evenings since.

I have been in Strathbogie also, and seen some of the Lord's wonders there. He that hath the key of David has opened a door there, for the salvation of many souls. I am still as anxious as ever that God's work should be pure, and unmixed with error and satanic delusions; and, therefore, when I pray for the revival of God's work, I always add that it may be pure and permanent. I have seen two awakened since I came home, with the use of hardly any means. If they shall turn out real conversions, I think I shall never despair of any.

I trust that your own studies get on well, dear friend. Learn much of your own heart; and when you have learned all you can, remember you have seen but a few yards into a pit that is unfathomable. "The heart is deceitful above all things, and desperately wicked: who can know it?" (Jer. 17:9). Learn much of the Lord Jesus. For every look at yourself, take ten looks at Christ. He is altogether lovely. Such infinite majesty, and yet such meekness and grace, and all for sinners, even the chief! Live much in the smiles of God. Bask in His beams. Feel His all-seeing eye settled on you in love, and repose in His almighty arms.

Cry after divine knowledge, and lift up your voice for understanding. Seek her as silver, and search for her as for hid treasure, according to the word in Proverbs 2:4. See that verse 10 be fulfilled in you. Let wisdom *enter into your hearts,* and

knowledge *be pleasant to thy soul;* so you will be delivered
from the snares mentioned in the following verses. Let your
soul be filled with a heart-ravishing sense of the sweetness and
excellency of Christ and all that is in Him. Let the Holy Spirit
fill every chamber of your heart; and so there will be no room
for folly, or the world, or Satan, or the flesh. I must now commend you all to God and the word of His grace. My dear people are just assembled for worship. Alas! I cannot preach to
them tonight. I can only carry them and you on my heart to
the throne of grace. Write me soon.

————

To His Sabbath School Teachers, During a Week of Absence from Them

(Accompanied by notes on the Scripture lesson that was to be taught in the
classes that week.)

Kelso, February 24, 1841

I SEND YOU a few notes on the parable for next Sabbath
evening. May you find them profitable. You cannot tell
what a sweet comfort it is to me, when I am so far distant from
my flock, to know that you are in the midst of the lambs, speaking to God for them, and speaking to them for God. I thank
my God without ceasing for your work of faith, and labor of
love, and patience of hope. Be not weary in welldoing, dear
friends, for in due season we shall reap, if we faint not. Do not
be impatient—wait on the Lord. The blessing will come. Use
a few spare half-hours in seeking after the lambs on the weekdays. This will prove to the parents that you are in earnest. To
bring one child to the bosom of Christ would be reward in
eternity for all our pains. Oh, with what glowing hearts we
shall meet in heaven those whom God has used us as humble
instruments in saving! Meditate on Philippians 1:8. And may

the Lord meet with you and the lambs on Sabbath day, and bless you, and do you good.

Farewell, dear fellow laborers. Ever your affectionate friend and pastor, absent in body, not in spirit.

To a Society in Blairgowrie for Diffusing the Knowledge of the Truth

Advices.

Dundee, March 27, 1841

I WAS HAPPY indeed to receive your letter, and the rules of your Society, which interested me very much. I would have answered you sooner, but have been laid down by my heavenly Father on a bed of sickness, from which I am just recovering by His grace. Spared fig trees should bear much fruit; pray that it may be so with me. Luther used to say that *temptations, afflictions,* and *prayer,* made a minister. I do trust that your Society may be greatly blessed, *first,* in the comforting, enlivening, and sanctifying of your own souls, and *then* in bringing others to know the same fountain where you have found peace and purity. Let Jesus come into your meetings and sit at the head of the table. It is a fragrant room when the bundle of myrrh is the chief thing there.

Let there be no *strife* among you, but *who* to be lowest at His feet, *who* to lean his head most fully on His breast. Let all your conversation, meditation, and readings lead you to the Lamb of God. Satan would divert your minds away to questions and old wives' fables, which gender strifes. But the Holy Spirit *glorifies* Jesus—*draws* to Jesus—*makes you cleave* to the Lord Jesus with full purpose of heart. Seek advance of personal holiness. It is for this the grace of God has appeared to you. (See Titus 2:11, 12.) For this Jesus died; for this He chose you; for this He converted you, to make you holy men—living epistles of Christ—monuments of what God can do in a sinner's heart. You know what true holiness is. It is *Christ in you, the hope of glory.* Let Him dwell in you, and so all His features will shine in your hearts and faces. Oh, to be like Jesus! This is heaven, wherever it be. I think I could be happy among devils, if only the old man were slain in me, and I was made altogether like Jesus! But, blessed be God, we shall not be called to such a trial, for we shall not only be like Jesus, but be with Him to behold His glory.

Pray to be taught to pray. Do not be content with old forms that flow from the lips only. Most Christians have need to cast their formal prayers away, to be taught to cry, Abba. Arrange beforehand what you have to pray for. Do not forget *confession of sin,* nor *thanksgiving.* Pray to get your closed lips opened in intercession; embrace the whole world, and carry it within the veil. I think you might with advantage keep a small book in which you might mark down objects to be prayed for. I pray God to make you very useful in the parish and in the world. Do all things without murmurings and disputings. (See Phil. 2:14, 16.)

Live for eternity. A few days more, and our journey is done. Oh! fight hard against sin and the devil: the devil never sleeps. Be you also active for good. The Lord bless you and your dear minister. Pray for us. Pray for the dead parishes around you.

LETTERS TO A SOUL SEEKING JESUS—NO. I

Seek to know your corruption.

Dundee, 1841

ACCORDING to promise, I sit down to talk with you a little concerning the great things of an eternal world. How kind it is in God that He has given us such an easy way of communicating our thoughts, even at a distance! My only reason for writing to you is, that I may direct your soul to Jesus, the sinner's friend. "This man receiveth sinners." I would wish much to know that you were truly united to Christ, and then, come life, come death, you will be truly and eternally happy.

Do you think you have been *convinced of sin?* This is the Holy Spirit's work, and His first work upon the soul. (John 16:8; Acts 2:37.) If you did not know your body was dangerously ill, you would never have sent for your physician; and so you will never go to Christ, the heavenly Physician, unless you feel that your soul is sick even unto death. Oh! pray for deep discoveries of your real state by nature and by practice. The world will say you are an innocent and harmless girl; do not believe them. The world is a liar. Pray to see yourself exactly as God sees you; pray to know the worth of your soul. Have you seen yourself *vile,* as Job saw himself (Job 42:5, 6)? undone, as Isaiah saw himself (Isa. 6:1, 5)? Have you experienced anything like Psalm 51? I do not wish you to feign humility before God, nor to use expressions of self-abhorrence which you do not feel; but pray that the Holy Spirit may let you see the very reality of your natural condition before God!

I seldom get more than a glance at the true state of my soul in its naked self. But when I do, then I see that I am wretched, and miserable, and poor, and blind, and naked (Rev. 3:17). I believe every member of our body has been a servant of sin (Rom. 3:13, 18)—throat, tongue, lips, mouth, feet, eyes. Every faculty of our mind is polluted (Gen. 6:5). Besides, you have long neglected the great salvation; you have been gainsaying and disobedient. Oh, that you were brought to pass sentence on yourself, *guilty of all!* Hear what a dear believer writes of himself: "My wickedness, as I am in myself, has long appeared to me perfectly ineffable, and swallowing up all thought and imagination, like an infinite deluge, or mountains

over my head. I know not how to express better what my sins
appear to me to be, than by heaping infinite upon infinite, and
multiplying infinite by infinite. When I look into my heart and
take a view of my wickedness, it looks like an abyss infinitely
deep, and yet it seems to me that my conviction of sin is exceeding small and faint."

Perhaps you will ask, Why do you wish me to have such a
discovery of my lost condition? I answer, that you may be
broken off from all schemes of self-righteousness; that you may
never look into your poor guilty soul to recommend you to God;
and that you may joyfully accept of the Lord Jesus Christ, who
obeyed and died for sinners. Oh, that your heart may cleave to
Christ! May you forsake all, and follow Jesus Christ. Count everything loss for the excellency of the knowledge of Christ. You
never will stand righteous before God in yourself. You are
welcome this day to stand righteous before God in Jesus. Pray
over Philippians 3:7, 9. I will try to pray for you. Grace be
with you.

———

To a Soul Seeking Jesus—No. II

Seek the righteousness of Christ.

I WAS GLAD to hear of your safe arrival, and that your
health had not suffered by the voyage. I trust the Lord is
dealing gently with your frail body, so that your mind may get
leave freely to fix itself on Jesus Christ and Him crucified.
Above all, I pray that the Holy Spirit may sweetly and silently
open your heart, to relish the way of salvation through the
blood and obedience of Immanuel. Through this Man is
preached unto you the forgiveness of sins, and by Him all that
believe are justified from all things (Acts 13:38, 39).

You would be deeply concerned to hear that your roommate,
———, has been so suddenly and awfully called away. Should

it not be a solemn warning to you? Oh, that you may be even now clothed in the righteousness of Jesus, so that, if you were called away, you may meet God in peace, and hear Jesus say, "Enter thou into the joy of thy Lord." In yourself you never will stand righteous before Jehovah. Psalm 143:2 answers your case. "Enter not into judgment with me," must be your cry. In your nature, in your past life, in your breaking of the holy law, in your contempt and neglect of Jesus, in your indwelling sin, God can see nothing but what He must condemn. Oh, that you would be of the same mind with God about your own soul! Do not be afraid to look upon its loathsomeness; for God offers to clothe you in Jesus Christ. "By the obedience of *one* shall many be made righteous" (Rom. 5:19). There is only *One* in all the world on whose face God can look and say, "He is altogether lovely." Jesus is that One.

Now God is willing that you and I should *hide in Jesus*. I feel at this moment that He is my righteousness. "This is his name whereby he shall be called, The Lord our Righteousness" (Jer. 23:6). I feel that the love of God shines upon my guilty soul through Jesus. This is all my peace. Your tears will not blot out sin. They do nothing but weep in hell; but that does not justify them. Your right views of the gospel will not justify you; you must be covered with a spotless righteousness. Your change of heart and of life will not justify you; it cannot cover *past sins*—neither is it perfect. Your amended life is still fearfully sinful in Jehovah's sight, and yet nothing but perfect righteousness can stand before Him.

Jesus offers you this perfect righteousness; in Him you may stand and hear God say, "Thou art all fair, my love." There is no spot in me. Do you thus look to Jesus? Do you believe the record that God has given concerning Him? Do you receive Christ with open arms? Do you cry, "My Lord and my God—my Surety, my all?" Dear friend, do not tarry. Eternity may be near. *Now* is your best time, perhaps your only time, of closing with Christ. How many worlds would a lost soul in hell give for such an opportunity of cleaving to Christ as you have now! "He that hath the Son hath life." This is all my prayer and desire for your precious, precious soul.

————

To a Soul Seeking Jesus—No. III

Joy in believing.

I SEND YOU another line to tell you Jesus is *the way*. I would like much to hear how your weak body prospers, and whether your soul is resting under the apple tree (S.S. 2:3); but till some opportunity occurs, I must just content myself with committing your soul and body into the hand of Jesus, your faithful Creator (I Pet. 4:19). We are now looking forward to another communion season, and I am busy instructing young persons for that holy and blessed ordinance. I think you said you were a good deal impressed at our last communion, and wished that you had been one of those seated at the Table: perhaps you may never be permitted to sit at the Table on earth; perhaps your first communion may be in glory.

There is a text in Romans 15:13, which expresses all my desire for you: "Now the God of hope fill you with all joy and peace in believing, that you may abound in hope, through the power of the Holy Ghost." You see here who is the author of conversion—"the God of hope." He must open your heart to attend to the things that are spoken. The truths that are presented to you will not convert your heart; the God of hope must breathe on your heart and water it oft.

Then see how He gives you joy and peace—"in believing." When Jesus revealed himself to Thomas (John 20:28), Thomas cried out with joy, "My Lord and my God!" If Jesus reveals Himself to you in all the glory of His person, the completeness of His work, and the freeness of His love, you too will be filled with appropriating, joyful faith, and will cry, "My Lord and my God!" It is a difficult thing to explain what it is to believe—I suppose it is impossible. But when Jesus unveils His matchless beauty, and gives you a sweet glimpse of His matchless face that was buffeted and spit upon, then the soul joyfully clings to Him. This is believing, and this is joy and peace in believing.

The truest, purest joy flows from a discovery of Jesus Christ. He is the hidden treasure that gives such joy to the finder (Matt. 13:44). Do you think you have found that treasure? Touching question! for if not, you are poor indeed. But how much joy may you have in Christ? "The God of hope *fill* you with all joy." You need not be afraid to take the full joy that Jesus gives. If you really come unto Christ, you come unto the love of Jehovah, and that is a filling love. The love of the creature does not fill the heart; but God's love coming full upon the soul gives fullness of joy (I John 1:4). It is holy love, sovereign love. I have been interrupted several times in writing this little note. I will not be long in writing you again. Do decide the question of your eternity. One thing is needful: have you closed with the great Mediator? Have you a saving knowledge of Jesus? Then only will death lose its power, and the grave become the bed of peaceful rest.

> There is a land of pure delight,
>   Where saints immortal reign;
> Infinite day excludes the night,
>   And pleasures banish pain.

Lean all your care for time and eternity on Jesus; that is the softest of all pillows—the bosom of our guardian Immanuel.

To a Soul Seeking Jesus—No. IV

Taste that Christ is precious.

December, 1841

IT IS WRITTEN, *"Unto you who believe He is precious";* and if you are a child of God, you will know and feel what the words mean (I Pet. 2:7). At one time Christ was "like a tender plant" to you, and like "a root out of a dry ground." You saw "no form nor comeliness in him, no beauty that you should desire him." At that time you were at ease in Zion—you had no concern for your soul Do you remember that time? Is it otherwise with you now? Have you been pricked in your heart by the Holy Spirit? Have you been made to see how impossible it is for man to be just with God? And has the Spirit drawn away the veil from the fair face of Immanuel, and given you an unfeigned glance at the brow that was crowned with the thorns, and the cheek from which they plucked off the hair?

Has the Spirit opened a window into the heart of Jesus, and let you see the fountainhead of that love that "passeth knowledge"? Then you will be able to say, "To me *He is precious."* If you see plainly that all your standing before God is in Him, that He is your foundation-stone, your fountain, your wedding garment, then you will feel Him to be precious. Most people refuse to come to Christ. Read Luke 14:16-24. They all with one consent began to make excuse. Why is this? Just because they do not see and feel that He is precious. But oh! if you, my dear friend, feel that He is your only righteousness, your only fountain of living water, your High Priest, your Shepherd, your Advocate, then you will say, *"He is precious!"* You will never say, "Have me excused." I carry to you the sweet invitation, "Come, for all things are now ready." Jesus is ready to wash and clothe you in His own blood and righteousness. The Holy Spirit is ready to come into your heart and make it new. The Father is ready to put His arms around your neck and kiss you (Luke 15:20). The angels are ready to give thanks for you, and to love you as a sister for eternity.

Now, will you come, for *all things are ready?* Are you now saying in your heart, "I cannot but believe I am the chief of sinners, and Jesus offers to be my refuge, my Mediator, my all in all; I feel He is precious"? Oh! dear friend, I trust you do. This only will make you happy in living, and blessed in dying. This is a poor, dying world. Man that is born of a woman is of few days and full of trouble. There is no part here that death cannot take from us. But if you have Christ, you have the only imperishable portion! Oh, may the Holy Spirit give you a firm hold of Jesus! Then we shall meet in that sweet place, where there shall be no more death, neither sorrow nor crying, neither shall there be any more pain. The Lord deal kindly and gently with you, both soul and body. Farewell, dear friend.

To a Soul Seeking Jesus—No. V

Be found in Christ.

December 8, 1841

I SEND YOU another line to tell you of Him who is altogether lovely. I have a very dear boy in my parish, who is dying just now. He said to me the other day, "I have just been feeding for some days upon the words you gave me, 'His legs are like pillars of marble set upon sockets of fine gold' (S.S. 5:15); for (said he) I am sure He is able to carry me and all my sins." You may say the same, if your eyes have been opened to see the beauty, fullness, freeness, and compassion of the Lord Jesus. Nothing but the hand of God can open your eyes to see your lost condition as it truly is.

Flesh and blood cannot reveal Him unto you, but my Father. Oh! call upon Him to do this for you. A spiritual discovery of yourself and of Jesus is better than a million of worlds to you, and to me also.

Remember, you cannot be fair in yourself before God. Song of Solomon 1:6 must be all your prayer: *"Look not upon me."* Take yourself at your best moments, you are but a vile worm in Jehovah's sight, and so am I. Remember, you may be "perfect in Christ Jesus." Allow yourself to be found in Christ. Oh! what will come of you if you are found in yourself? Where will you appear? You will shrink back, and call on rocks and mountains to fall upon you and cover you. But if you are hiding in Jesus—if your eye and heart are fixed upon His wounds made by our sins—if you are willing to be righteous in His righteousness, to lie down under the stream of His blood, and to be clothed upon with the snowy fleece of the Lamb of God—then God will love you with His whole soul exceedingly. The pure, full love of God streams through the blood and obedience of Jesus to every soul that is lying under them, however vile and wretched in themselves.

Have you tried—have you tasted the holy love of a holy God? Thy love is better than wine. It is better than all creature love or creature enjoyments. Oh! do not live—oh! do not die, out of this sweet, sweet, sin-pardoning, soul-comforting love of God! Remember, Jesus is quite willing to gather you under His wings (Matt. 23:37). Put that beyond all doubt. Remember also, the present is your only time to be saved (Eccles. 9:10). There is no believing, no repenting, no conversion in the grave—no minister will speak to you there. This is the time of conversion. We must either gain you now, or lose you forever. Oh, that you would use this little time! Every moment of it is worth a world. Your soul is very dear to me—dearer far to Jesus. Look to Him and you will be saved.

To a Soul Seeking Jesus—No. VI

Go up, leaning on Jesus.

I HAVE HEARD OF YOU from ——, and have been praying for you, that your eye may rest on Jesus, and that your soul may lie in perfect peace under His blood shed for the sins of many. I have been thanking my Father, too, for dealing so bountifully with you. "He is the Father of mercies, and the God of all comforts." I will give you a sweet verse to meditate upon: "Who is this that cometh up from the wilderness, leaning upon the beloved?" (S.S. 8:5). Do you think this is your position?

Truly this world is a wilderness if you have seen it rightly. It is a place of guilt and shame. Every natural heart is a wilderness—a dead place without a drop of living water; and then all natural hearts put together make up a wilderness world. The whole world lieth in wickedness. There are few that know and love Jesus, and these few are panting to get more of the living water. But if you have truly fled to Jesus, you are coming up from the wilderness. Now is our salvation nearer than when we believed. "The night is far spent, the day is at hand."

Have you found Jesus truly? Do you feel willing to be all vile, all hell-deserving in yourself, and to let God's dear Son be all your shield and righteousness? Oh! make sure of this. Never mind what *man* thinks of you. I would not give a straw for the opinions of men, as to whether I was safe or no. It is not what man thinks of us that will cover us on the judgment day. Oh no! You must be in Jesus, sitting at His feet, allowing Him to wash your stains away, allowing Him to enwrap your guilty soul in divine righteousness.

If you were lying at the bottom of the sea, no eye could see your deformities: so when the infinite ocean of Immanuel's righteousness flows over the soul, you are swallowed up as it were in Christ. Your blackness is never seen, only His fairness; and thus a God of truth can say, "Behold thou art fair; behold thou art fair, my love. Thou art all fair, my love; there is no spot in thee" (S.S. 4:1-7). Keep this always in memory; and when guilt comes on the conscience, as it will, lie down again beneath the righteousness of Jesus. Never lose sight of this.

Jesus must be seen by the Father instead of our guilty soul. It is no change in our black soul that is to be our covering. You must leave self, and stand in your Elder Brother. Hide behind Him. Let the Father's eye fall on Him, not on you. This is what Jesus wants. He died to be a shelter for such as you. This is what the Father wants; for He is not willing that any should perish. If you are seen by the Father a naked, guilty sinner, you must die; there is no help for it.

But if Jesus appear for you—if you hide in His wounds like the dove in the clefts of the rock, and under His snowy raiment—then the Father Himself loveth you, and now you are coming up from the wilderness. Every hour that strikes, that is an hour less between you and glory. Oh! do not grieve to part with the world if you are in Christ: an hour with Christ will make up for all your griefs and pains. Half an hour in the presence of our God will make us forget a lifetime of agony. "Leaning on her beloved!"

Is this the position of your soul? Do you feel empty, weak, and helpless; and do you see Him mighty to save, able to save to the uttermost? "His legs are like pillars of marble." This is Christ's glory, that He justifies sinners who have no righteousness, and sanctifies souls that have no inborn holiness. Let Jesus bear your whole weight. Remember, He loves to be the only support of the soul. He is a jealous Saviour. He wants to be entirely trusted.

There is nothing that you can possibly need but you will find it in Him. *All my springs are in thee.* Do you want

righteousness? He has the spirit of a weaned child to give you
(Ps. 131). Do you want love? He is the fountain of love: all
the promises of God in Him are yea and in Him amen. I
am sure, if you get a glimpse of Him, you would lay your
head in His breast and die there. May the Spirit anoint your
eyes to see Him more and more, and soften your heart to lean
on Him. Those that have leaned on Him through the wilderness shall sit with Him on the throne (Rev. 3:21). Farewell,
dear soul! the Lord feed you sweetly, as He feeds the flowers,
by silent drops of dew. _____

To the Members of a Prayer Meeting

Parable of the sower.

IT HAS BEEN a matter of great joy to me to hear that
you meet together from time to time to read the Word of
God and pray—to pray for a blessing on yourselves and
families, that you may be brought to the saving knowledge of
the Lord Jesus Christ, and to pray for ministers, that they
may be filled with the Holy Spirit, and made insatiably greedy
for the salvation of souls, and that the Word of God preached
on the Sabbath may rise and be glorified till the whole world
bow the knee at the name of Jesus.

Oh, you that have had your eyes opened to see your lost
condition by nature and by wicked works, you that have been
drawn by the Father to believe in Jesus, to wash in the blood
of the Lamb, and to put on the righteousness of God—oh!
pray with all your heart that your dear friends may be brought
to take the peace you feel, that your enemies may be brought
to the same Saviour, and that all the world may be brought
to know Him, whom to know is life eternal.

If you look at Matthew 13:3-9, you will see how much of
our preaching is in vain, and what need there is to pray that
God would open the hearts we speak to.

Many among you, I fear, are like the hard wayside, so that, when the seed falls, it cannot get into your hearts, and the devil plucks it all away (v. 3, 4). Is it not true that some of your hearts are like the footpath, trodden all the week by wicked thoughts? *"Free passage this way"* is written over your hearts—common worldly thoughts—busy, covetous desires of money—malicious thoughts—impure, abominable thoughts. Oh, who can tell what a constant thoroughfare of wicked imaginations is passing night and day through every unconverted mind! Oh, look at Genesis 6:5, and weep over the Bible description of your own hard hearts.

Now, when you come to the church on Sabbath, your heart is like a footpath; the seed cannot fall in, it lies upon the surface. You do not understand the minister. Perhaps he preaches of the desperate wickedness of the heart, and the danger you are in of going to hell if you be not born again. You feel it to be a dry subject, and turn your head away. Perhaps he is preaching of the love of Jesus, in tasting death for every man; and that He will in no wise cast the vilest sinner out. Still you feel no interest, and perhaps you fall asleep during the sermon. Oh, you are the wayside hearers, the devil plucks all the seed away.

When you turn your back on the church, you turn your back on divine things; and before you have got halfway home, the devil has carried off every word of the sermon. Yea, often, I fear, before you have got a sight of your own cottage, or the trees before the door, the devil has filled your hearts with abominable, worldly thoughts, and your tongue with evil talk, unworthy of the Sabbath. O Satan, Satan! what a cunning fiend thou art! Even when the hard hearts will not receive the Word, thou wilt not suffer it to remain; lest it should come back in a time of sickness or danger, thou carriest all away.

Dear believers, pray that it be not so with you, nor with

your friends; pray for a soft heart and a retentive memory; and often speak together of the sermons you hear, and get them harrowed into your hearts, that Satan may be cheated, and your soul saved.

Many, I fear, among you, are receiving the seed into stony places (Matt. 13:6)—receiving the Word for a while, but soon withering away in time of persecution. I fear there may be some among you who are charmed with something about the gospel, instead of cleaving in heart to Christ. I can imagine that some of the wounded Israelites, that were bitten by the serpent, were much taken with Moses, as he held up the brazen serpent, instead of looking at the serpent itself. Many are fond of ministers, who are not fond of Christ. Read over Ezekiel 33:30-32, and pray that this be not your case.

Now, I will give you two marks, by which you may know whether you are one of these unfruitful hearers. *First,* The *rocky heart* will remain the same. If you find that your liking to the gospel is from the surface, from curiosity, or fancy, or love to a minister—if you find that your rocky heart has never been broken by conviction of sin, has never melted to flow towards Jesus—then you are an empty professor; you have a name to live, while you are spiritually dead.

Second, You will endure for a while. A really converted soul is like a branch. "I am the vine, ye are the *branches.*" It will cleave to it summer and winter. But if you have only a mock conversion, you will wither away when persecution comes. God knows how soon days of trial may come in Scotland. Be ye therefore ready. He that endureth to the end shall be saved. I fear, dear friends, that many of you receive the seed among thorns (Matt. 13:7). Look into your heart and see, when you read your Bible in the morning, how many cares and anxieties are dancing before your eyes, so that you can hardly see the page you are reading. How often you come to the house of God, and you see the minister preaching of eternal things with all his might; but your heart is stuffed full of cares, and plans, and pleasures. Alas, alas! the world has got the first hold of your heart, and so you can think of nothing else. What will it profit you if you gain the whole world and lose your own soul?

One thing is plain, that thorns and wheat cannot grow on the same spot of ground; so that, if you will keep to your thorns, you must burn with them. Oh, dear souls, if you got but a glimpse of the beauty of Jesus, you would leave all and follow Him! If you got but a taste of the sweetness of forgiveness, you would count everything else but loss for the excellence of the knowledge of Christ. See how Matthew did (Matt. 9:9). He was once as worldly as yourselves, and as greedy of money as any one of you; and yet a word from the sweet mouth of Christ made him leave all. Read that sweet command of Christ (Matt. 10:37, 38). Oh! pray to be made willing to leave all for Christ. He is kinder than father or mother—more precious than son or daughter. Take up your cross, then, and follow Him.

Last of all, I trust there are some among you like the good ground (Matt. 13:8), who receive the Word into a heart broken up by the Spirit of God, watered by prayer, and who bear fruit unto *life eternal*. Have you had your hearts broken, dear friends? Has God ploughed up your hard, un-believing hearts? Have you had real concern for your perish-ing soul? Have you been driven to your knees? Have you ever wept in secret for your sins? Have you been made to tremble under your load of guilt? Do you come thus to the house of God, *your heart like an open furrow, waiting for the seed?* Inquire earnestly whether the fallow ground of your heart has ever been broken up (Jer. 4:3). *A broken heart alone can receive a crucified Christ.*

Have you understood the gospel? Have you believed the

record that God has given concerning His Son? Do you feel that it is true that God is love? that Christ has died, the just for the unjust? that He is beckoning you to come to Him? Do you believe on the Son of God? He that believeth shall be saved; he that believeth not shall be damned (Mark 16:16).

Do you bear fruit? Without holy fruit all evidences are vain. How vain would it be to prove to a farmer that his fields were good and productive, if they produced no corn! You might say to him, "Neighbor, your land is good; the soil is dry and well trenched." "Oh! but," he would say, "where is the yellow grain—where are the full ears falling before the sickle of the reaper?" Dear friends, you have awakenings, enlightenings, experiences, a full heart in prayer, and many due signs; but if you want holiness, you will never see the Lord. If you are a drinker, a swearer, a liar, a lascivious talker, a wanton, a slanderer, you are in the broad way that leads to destruction.

Read Matthew 7:21-23, and pray that you may not be deceiving your own souls. Dear believers, pray that you may bear fruit an hundredfold. Do not be content with bearing thirtyfold or sixtyfold; pray to be *sanctified wholly* (I Thess. 5:23). Pray that the whole lump may be leavened (Matt. 13:33). Pray that, day or night, in company or alone, Sabbath and weekday, you may adorn the doctrine of God our Saviour in all things. I often pray for you all, and desire that in secret, and in your families, you will not forget me.

To E. R.

A sight of corruption drives to Christ.

Dundee, 1842

I SEND YOU A HURRIED LINE, and may the Spirit accompany it with His divine power to your heart! It is a good thing to be shown much of the deceitfulness and desperate wickedness of your heart, provided it lead you to the Lord Jesus, that He may pardon and subdue it. Slightness and carnal ease are much more to be dreaded than discoveries of our leprosy.

The groans and triumphal song of a believer are not far separated, as you may see in Paul, Romans 7:24, 25: "O wretched man," and "I thank God," all in one breath! David felt the same (Ps. 73). At one verse he feels himself a fool and a beast in the sight of a holy God, and in the very next verses he is cleaving to Christ with a song of unspeakable joy (vv. 22-24). Ah! there is a sweet mystery here—bitter herbs along with our passover Lamb. It is sweet to see ourselves infinitely vile, that we may look to Jehovah our Righteousness, as all our way to the Father.

The sweet psalmist of Israel felt this on his dying bed: "Although my house be *not so* with God; yet hath He made with me an everlasting covenant" (II Sam. 23:5). His house had been the scene of many a black sin; and now, when dying, he could not but confess that it was not right with God. Not a day he had lived appeared clean—not a moment. So may you say in the house where you live, and looking at the pollutions of your own heart: "Although my house be not so with God"—although my heart and life be not so, yet hath He made with me an everlasting covenant, ordered in all things and sure.

God makes that covenant with you, when He brings you to

lay hold on Jesus as your Surety—your curse-bearing, law-fulfilling Surety. Then you are brought into the bond of the everlasting covenant, and all its blessings are yours—pardon, righteousness, consolation, grace upon grace, life, love, the spirit of supplications—all are yours, and you are Christ's, and Christ is God's.

Pray to be made like Caleb, who had another spirit, and followed the Lord fully. Follow Christ all the day. He is the continual burnt offering in whom you may have peace. He is the Rock that follows you, from whom you may have constant and infinite supplies. Give yourself wholly away to Him. You are safe in no other keeping but in the everlasting arms of Jehovah Jesus.

Keep yourself from other men's sins. Do not go *to the end of the string,* that is, going as far as you can in dallying with temptation without committing open sin. Remember that it is our happiness to be under grace, and every sin will be bitterness in the end, and will take something out of your eternal portion of glory.

Grace be with your dear and much honored minister, and with all that love Christ in sincerity. Never cease to pray for the parish, and for all parishes, that God would pour down His life-giving Spirit, to the conversion of perishing sinners and the glory of His own great name. I will remember you on the twelfth of June.—May the Lord remember us.

To J. T.

To a young boy anxious about his soul.

Collace, January 27, 1842

I WAS VERY GLAD to receive your kind note, and am glad to send you a short line in return, although my time is much taken up. You are very dear to me, because your soul

is precious; and if you are ever brought to Jesus, washed and
justified, you will praise Him more sweetly than an angel of
light. I was riding in the snow today where no foot had
trodden, and it was pure, pure white; and I thought again
and again of that verse: *"Wash me, and I shall be whiter than
snow."* That is a sweet prayer—make it your own. Often go
alone and look up to Jesus, who died to wash us from our sins,
and say, *"Wash me."*

Amelia Geddie was one day dressed in a new white frock,
with red ribbons in her bonnet, and someone said to her, "No
doubt you will think yourself very trim and clean?" "Ah! no,"
she said, *"I will never think that until I have the fine white
robe of my Redeemer's righteousness put upon me."* I am
glad, my dear boy, you think that God is afflicting you to
bring you to Himself. It is really for this that He smites you.
His heart, His hand, and His rod, are all inscribed with love.
But then, see that He does bring you to *Himself.* Do not
delay. The lake of fire and brimstone stretches beneath every
soul that lives in sin. "There is no peace, saith my God, to
the wicked." If the Lord Jesus would but draw the curtain
and let you see His own fair face, and His wounded side, and
how there is room for the guiltiest sinner in Him, you would
be drawn to Jesus with the cords of love.

I was preaching in Perth last Sabbath. When I came out,
a little girl came up to me, I think about three or four years
old. She wanted to hear of the way to be saved. Her mother
said she had been crying the whole night before about her soul,
and would take no comfort till she should find Jesus. Oh!
pray that the same Spirit may waken you. Remember, Johnnie,
you once wept for your soul too, and prayed and sought Jesus.
Have you found Him? or have you looked back, like Lot's wife,
and become a hard, cold pillar of salt? Awake again, and
call upon the name of the Lord. Your time may be short,
God only knows. The longest lifetime is short enough. It is

all that is given you to be converted in. They are the happiest
who are brought soonest to the bosom of Jesus.

Write me again. At present I must draw to a close. Give
my kindest remembrances to your mamma, and to A. when
you write. Tell him to write me. May you all meet at the
table of Jesus above; and may I be there too, a sinner saved
by grace.

_____

To A. T.

On the death of his brother, the little boy to whom the preceding letter
was written.

St. Peter's, March 1, 1842

I DID NOT THINK I was to have answered your kind
letter in the time of bitter grief. But so it pleases Jehovah,
whose will must be our will, if we would be happy. It is good
for you to bear the yoke in your youth. This is the way God
trains His saints, and especially His ministers. I saw your dear
little brother twice on his dying bed, and indeed I could not
believe he was dying, except that his calm eye was directed to
the hills of Immortality, and he seemed already to breathe
some of the atmosphere of the world of sinless joy. I do
trust and believe that he was a saved boy. You know I am
rather slow of coming to this conviction, and not fond of
speaking when I have not good evidence; but here, I think,
God has not left us in doubt.

At Blairgowrie he used several times to speak to me about
divine things, and the tear would gather in his eye when he
said that he feared he had never been brought to Jesus. Once,
when he had a sore throat, he told me he was not ready to die.
But now he was quite different. The veil seemed to be lifted
away from his heart, and he saw divine things simply and fully.

Over and over he told me that he was not afraid to die, for
Christ had died. "How kind it was in God to send Jesus to

die for sinners." He seemed tranquil and happy, even when
the pain came on in his head and made him knit his brows.
You have reason to mingle praise with your tears. Do not
sorrow as one who has no hope. Only seek a right improvement of this bereavement. He is not lost, but gone before,
and we shall soon put off this clay cottage also. And soon we
and he, made new, body and soul, shall meet the Lord in the
air, and so be forever with the Lord. I was at your house on
Sabbath night, and saw them all—sorrowful, yet rejoicing.
Your dear little brother lies like a marble statue in the peaceful sleep of death, till Jesus' voice shall waken him. Happy
boy! he shall hunger no more, neither thirst any more, neither
shall the sun light on him, nor any heat. The days of his
mourning are ended, and his eternity of love and holy joy is
begun.

Improve this sharp wind, dear A., for you will soon lose the
benefit, if not carefully sought after. Search out the Achan in
your heart at such an hour. Let affliction strike heavy blows at
your corruptions, your idolatries, and self-pleasing and *worldly
schemes*. Learn much of Christ at such an hour. Study Him at
the grave of Lazarus (John 11); and at the gate of Nain (Luke
7); and also within the veil (Rev. 1:18). Do not be
ashamed to grieve deeply; but let your sadness find relief in
the bosom that was pierced with the spear.

"Is any afflicted? let him pray." Strange, Satan often tempts
us to restrain prayer at such a time. Be very gentle towards
the souls of your kindred now.

Remember D. and H. at the throne of grace. If God had
taken them, where would they have been? Learn also that
ministers must care for lambs. "Preach the gospel to every
creature."

Pray for me, also, that I may do so, that I may be made a
better man and a more faithful pastor of old and young.

———

To Rev. H. Bonar, Kelso

Ministerial arrangements. Breathings after holiness.

August 18, 1842

I LAID ASIDE YOUR NOTE, and cannot find it again. I think you asked me for the second Sabbath of November, on my way back from London. I fear I must not do it, but abide by my former arrangement. Mr. Hamilton presses me hard to stay two Sabbaths, and I would have agreed, but am to elect elders on the second Sabbath of November. According to the new law of the church, the signed lists are read in a meeting of session on the third Sabbath after the intimation is given, so that I will need to be back, even though I should need to be in Edinburgh the week after. If spared then, I shall hold to our former arrangement.

We have had a very sweet season here during the concert, which was also our communion week. Andrew, Candlish, Cormick, Cumming, Milne, and Graham from Ireland, all assisted me. We had meetings every morning.

Your scheme was very helpful; I enclose mine. About seven hundred people attended each morning; and on the fast-day, and Sabbaths too. Several souls have been deeply awakened.

I have great desire for personal growth in faith and holiness. I love the Word of God, and find it sweetest nourishment to my soul. Can you help me to study it more successfully? The righteousness of God is all my way to the Father, for I am the chief of sinners; and were it not for the promise of the Comforter, my soul would sink in the hour of temptation.

Did you observe that the Charlinch Revival took place in the week of the concert for prayer last year?

The trials of the church are near. May we be kept in the shadow of the Rock. Farewell! May Jesus shine on you.

To Rev. R. Macdonald, Blairgowrie

Inward life. Words of counsel.

Dundee, 1842

THIS IS Friday evening, and I do not know what to preach on Sabbath next, else I would have written you at greater length; but as I am to see you so soon face to face, there is the less need of communing with ink and pen.

I hope your health keeps good, and your labors abundant; that you have a continued interest in the blood which speaketh peace, a sense of forgiveness and acceptance in the Beloved; that you feel "his right hand under your head," and the power of His indwelling Spirit dwelling in you and walking in you. These sweet experiences alone make the minister's life calm and serene, like this autumnal evening. Ah! how easy it is to speak or write about them! What a different thing to feel them! It is my constant desire, and yet I am constantly disappointed. I think I never was brought to feel the wickedness of my heart as I do now. Yet I do not feel it as many sweet Christians do, while they are high above it, and seem to look down into a depth of iniquity, deep, deep in their bosoms. Now, it appears to me as if my feet were actually in the miry clay, and I only wonder that I am kept from open sin. My only refuge is in the word, "I will put my Spirit within you." It is only by being made a partaker of the *divine nature* that I can escape the corruption that is in the world through lust.

All things go on here much as they did. I cannot say that my sermons are much shorter, though I have tried to shorten them. My meeting is still an hour and a half, nor do I see how I can shorten it. It is very well attended. A stranger started up and prayed one evening. I did not interrupt him, or take notice of it, but have thought it best to forbid it. None but ordained servants should speak in churches.

I hope you have got all your preparations well forward. Deal faithfully by all that speak to you for the communion, especially the young. If you would have a clear conscience, none but those who are seeking really to close with Jesus Christ should be allowed to take the bread and wine, if a word of yours can help it.

Be decided in keeping back the scandalous. Stir up your elders to this. They are very apt to be remiss. May you have much grace given you at this time, and peace—droppings of the Spirit, and refreshings of peace in the heart. I invite all who have any wish to speak to their minister before communicating, to do so. May you have much fruit at this time that shall appear many days hence! I have been surprised to find even a poor table service blessed. Expect much, and much will be given. Pray for me, for I am all but desolate.

———

To One of His Flock, Who Had Been Appointed to the Charge of a Girls' School in the Country

Do what you can.

Collace, July 25, 1842

I HAVE BEEN LAID ASIDE for a short time, and did not receive your letter till it was too late to send the communicant's line, which you desired. I have no doubt Mr. B. would give you a token, however, even without a line. I am truly glad to hear that you are so fully employed, and earnestly trust that your labors may be owned by God. Souls are perishing every day, and our own entrance into eternity cannot be far distant. Let us, like Mary, "do what we can," and no doubt God will bless it, and reward us openly. Sit under a living ministry if you can. Seek much personal holiness and likeness to Christ in all the features of His blessed character.

Seek to be lamblike, without which all your efforts to do good to others will be as sounding brass or a tinkling cymbal.

Pray for dear St. Peter's, that the dew may never cease to fall there; continue in prayer, and watch in the same with thanksgiving.

———

To One Awakened

Call upon a soul to choose Jesus.

Dundee, September, 1842

I WAS GLAD INDEED to see, by the line you sent me, that though your mind is dark and troubled, you have not gone back to the world. Ah, it is a false, deceiving world! It smiles only to betray. Fain would I lead you to taste the peace that passeth understanding, and that is only to be found in Jesus. You are quite wrong in thinking that I do not understand your misery. I know it well. It is true Jesus does give me peace. He washes me from all sin in His own blood. I often feel Him standing by my side and looking down upon me, saying, "Thou art mine."

Yet still I have known more misery than you. I have sinned more deeply than you. I have sinned against more light and more love, and yet I have found mercy; why may not you? Remember what James Covey said: "Tell poor sailors that none of them need to despair, since poor blaspheming Covey found mercy."

I was interrupted just while writing this, by a very little girl coming to ask, "What must I do to be saved?" Poor thing, she has been weeping till I though her heart would break. She lives several miles off; but a companion was awakened and told her, and ever since she has been seeking Christ with all her heart. I was telling her that sweet verse:

"Christ Jesus came into the world to save sinners, of whom I am the chief" (I Tim. 1:15). It will answer you also, dear friend.

Christ Jesus was God's dear Son. He made all things—sun, moon, and stars, men and angels. He was from all eternity in the bosom of the Father, and yet He came into the world. He did not say, "I will keep my throne and my happiness, and leave sinners to die and perish in their sins." No; "He came into the world." He became a babe, and was laid in a manger, for there was not room in the inn. The inn was like your heart; it was filled with other lodgers, and had no room for Jesus. He became "a man of sorrows, and acquainted with grief." He bore our sins in His own body on the tree. While we were sinners, "Christ died for us." Why did He do all this? Ah! it was to save sinners. Not to save good people, not to save angels, but sinners.

Perhaps you will say, "But I am too bad a sinner"; but Paul says, "of whom I am the chief." Paul was the chief of sinners, and yet he was saved by Christ. So Christ is willing and able to save you, though you were the chief sinner on the face of the earth. If Christ came into this world and died to save such as you, will it not be a fearful thing if you die without being saved by Him? Surely you have lived long enough without Christ. You have despised Jesus long enough.

What has the world done for you, that you love it so much? Did the world die for you? Will the world blot out your sins or change your heart? Will the world carry you to heaven? No, no! You may go back to the world if you please, but it can only destroy your poor soul. "She that liveth in pleasure is dead while she liveth" (I Tim. 5:6). Read these words in your Bible, and mark them; and if you go back, that mark will be a witness against you before the great white throne, when the books are opened. Have you not lived long enough in pleasure?

Come and try the pleasures of Christ—forgiveness and a new heart. I have not been at a dance or any worldly amusement for many years, and yet I believe I have had more pleasure in a single day than you have had all your life. You will ask, In what? In feeling that God loves me, that Christ has washed me, and in feeling that I shall be in heaven when the wicked are cast into hell. "A day in thy courts is better than a thousand" (Ps. 84:10).

I do not know what is to be the result of your anxieties. I do not know whether you will be drawn to Christ, or driven back into the whirlpool of a perishing world; but I know that all will soon be settled for eternity. I was in a very wicked family today, where a child had died. I opened my Bible, and explained this verse to them over the coffin of their little one: "It is appointed unto men once to die, but after this the judgment" (Heb. 9:27). Solemn words! we have only once to die, and the day is fixed. If you die wrong the first time, you cannot come back to die better a second time. If you die without Christ, you cannot come back to be converted and die a believer—you have but once to die. Oh! pray that you may find Christ before death finds you. "After this the judgment." Not, after this, purgatory. No further opportunity to be saved: "after this the judgment." As death leaves you, so judgment finds you. If you die unsaved, you will be so in *the judgment*. May I never see you at the left hand! If I do, you will remember how I warned you, and prayed for you, and besought you to come to the Lord Jesus.

Come to Jesus, He will in no wise cast you out.

To a Soul Inquiring After Jesus

The wise men. Guilt in us, righteousness in Jesus.

St. Peter's, Monday, September 18, 1842

I DO NOT and cannot forget you; and though it is very late, I have to write you a few lines to say, Follow on to know Jesus. I do not know if you can read my crooked writing, but I will make it as plain as I can. I was reading this morning, Luke 2:29, what old ·Simeon said when he got the child Jesus into his arms: "Now lettest thou thy servant depart in peace, according to thy word: for mine eyes have seen thy salvation." If you get a firm hold of the Lord Jesus, you will be able to say the same.

If you had died in your ignorance and sin, dear soul, where would you have been this night? Ah! how shall we sufficiently praise God if He really has brought you to the blood of the Lord Jesus Christ! If you all are really brought to Christ, it will be something like the case of the wise men of the East (Matt. 2). When they were in their own country, God attracted their attention by means of a star. They followed it, and came to Jerusalem, saying, "Where is he that is born King of the Jews? . . . for we are come to worship him." Herod and Jerusalem were troubled at the saying. No one was seeking Christ but the wise men. The world thought they were mad; but soon they saw the star again, and it led them to the house where the infant Saviour lay, His robe of state a swaddling band, His cradle the manger. Yet they kneeled down and called Him, "my Lord and my God," they got their own souls saved, and gave Him gifts, the best they had, and then departed into their own country with great joy in their hearts, and heaven in their eyes.

So it may be with you. The most around you care not for Jesus. But you are asking, "Where is He? We are come to

be saved by Him." None around you can tell. They think
you are going out of your mind. But God is leading you to
the very spot where the Redeemer is—a lowly, despised, spit-
upon, crucified Saviour. Can this be the Saviour of the world?
Yes, dear soul; kneel down and call Him your Redeemer. He
died for such as you and me. And now you may go away into
your own country again, but not as you came. You will carry
with you joy unspeakable and full of glory.

A young woman called upon me on Wednesday last, whom
I had never seen before. She said she was a stranger from
another part of Scotland; she came to this town about a year
ago, and attended St. Peter's, and there for the first time
learned that she was a sinner and needed Christ. About four
weeks ago she found rest and joy at the Saviour's feet. I said
to her, "Then you will bless God that He brought you from
your own country to this place." She said, "I often do that."
Another woman came the same evening, whom I had never
seen. She said she had been married eight years to a wicked
husband. One of her neighbors had brought her to our church,
and now she feels that Christ has saved her soul.

Thus the work goes on: "The Lord added to the church
daily such as should be saved. A young woman was with me
tonight in great distress. She said, "I have a wicked heart
within me that would sink a world." I said, "I am thankful
to hear you complain of your wicked heart, dear friend, it is
unsearchably wicked. There is not a sin committed on earth
or in hell but has its spring and fountain in your breast and
mine. You are all sin, your nature is sin, your heart is sin,
your past life is sin, your prayers are all sin." Oh, that you
would despair of being righteous in yourself! Then take the
Lord Jesus for your righteousness. In Him is no sin. And He
stood for us, and offers to be your shield, your way to the
Father.

You may be righteous in Christ with a perfect righteousness, broad as the law, and pure as the light of heaven. If you had an angel's righteousness, you might well lay it down and put on Jesus. The robe of a blood-washed sinner is far whiter than that of an angel. Do not fear the frown of the world. When a blind man comes against you in the street, you are not angry at him; you say he is blind, poor man, or he would not have hurt me.

So you may say of the poor world, when they speak evil of Christians, they are blind. If they knew their sin and misery, and the love of Jesus, they would cleave to Him also. Fear not them which kill the body, and after that have no more that they can do. Keep close to the Lord Jesus. He is greater than all that can be against you; He is the Shepherd of His sheep; He will defend you from wolves. Pray for the Holy Spirit, dear friend. Ask Him to come into your heart, and abide there. It is a mean dwelling for such a guest. Still He will make it clean and holy by dwelling in it. Ask Him to teach you to pray (Rom. 8:26, 27). He will give you "groanings that cannot be uttered." Ask Him to change your heart and make it like that of Jesus. Ask Him to write the law upon your heart, and to keep you in every time of need. I fear you are weary of my long sermons. Remember, if you are not saved, I will be a witness against you in the judgment day.

> Come, ye weary, heavy laden,
>   Lost and ruined by the Fall;
> If ye tarry till you're better,
>   You will never come at all.
> Not the righteous—sinners Jesus came to call.

Farewell! Write me soon all your heart.

———

To a Soul Inquiring After Jesus

Trials from a blind world. How the death of Christ is an atonement.

London, November 5, 1842

I PRAY FOR YOU that your faith may not fail. Hold fast by Jesus for a little while, and then we shall be forever with the Lord, where the unbelieving will never be. I got safely up to town without stopping. The young man in the coach with us was Lord P. He and I were alone all night in the railway carriage, and I would fain have told him the way to be saved, but when morning dawned I lost him. I preached twice on Thursday, and once last night, and now I am preparing for tomorrow. I feel, like John the Baptist, the voice of one crying in the wilderness. The mad world presses on like a bird hasting to the snare. They do not know that the dead are there, and her guests are in the depths of hell.

I thank God without ceasing when I remember you all— how God opened your eyes and hearts, and made you flee from the wrath to come, and believe the record which God hath given concerning His Son. "Fear none of those things which thou shalt suffer. . . Be thou faithful unto death, and I will give thee a crown of life" (Rev. 2:10). Do not be surprised if worldly people mock you, and say all manner of evil against you falsely. Jesus told you it would be so. "If you were of the world, the world would love its own." You have been long enough of the world. Did the world ever hate you then? So now, when you have come out from among them, and are cleaving to Jesus, do you think they will love you? Remember Jesus loves you. God is for you, and who can be against you? Remember, all who have gone to heaven before you suffered the same things: "These are they that came out of great tribulation" (Rev. 7:14).

You wish to understand more about Christ's death being an

atonement. I shall try to explain. The curse which Adam by
his sins brought upon us all was this, "Thou shalt surely die"
(Gen. 2:17). This included the death of the body, the death
of the soul, and the eternal destruction of both in hell. This
is the curse that hangs over every unpardoned sinner. And
our sins have only added certainty and weight to the awful
curse, for the "wages of sin is death." Now, when the Son
of God said He would become our Surety and Saviour, the
Father said, "Thou must die for them" (see John 10:17, 18):
"I lay down my life. . . This commandment have I received
from my Father."

It is true, Christ did not suffer eternal destruction in hell;
but He was a person so glorious and excellent—God's own
Son—that His short sufferings were equal in value to our
eternal agonies. So that, in the eye of law, and in God's account, Jesus has suffered all that you and I were condemned
to ˙suffer. Hence that sweet, sweet passage, "Comfort ye,
comfort ye . . . for she hath received (in Christ) of the
Lord's hand double for all her sins" (Isa. 40:1, 2). Christ's
dying for us is as much in God's account as if we had twice
over borne the eternal agonies of hell. Hence that sweet song
which God enabled you and G. to sing: "I will praise thee;
though thou wast angry with me, thine anger is turned away,
and thou comfortedst me" (Isa. 12:1). Hence also that triumphant question, "Who is he that condemneth? It is Christ
that died" (Rom. 8:34).

Keep looking, then, to Jesus, dear soul, and you will have
the peace that passeth all understanding. Whenever Satan ac-
cuses you, send him to the stripes of the Lord Jesus. Deal
gently and tenderly with your unconverted friends. Remember
you were once as blind as they. "He was despised, and we
esteemed Him not" (Isa. 53). Honor your mother in the
Lord. Give her all reverence and obedience in things not
sinful. Ask —— to read and pray over Matthew 18:3-6.

I would love much to visit the cottage on my return, but I fear I shall be kept in town till Friday, so that I must travel night and day on the way home. The Lord bless you, and keep you cleaving to Christ the true vine. You have found the pearl of great price. Go and sin no more. "If any man draw back, my soul shall have no pleasure in him." God is able to keep you from falling. In His dear arms I leave you.

────────

To a Soul That Had Begun to See Christ

What you want in yourself is to be found in double measure in Christ.

Dundee, November, 1842

WHY did you not write me a few lines? It would be occupation for you, and your soul might find rest, even when pouring itself out to another. I do trust you are seeking hard after Him whom your soul loveth. He is not far from any one of us. He is a powerful and precious Saviour, and happy are they who put their trust in Him. He is the Rose of Sharon, lovely to look upon, having all divine and human excellences meeting in Himself; and yet He is the Lily of the Valley, meek and lowly in heart, willing to save the vilest. He answers the need of your soul. You are all guilt; He is a fountain to wash you. You are all naked; He has a wedding garment to cover you. You are dead; He is life. You are all wounds and bruises; He is the Balm of Gilead. His righteousness is broader than your sin, and then He is so free. Remember the word we read at the well: "Whosoever will, let him take the water of life freely."

Look at Isaiah 40:1, 2: "Comfort ye, comfort ye my people." If you receive Christ as your Surety, you have realized double punishment for all your sins. The sufferings of Christ for us were as honoring to God as if we had suffered eternal punishment thrice over. If you will only open your arms to receive Christ as your Surety, then your iniquity is pardoned. You will taste immediate forgiveness. Your warfare with the law and an accusing conscience will be immediately accomplished. If you will only lay hold on Christ now, you will feel the force of that sweet command, "Comfort ye, comfort ye"; double comfort, double peace, for in Jesus you have suffered double wrath.

Pray over that verse; and may He who first made the light to shine out of darkness shine into your heart, to let you see the way of salvation clearly. Soon may you sing: "Thou wast angry with me; but thine anger is turned away, and thou comfortedst me." Oh, to grace how great a debtor! You are always in my prayers, that God would reveal Himself unto you. Oh, the joy of being able to say, "My beloved is mine, and I am his!"

———

To Rev. P. L. Miller, Wallacetown

A word in season to the weary.

September 14, 1842

WHEN I last saw Horatius, I agreed not to ask him at all at the autumn communion, but only in the spring. I know not well where to look, as A. is to undertake the Edinburgh communion.

Don't be cast down, except for sin. Lie low in self, and set both feet on the Rock of Ages. The sun, by one blink, can give a smile to nature; so can the Lord's face give life to our dark souls. Numbers do not prove life always. Remember the well of Sychar. Get much of the hidden life in your own soul; soon it will make life spread around.

Try prayer, when preaching fails. He can turn the water into wine. Farewell!

To Rev. J. Milne, Perth

Another word in season to a brother.

September 24, 1842

I LONG AFTER YOU in the bowels of Jesus Christ. If I make you sorry, who is he that maketh me glad, but the same who is made sorry by me? I often try to carry you to Jesus, as the four friends did the palsied man, and I have been longing to hear you say that His word to you was, "Be of good cheer, thy sins be forgiven thee"; and then, "Arise and walk." I wonder often God does not hide His face from me and lay me low, yet He restores my soul after many falls. He holds me by my right hand, and I believe will bring me to glory, though the weakest and most inconstant of all His saved ones. We shall praise more loudly than other men, and love more ardently, and gaze upon His wounds more wistfully, and say, He gave Himself for us. Cheer up, brother, and tell poor sinners what Jesus can do; for if He could not save the vilest of them all, we had never preached the good news.

If I could be with you, how gladly would I, but I do not see my way. I have promised to be in London the first Sabbath of November, which will take me soon away, and for a long time, from this poor flock.

Will you come to me on Monday the seventeenth, the last day of the concert for prayer? I think of printing a similar tract to last year's, or perhaps the same, with improvements. Suggest something.

This is Saturday, and I am empty. Oh, for fullness out of Him! Why do we not take all out of Jesus?

To Rev. J. Milne, Perth

Breathings of heart.

December 13, 1842

WE ARE TO HAVE the communion, if God permit, on January 1, 1843. A. B. is to be with me. Could you come down on the Thursday or Friday previous, and give us a good and comfortable word in the evening—either, or both if you prefer?

I preach at Newtyle tonight, and tomorrow evening at Lintrathen in a barn, and on Thursday at Kirriemuir. Pray for me, for I am a poor worm, all guilt and all helplessness, but still able to say, In the Lord have I righteousness and strength. When shall the day break and the shadows flee away? When that which is perfect is come, then that which is in part shall be done away. I long for love without any coldness, light without dimness, and purity without spot or wrinkle. I long to be at Jesus' feet, and tell Him I am all His, and ever will be.

To One Who Had Lately Taken Up the Cross

Kept by God—meeting with God.

St. Peter's, January 31, 1843

I WAS GLAD INDEED to hear that you are prospering, and that you do not repent having made Moses' choice (Heb. 11:24, 25), of which I used to tell you so often. Happy is that people whose God is the Lord. You remember what Ruth said when she cleaved to Naomi—"Thy people shall be my people, and thy God my God." I have not got your note by me, and it is late, but I will answer it tomorrow. I only write a line tonight to strengthen your faith, "that I may be comforted together with you, by the mutual faith both of you and me"

(Rom. 1:12). I have been remaining quiet since I wrote you last, that I may gather strength for the North. I expect hard service, but I hope Jesus will be with me. You remember the sweet promise Jacob got at Bethel while he slept at the foot of that wondrous ladder: "Behold, I am with thee, and will keep thee in all places whither thou goest; for I will not leave thee until I have done that which I have spoken to thee of." That promise is to you and me as truly as to Jacob. Therefore do not fear though you may be taken among those who are strangers to Jesus and His love.

There is a sweet promise (Ezek. 11:16). I have felt its preciousness in foreign lands. Jesus Himself will be our sanctuary not made with hands. I was preaching on Thursday last on Revelation 19:12: "On his head were many crowns," trying to teach them the kingly office of the Lord Jesus. It was a very solemn night. On Sabbath I lectured on Hebrews 9: 9, 10, and preached in the evening on Isaiah 49:5: "Though Israel be not gathered"; showing that however many will be lost by unbelief, still Christ would not lose one beam of His glory. If all the world were blind, and said the sun was dark, that would not take away one bright ray from it. It was a very awful subject, and my heart yearned over poor lost sinners. Four little girls have come since, asking, "What must I do to be saved?" Three of them were awakened before, and one very lately. A widow came last night whom I never saw before, to tell me that she had found the Lord Jesus. Tonight we have been at a large meeting about the tracts which are distributed monthly to every house in town—a very sweet society.

It is now late, and I am talking a little while with you as we used to do before retiring. Did you read Genesis 32 today? What a solemn chapter! Do you ever come to a spot you can call Mahanaim, where the angels of God meet you? I trust you are one of the heirs of salvation, and that the angels are sent forth to minister to you. Unconverted souls have no such

privilege. You see Jacob was going on God's errand, at God's
command (see 31:3), when the angels of God met him. Oh,
it is sweet to go on God's errands! How long we went Satan's,
and the world's, and our own, "serving divers lusts and pleasures!"

Do you not feel your heart lighter now as you walk on the
narrow way? Is not a Christian's darkest hour calmer than the
world's brightest? Is not Jacob's prayer in his distress an interesting one? He puts God in remembrance of His promise.
This is what we should do: "The Lord which said unto me."
And "Thou saidst, I will surely do thee good" (Gen. 32:9-12).
God commands us to do this: "Put me in remembrance" (Isa.
43:26). It is a blessed way of praying, to pray upon a promise,
and to plead, "Do as thou hast said." You remember *Faith's
Plea,* a little book Miss C. gave you. Who do you think the
man was that wrestled with Jacob? Was it not Jesus, the sinner's Friend? At the daybreak Jacob began to see His blessed
features, and when his thigh was out of joint he could do
nothing but hang upon Him. This is what you and I should do.
Say, "I will not let thee go except thou bless me." Are there
not some spots that you can call Peniel, where you have met
Jehovah-Jesus face to face? When you do get into His presence, oh, do not weary of it; do not soon let go your hold. I
am sure we lose much by our slight hold on Jesus.

I was telling an interesting story tonight. Thirty thousand
Spaniards lately came over the Pyrenees into France, to escape
the civil wars. Some Geneva youths determined to take the
opportunity of providing them with Spanish Testaments. The
London Society granted them ten thousand copies. With these
they set off and distributed freely. But the Spanish priests had
come over, and would not allow the Spaniards to receive or
keep them. Many were burned or torn; they called them "The
Plague." One Spanish youth bought a Testament—kept it,
read it, believed on Jesus; and when his countrymen returned

to Spain, he stayed behind to hear more of these wonders of redeeming love. Was not this one precious soul worth all the expense and trouble a thousand times over? "Be not weary in well-doing, for in due season we shall reap if we faint not."

Be active for God; you have lost much time already. Do nothing rashly, nothing unfeminine: give no just cause for reproach, but do not fear ridicule or proud men's sneers. If they knew what you know, they would rather inquire, "Oh, that I knew where I might find Him!" Meanwhile, good night. May He who never slumbers nor sleeps watch over you all, and keep you till your dying day! May Jesus be near you, and make you His own!

I fear I must not visit Kelso this season. I leave for the North on Monday, and do not expect to be home till the twenty-fifth. I fear this cuts off all hope of my visiting R—— the time you mention. I do hope to be in England early in the summer, but before that I do not see my way. But I shall gladly leave myself in Jehovah's hand. Present duty is ours; neither must we consult our mere wishes. If I hear from you before I leave, I shall try and send you another line. I am glad you teach in the classes, and I think I see you telling all you know. Remember Paul; when his heart was changed, for thirty years he did nothing else than serve Jesus. He labored away in the service of Him who died for him, and plucked him from the burning. It is interesting to notice also, how often Paul told them of his own conversion. He told it to the Jews (Acts 22); then to Agrippa (Acts 26); then to the Galatians (Gal. 1:13-16); then to the Philippians (Phil. 3:4). I think this is an example for us to do the same, cautiously and wisely. John Newton once preached in Newgate to the prisoners. He chose I Timothy 1:15 for his text, and told them his own history, so that they wept and he wept.

Pray for me still, that my way may be made plain. This is one of the blessings of having spiritual children, that you will

surely pray for me. Do not cease to pray for——, that her
eyes may be opened to see her true condition, and that she
may call upon Jesus before it be too late. I must now leave you
and write a little to others. I preach at Wallacetown tonight.
May the Master be there! Oh, He is a sweet Master! One smile
from Jesus sustains my soul amid all the storms and frowns of
this passing world. Pray to know Jesus better. Have no other
righteousness, no other strength, but only Jesus. Soon we shall
see Him coming in the clouds of heaven. May you be kept
faithful to death.

————

To M.B.,

To one of his flock who had felt deserted in soul.

Peterhead, February 7, 1843

I WAS VERY HAPPY to hear from you. I grieve to hear of
your sorrow; but Job's sorrow was deeper, and David's also
(Ps. 42). If you cannot say, "I found him whom my soul
loveth," is it not sweet that you can say, "I am sick of love"—
He is my Beloved still, though He has withdrawn Himself and
is gone for a time?

Seek into the cause of your declension. See that it be not
some Achan in your bosom, some idol set up in the corner of
your heart. See that it be not some allowed sin, an unlawful
attachment that is drawing you away from the bleeding side of
Jesus, and bringing a cloud between you and the bright Sun
of Righteousness. When you find out the cause, confess it and
bewail it in the ear of a listening God. Tell Him all; keep
nothing back. If you cannot find out the cause, ask Him to tell
it you. Get it washed in the blood of Jesus; then get it sub-
dued (Micah 7:19). None but the Lord Jesus can either pardon or subdue. Remember not to rest in a state of desertion.

"I will rise now and go about the city." And yet do not think
that you have some great thing to do before regaining peace
with God. The work on which peace is given has all been done
by Jesus for us. "The word is nigh thee." Christ is the end of
the law for righteousness to every one that believeth.

The sunshine is always sweeter after we have been in the
shade; so will you find Jesus in returning to Him. True, it is
better never to wander; but when you have wandered, the
sooner you return the happier you will be. "I will go and return to my first husband; for then it was better with me than
now" (Hos. 2:7).

Do not delay, but humble yourself under His mighty hand,
and He will exalt you in due season. I have been speaking
tonight in this place to a large and attentive audience on
Zechariah 9:9. May you be enabled to apply it. Remember me
to Mrs. K——, and also to all your fellow servants whom I
know and love in the truth. Tell N—— C—— to make sure
that she is in Christ, and not to take man's word for it. Tell
E—— L—— to abide in Jesus; and tell her brother to take
care lest he be a rotten branch of the true vine. Tell W——
J—— to be faithful unto death.

I have no greater joy than to know that my children walk in
the truth.

————

TO THE REV. ALEX. GATHERER, DUNDEE

During his visit to the North.

Ellon, February 20, 1843

I WAS GLAD to hear from you in this far-off land. I am
deeply grieved to hear that fever still prevails. God is
pleading hard with my poor flock. I am glad to hear of your
preaching on such precious texts, and hope they were blessed to

many. Never forget that the end of a sermon is the salvation of the people. I feel more and more that it is God's cause in which we are embarked. King Jesus is a good master. I have had some sweet seasons of communion with an unseen God, which I would not give for thousands of gold and silver. May you have much of His presence with you!

To One Who Had Met with a Bereavement

March 8, 1843

I KNOW you will be wearying to hear from me; but it has scarcely been in my power till now, I have had so many things to do since my return. I trust Jesus is making known to you His power to calm the soul in the deepest trials. "Where is your faith?" He said to the disciples; and He says to you, "All things are possible to him that believeth."

I was much afflicted for your sakes to read the solemn letter you sent me. Do you remember the words, "He must needs go through Samaria"? We are getting new light upon their meaning.

I was reading today about godly sorrow, and the sorrow of the world. Do you know the difference between these two?

Had this blow come upon you in your unconverted state, it would have wrought, perhaps, only the sorrow of the world—carnal sorrow that drives us away from God and makes us murmur and complain of His dealings, like Pharaoh who turned harder every blow that Gód struck—even the loss of his first-born only hardened him. But godly sorrow, or more literally, "sorrow towards God," grief that brings us to the feet of God, worketh repentance unto salvation, not to be repented of. It is used as an instrument to bring the humbled soul to cleave to Jesus. Oh, may it be so with you!

Humble yourselves under the mighty hand of God, and He

shall exalt you in due season. Improve the season while it lasts. The farmer improves the seedtime, to cast in the seed into the furrows. Now, when God has made long the furrow by the plough of affliction in your heart, oh see that you let the sower sow the good seed deep in your heart. I trust H. B. may be made a great blessing and comfort to you next Sabbath. May you all be enabled to meet with Jesus at His own table, and to tell Him all your sorrows there, and ask grace to keep you in the evil day.

I would like well to be with you; but in body this may not be. In heart I am often with you, because I can say what I was reading today: "Ye are in my heart to live and to die with you" (II Cor. 7:3).

I preached twenty-seven times when I was away, in twenty-four different places. I was very, very tired, and my heart has beat too much ever since, but I am wonderfully well. I have "fightings without and fears within" just now. Do pray earnestly for me—as indeed I know you do. I wish you had been with me last night. When I was away, the people agreed to meet twice a week in the lower schoolroom to pray for me; and now that I have come back, we have continued the meetings. The school is quite crammed. Such sweet, loud singing of praise I never heard, and many tears.

I stood by a poor socialist in the agonies of death today. He was quite well yesterday. He anxiously wished me to come and pray. Oh, to be ready when the Bridegroom comes!

Farewell. Peace from above fill your soul.

ANOTHER TO ONE BEREAVED

Betake yourself to Him that is ever the same.

March 9, 1843

I DID NOT THINK I would have been so long in answering you in your time of sorrow, but I have been more than occupied. I earnestly trust that this sad bereavement may be greatly blessed by God to you. Pray that you may not lose this precious opportunity of giving your hand and heart forever away to the Lord Jesus. May Hosea 2:14 be fulfilled in you all: "Behold, I will allure her, and *bring her into the wilderness, and speak comfortably unto her*"; and that clear promise: "I will cause you to pass under the rod, and I will bring you into the bond of the covenant" (Ezek. 20:37). This solemn event shows you what I always used to tell you, *how short* your life is, what a vapor, how soon the joys that depend on the creatures may be dried up; that "one thing is needful," and that Mary was wise in choosing *the good part that cannot be taken away from her.*

You remember the first night you were in St. Peter's I showed you this preaching from Psalm 16:6: "The lines have fallen to me in pleasant places, and I have a goodly heritage." I am indeed more than ever anxious about you, that you receive not the grace of God in vain. It is the furnace that tries the metal, and it is affliction that tries the soul whether it be Christ's or not. I am jealous over you with a godly jealousy, lest the furnace should show you to be reprobate silver. Do let me hear how your soul truly is, whether you can see the hand of a Father in this bereavement, and whether you are more than ever determined, through grace, to be the Lord's. How sweet that *Jesus ever liveth!* He is the same yesterday, and today, and forever.

You will never find Jesus so precious as when the world is one vast howling wilderness. Then He is like a rose blooming in the midst of the desolation, a rock rising above the storm. The Bible, too, is more full of meaning. Have you ever prayed over that verse: *"He doth not afflict willingly?"* (Lam. 3:33). O precious book, that conveys such a message to the mourner's dwelling! And does not trial bring more meaning out of that verse: "We know that *all* things work together for the good of them that love God, to them who are the called according to his purpose" (Rom. 8:28)? The Bible is like the leaves of the lemon tree—the more you bruise and wring them, the sweeter the fragrance they throw around. "Is any afflicted? let him pray." Do you not find that prayer is sweeter now? The soul finds vent for its feelings toward God. *"Call upon me in the day of trouble:* I will deliver thee, and thou shalt glorify me." When I had my fever abroad, Mr. Bonar whispered that verse into my ear. I had nearly lost all my faculties —I could remember nothing except that I was far from home; but that verse kept sounding in my ears when I was nearly insensible: "I called, and he delivered me."

Are you preparing to go to the Lord's Table next Lord's day? May you indeed have the wedding garment—righteousness without works—and see the King in His beauty, and give yourself away to Him, saying, "I am my beloved's, and my beloved is mine!" It should be a solemn sacrament to you. I can add no more. Write me soon, dear G——, and tell me all that is in your heart, and whether the voice of the Comforter does not say, Be still! when death has left so deep a silence in your family.

To One Complaining of the Plagues of the Heart

Passing on to glory.

St. Peter's, March 8, 1843

I SEND A FEW LINES to you in answer to yours. You complain of the plague of your own heart, and so you will till you die. You know little yet of its chambers of imagery. All that is ours is sin. Our wicked heart taints all we say and do; hence the need of continual atonement in the blood of Jesus. It is not one pardoning that will serve the need of our souls. We must have daily, hourly pardons. I believe you are in the furnace, but for a short time. Soon the Bridegroom will come, and we shall be with Him, and like Him, and God shall wipe away all tears from our eyes. I burst through all the cobwebs of present things, and, His Spirit anointing my eyes, look at Jesus as one beside me. Blessed Elder Brother, with two natures—God and man—ever-living, never-dying, never-changing!

I was preaching last Sabbath on Hebrews 9:13, 14: "He through the eternal Spirit offered himself." It was very sweet to me. In the afternoon I preached on Revelation 2:4, 5: "I have this against thee, that thou has left thy first love." I fear many of my people have done so; therefore it was very suitable. Several I see have felt it very deeply. In the evening I preached on Psalm 78:41: "They turned back, and tempted God, and limited the Holy One of Israel"—on the sinfulness of limiting God. It was a very sweet and solemn day.

Meantime, stay your soul on God. "Thou wilt keep him in perfect peace whose mind is stayed on thee, because he trusteth in thee." A few more trials, a few more tears, a few more days of darkness, and we shall be forever with the Lord! "In this tabernacle we groan, being burdened." All dark things shall yet be cleared up, all sufferings healed, all blanks supplied, and we shall find fullness of joy (not one drop wanting)

in the smile and presence of our God. It is one of the laws of
Christ's kingdom, "We must through much tribulation enter
into the kingdom of God." We must not reckon upon a smooth
road to glory, but it will be a short one. How glad I am that
you have "received the word in much affliction, with joy of the
Holy Ghost"! Cleave closely to Jesus, that you may not have
to say in a little, "Oh that I had affliction back again to quicken
me in prayer, and make me lie at His feet!"

> Trials make the promise sweet,
>   Trials give new life to prayer;
> Trials bring me to His feet,
>   Lay me low, and keep me there.

This land will soon be strangely convulsed, if God prevent
not. The plans now preparing for carrying the gospel into
every corner of the land are sweet indeed. If I be spared and
strengthened, I go to London toward the end of April. My
stay must be very short. It is also intended to send me to the
General Assembly in May. My poor flock, how I yearn over
them! So many of them careless, and judgment at the door!
Mr. Burns comes to me tomorrow.

I must add no more, as I have work before me. May you experience more and more, that "when he giveth quietness, none
can make trouble"—even as you once experienced the other,
"When he hideth his face, who then can behold him?" Soon
we shall see Him as He is; then our trials shall be done. We
shall reign with Him, and be entirely like Him. The angels
will know us by our very faces to be brothers and sisters of
Jesus.

Remember Jesus *for us* is all our righteousness before a holy
God, and Jesus *in us* is all our strength in an ungodly world.
Persevere even to death; eternal life will make up for all.
Remember Barnabas' advice, "Cleave to the Lord"—not to
man, but to the Lord. May He perfect all that concerneth you.
Do not fear the face of man. Remember how small their
anger will appear in eternity.

BIBLE MESSAGES

Those who had an opportunity of hearing Mr. McCheyne at those times when his soul was most enlarged, and his lips fresh touched with the live coal, will be ready to remark that some of his most impressive Sermons (*e.g.*, "The Great White Throne") are not here. This is true; and the reason is, that they were not found in his manuscripts. I might indeed have given full notes from the records of hearers; but it was far better to adhere to what was found in his own handwriting, that so the reader may be sure that, if he has not before him the discourses as they were delivered, he has at least what passed through the author's soul.

BIBLE MESSAGES

MESSAGE I

"Jesus saith unto him, I am the way, the truth, and the life; no man cometh
unto the Father but by me."—John 14:6.

IT IS THE SAYING of an old divine, that God often orders
it that when He is in hand with the greatest mercies for us,
then we are most of all sinning against Him; which He doth to
magnify His love the more.

In the words I have read, we find an example of this. At no
time did the heart of Jesus overflow with a tenderer and more
sovereign love to His disciples, than when He said, "Let not
your heart be troubled." They were troubled by many things.
He had told them that He was going to leave them; He had
told them that one should betray Him, that another should
deny Him, that they should all be offended because of Him
that very night; and perhaps they thought He was going from
them in anger. But whatever the cause of their trouble was,
Jesus' bosom was like a vessel full to overflowing, and these
words were the overflowing drops of love: "Let not your heart
be troubled: ye believe in God, believe also in me."

Surely such words of confiding tenderness were never whispered in this cold world before; and oh then, think how cold,
how dark, how dull is the question with which Thomas breaks
in upon the heavenly discourse: "Thomas saith unto him, Lord,
we know not whither thou goest; and how can we know the
way?" And yet how condescendingly does Jesus bear with their

cold-hearted dullness! How lovingly does He begin the very
alphabet of salvation with them, and not only answers, but
overanswers Thomas—gives him more than he could ask or
think. He asked about the way and the place; but Christ answers, "I am the way, the truth, and the life: no man cometh
unto the Father but by me." Regarding this, then, as a complete description of the gospel salvation, let us go over the
different parts of it.

I. *Christ is the Way.*—"I am the way; no man cometh,"
and so forth. The whole Bible bears witness that by nature we
have no way to the Father. We are by nature full of sin, and
God is by nature infinitely holy, that is, He shrinks away from
sin. Just as the sensitive plant, by its very nature, shrinks away
from the touch of a human hand, so God, by His very nature,
shrinks away from the touch of sin. He is everlastingly separate
from sinners; He is of purer eyes than to behold iniquity.

1. This was impressively taught to Adam and the patriarchs.
As long as Adam walked holily, God dwelt in him, and walked
in him, and communed with him; but when Adam fell, "God
drove the man out of paradise; and he placed at the east of the
garden of Eden, cherubim and a flaming sword, which turned
every way to keep the way of the tree of life." This flaming
sword between the cherubim was a magnificent emblem of God
—the just and sin-hating God. In the bush, He appeared to
Moses as a consuming fire; in the temple, He appeared between
the cherubim in the milder glory of the Shekinah; but here He
appeared between the cherubim as a sword, a just and sin-
hating God.

And I beseech you to remark, that this flaming sword turned
every way to keep the way of the tree of life. If it had not
turned *every way*—if it had left some footpath unglared across
—then Adam might have stolen in by that footpath, and made
his own way to the tree of life. But no: whatever avenue he
tried, however secret, however narrow, however steep and diffi-

cult, however silently he crept along, still this flaming meteor met him, and it seemed to say, "How can men be just with God? by the deeds of the law there shall no flesh living be justified." Well might Adam sit down, wearied with the vain search for a pathway into life; for man by nature has no way to the Father.

But Christ says, "I am the way." As He says in Psalm 16, "Thou wilt show me the path of life." No man could find out this path of life; but Jesus says, "Thou wilt show it me: in thy presence is fullness of joy; at thy right hand are pleasures for evermore." *Jesus pitied* the poor sons of Adam vainly struggling to find out a way into the paradise of God, and He left the bosom of the Father, just that He might open up a way for us into the bosom of the Father. And how did He do it? Was it by escaping the vigilance of the flaming sword? No; for it turned every way. Was it by exerting His divine authority, and commanding the glittering blade to withdraw? No; for that would have been to dishonor His Father's law instead of magnifying it. He therefore became a man in our stead—yea, became sin. God caused to meet on Him the iniquities of us all. He advanced in our stead to meet that fiery meteor, He fell beneath its piercing blade; for He remembered the word of the prophet, which is written: "Awake, O sword! against my shepherd, and against the man that is my fellow, saith the Lord of hosts."

And now, since the glittering blade is bathed in the side of the Redeemer, the guiltiest of sinners—whoever you be, whatever you be—may enter in over His bleeding body, may find access to the paradise of God, to eat of the tree of life, and live forever. Come quickly—doubt not; for He says, *I am the way.*

2. The same fact—that man has by nature no way to the Father—was impressively taught to Moses and the people of Israel.

When God condescended to dwell among the children of
Israel, He dwelt peculiarly in the Holiest of all—the innermost
apartment of the Jewish Temple. There the visible token of His
presence rested between the cherubim, at one time described
to us as a light inaccessible and full of glory, at another time as
a cloud that filled the Temple. But this innermost apartment, or
Holiest of all (or secret place, as it is called in the Psalms),
was separated from the holy place by a curtain or veil; and
through that veil no man was allowed to pass, lest he should
die, except the high priest, who entered in once in the year,
not without blood. Now, no picture could express more plainly
that the way into the Holiest was not made manifest, that no
sinful man has any way of coming into the presence of God.

But Jesus says, "I am the way." Jesus was grieved that we
were shut out from the Holiest of all—from the presence of
God; for He knew by experience that in that presence there is
fullness of joy. But how did He open the way? Did He pull
aside the veil, that we might steal in secretly and easily into
the presence of the Father? No; but He offered Himself an
offering to satisfy divine justice and reconcile us to God. "He
said, It is finished, and bowed his head and gave up the ghost.
And, behold, the veil of the temple was rent in twain, from
the top to the bottom." It is finished: the punishment of the
law is borne, the demands of the law are answered, the way is
finished, the veil is rent from the top to the bottom! Not a
shred of the dreadful curtain now remains to intercept us. The
guiltiest, the vilest sinner of you all, has now liberty to enter in
through the rent veil, under the light of Jehovah's countenance, to dwell in the secret of His Tabernacle, to behold His
beauty, and to inquire in His Temple.

And now, my friends, is this your way of coming to the Father? Christ says, "I am the way; no man cometh unto the
Father but by me." If, then, you will still keep to your own
way, whatever it be—whether it be the way of tears, or pen-

ances, or vows of amendment, or hopes that God will not deal strictly—if you will not be warned, you will find in the judgment day that the cherubic sword turned every way, and that you are left a prey to the consuming fire.

But oh! if there be one soul that can find no peace in any self-righteous way, if there be one of you who find that you are lost in yourself, behold, Christ says to you, "I am *the* way," as He says in another place, "I am *the* door." It is a full, free, and open way, and it is a way for sinners. Why wait a moment longer? There was once a partition wall between you and God; but Christ hath cast it down. God was once angry; but His anger is turned away from this blessed path. In Christ He is ever well pleased.

II. *Christ is the Truth.*—The whole Bible and the whole of experience bear witness that by nature we are ignorant of *the truth.* No doubt there are many truths which an unconverted man does know. He may know the truths of mathematics and arithmetic—he may know many of the common everyday truths; but still it cannot be said that an unconverted man knows *the truth,* for Christ is the truth. Christ may be called the keystone of the arch of truth. Take away the keystone of an arch, and the whole becomes a heap of rubbish. The very same stones may be there; but they are all fallen, smothered, and confused, without order, without end. Just so take Christ away, and the whole arch of truth becomes a heap of rubbish. The very same truths may be there; but they are all fallen, without coherence, without order, without end.

Christ may be called the sun of the system of truth. Take away the sun out of our system, and every planet would rush into confusion. The very same planets would be there; but their conflicting forces would draw them hither and thither, orb dashing against orb in endless perplexity. Just so take Christ away, and the whole system of truth rushes into confusion. The same truths may be in the mind, but all conflicting and jarring in inextricable mazes; for "the path of the wicked is as darkness; they know not at what they stumble." But let Christ be revealed to an unconverted soul—let it not be merely a man speaking about Christ unto him, but let the Spirit of God reveal Him—and there is revealed, not a truth, but *the truth*. You put the keystone into the arch of truth; you restore the sun to the center of the system. All truth becomes orderly and serviceable in that mind.

Now he knows the truth with regard to himself. Did the Son of God really leave the bosom of the Father to bear wrath in our stead? Then I must be under wrath. Did the Lord Jesus become a servant, that He might obey the will of God instead of sinners? Then I must be without any righteousness, a child of disobedience.

Again, knowing Christ, he knows the truth with regard to God. Did God freely give up His Son to the death for us all? Then, if I believe in Jesus, there is no condemnation to me. God is my Father, and God is love.

My friends, have you seen Christ, who is the truth? Has He been revealed to you, not by flesh and blood, but by the Spirit of our God? Then you know how true it is that in Him "are hid all the treasures of wisdom and knowledge," that He is the "Alpha and Omega," the beginning and the ending of all knowledge. But if you have not seen Christ, then you know nothing yet as you ought to know; all your knowledge is like a bridge without a keystone, like a system without a sun. What good will it do you in hell that you knew all the sciences in the world, all the events of history, and all the busy politics of your little day? Do you not know that your very knowledge will be turned into an instrument of torture in hell? Oh, how will you wish in that day that you had read your newspaper less and your Bible more, that with all your getting, you had got understanding, that with all your knowledge, you had known the Saviour, whom to know is life everlasting!

III. *Christ is the Life.*—The whole Bible bears witness that by nature we are dead in trespasses and sins, that we are as unable to walk holily in the world, as a dead man is unable to rise and walk.

Both Scripture and experience alike testify that we are by nature dead in trespasses and sins; and yet it is not a death in which we are wholly inactive, for in it we are said to walk according to the course of this world, according to the prince of the power of the air.

This truth is taught us impressively in that vision of the prophet Ezekiel, where he was carried out by the Spirit, and set down in the midst of an open valley full of dry bones; and as he passed by them round about, behold, there were very many in the open valley, and lo! they were very dry.

Just such is the view which every child of God gets of the world. The dry bones are very many, and they are very dry; and he asks the same question which God asked of Ezekiel: "Can these bones live?" Oh yes, my friends; and does not experience teach you the same thing? True, the dead cannot know that they are dead; and yet, if the Lord touch your heart, you will find it out. We prophesy to dry bones; for this is the Lord's way; while we prophesy, the breath enters in. *Look back over your life, then.* See how you have walked according to the course of this world. You have always been like a man swimming with the stream, never like a man swimming against the current. *Look into your heart,* and see how it has turned against all the commandments: you feel the Sabbath to be a weariness, instead of calling it a delight and honorable.

If ever you tried to keep the commandments of God, if ever you tried to keep your eyes from unlawful desires, your tongue from words of anger or gossiping or bitterness, your heart from malice and envy and covetousness, if ever you have tried this— and I fancy most unconverted men have tried it—if ever you have tried this, did you not find it impossible? It was like

raising the dead. Did you not find a struggle against yourself?
Oh how plain that you are dead—not born again! Marvel not
that we say unto you, Ye must be born again. You must be
joined to Christ, for Christ *is the life*.

Suppose it were possible for a dead limb to be joined into a
living body so completely that all the veins should receive the
purple tide of living blood, suppose bone to join to bone, and
sinew to sinew, and nerve to nerve, do you not see that that
limb, however dead before, would become a living limb? Before, it was cold and stiff and motionless, and full of corruption; now it is warm and pliable, and full of life and motion.
It is a living limb, because joined on to that which is life.
Or, suppose it possible for a withered branch to be grafted into
a living vine so completely that all the channels should receive
the flow of the generous sap, do you not see that that branch,
however dead before, becomes a living branch? Before, it was
dry and fruitless and withered; now, it is full of sap, of life,
and vigor. It is a living branch, for it is joined to the vine,
which is its life. Well, then, just in the same way, Christ is the
life of every soul that cleaves to Him. He that is joined to the
Lord is one spirit. Is your soul like a dead limb—cold, stiff, motionless, and full of corruption? Cleave you to Christ, be joined
to Him by faith, and you shall be one spirit, you shall be made
warm and vigorous and full of activity in God's service.

Is your soul like a withered branch—dry, fruitless, and withered, wanting both leaves and fruit? Cleave you to Christ; be
joined to Him, and you shall be one spirit. You will find it
true that Christ is the life; your life will be hid with Christ in
God. You will say, "I live; yet not I, but Christ liveth in me;
and the life which I now live in the flesh, I live by the faith of
the Son of God, who loved me, and gave himself for me."

Remember then, my unbelieving friends, the only way for
you to become holy is to become united to Christ. And remember you, my believing friends, that if ever you are relaxing

in holiness, the reason is, you are relaxing your hold on Christ. "Abide in me, and I in you; so shall ye bear much fruit. Severed from me, ye can do nothing."

DUNDEE, 1836.

MESSAGE II

"Consider the Apostle and High Priest of our profession, Christ Jesus."—
Hebrews 3:1.

WHEN A TRAVELER passes very rapidly through a country, the eye has no time to rest upon the different objects in it, so that, when he comes to the end of his journey, no distinct impressions have been made upon his mind; he has only a confused notion of the country through which he has traveled.

This explains how it is that death, judgment, eternity, make so little impression upon most men's minds. Most people never stop to think, but hurry on through life, and find themselves in eternity before they have once put the question, "What must I do to be saved?" More souls are lost through want of consideration than in any other way.

The reason men are not awakened and made anxious for their souls is that the devil never gives them time to consider. Therefore God cries, Stop, poor sinner, stop and think. Consider your ways. "Oh that you were wise, that you understood this, that you considered your latter end!" And, again He cries, "Israel doth not know, my people doth not consider."

In the same way does the devil try to make the children of God doubt if there be a Providence. He hurries them away to the shop and market. Lose no time, he says, but make money. Therefore God cries, Stop, poor sinner, stop and think; and Jesus says, "Consider the lilies of the field, how they grow . . . consider the ravens, which have neither storehouse nor barn."

In the same way does the devil try to make the children of

God live uncomfortable and unholy lives. He beguiles them
away from simply looking to Jesus: he hurries them away to
look at a thousand other things, as he led Peter, walking on
the sea, to look round at the waves. But God says, Look here,
consider the Apostle and High Priest of your profession; look
unto Me and be ye saved; run your race, looking unto Jesus;
consider Christ, the same yesterday, today, and forever.

I. *Believers should live in daily consideration of the greatness and glory of Christ.*

1. There was once a time when time was not—when there
was no earth, neither sun, nor moon, nor star; a time when you
might have wandered through all space, and never found a
resting-place to the sole of your foot, when you would have
found no creatures anywhere, but God everywhere; when there
were no angels with golden harps hymning celestial praises,
but God alone was all in all.

Question—Where was Jesus then?

Answer—He was with God. "In the beginning was the
Word, and the Word was with God." He was near to God,
and in perfect happiness there. "The Lord possessed me in
the beginning of his way, before his works of old. Then I
was by him as one brought up with him; and I was daily his
delight, rejoicing always before him." He was in the bosom of
God: "The only begotten Son which is in the bosom of the
Father." He was in perfect glory there: "O Father, glorify
thou me with thyself, with the glory which I had with thee before the world was!"

Question—What was Jesus then?

Answer—He was God. The Word was with God, and "was
God." He was equal with the Father. "He thought it not rob-
bery to be equal with God." He was rich. He was the bright-
ness of His Father's glory, and the express image of His
person.

Now, brethren, could I lift you away to that time when God

was alone from all eternity; could I have shown you the glory of Jesus then—how He dwelt in the bosom of the Father, and was daily His delight; and could I have told you, "That is the glorious Being who is to undertake the cause of poor lost sinners; that is He who is going to put Himself in their room and stead, to suffer all they should suffer, and obey all they should obey; consider Jesus, look long and earnestly, weigh every consideration in the balance of the soundest judgment; consider His rank, His nearness, His dearness to God the Father; consider His power, His glory, His equality to God the Father in everything; consider, and say do you think you would entrust your case to Him? do you think He would be a sufficient Saviour?" Oh, brethren, would not every soul cry out, He is enough—I want no other Saviour?

2. Again, there was a time when this world sprang into being—when the sun began to shine, and earth and seas began to smile. There was a time when myriads of happy angels springing into being, first spread their wings, doing His commandments—when the morning stars sang together, and all the sons of God shouted for joy.

Question—What was Jesus doing then?

Answer—"Without him was not anything made that was made. . . By him were all things created that are in heaven, and that are in earth, visible and invisible, whether they be thrones, or dominions, or principalities, or powers: all things were created by him and for him." Oh, brethren, could I lift you away back to that wonderful day, and show you Jesus calling all the angels into being, hanging the earth upon nothing; could you have heard the voice of Jesus saying, "Let there be light, and there was light"; and could I have told you, "That is He who is yet to undertake for sinners; consider Him, and see if you think He will be a sufficient Saviour; look long and earnestly"; good news, good news for sinners, if this mighty Being undertakes for us! I can as little doubt the sureness and completeness

of my salvation as I can doubt the sureness of the solid earth
beneath my feet.

3. But the work of creation is long since passed. Jesus has
been upon our earth. And now He is not here—He is risen.
Eighteen hundred years and more have passed since Christ was
upon the earth.

Question—Where is Jesus now?

Answer—"He is set down at the right hand of the Majesty
on high." He is upon the throne with God in His glorified
body, and His throne is forever. A scepter is put into His hand
—a scepter of righteousness, and the oil of gladness is poured
over Him. All power is given to Him in heaven and on earth.

Oh, brethren, could you and I pass this day through these
heavens, and see what is now going on in the sanctuary above;
could you see what the child of God now sees who died last
night; could you see the Lamb with the scars of His five deep
wounds in the very midst of the throne, surrounded by all the
redeemed, everyone having harps and golden vials full of
odors, could you see the many angels round about the throne,
whose number is ten thousand times ten thousand, and thousands of thousands, all singing, "Worthy is the Lamb that was
slain"; and were one of these angels to tell you, "This is He
that undertook the cause of lost sinners; He undertook to bear
their curse and to do their obedience; He undertook to be the
second Adam—the man in their stead. And lo! there He is
upon the throne of heaven; consider Him; look long and
earnestly upon His wounds—upon His glory—and tell me, do
you think it would be safe to trust Him? do you think His
sufferings and obedience will have been enough?" Yes, yes,
every soul exclaims, Lord, it is enough! Lord, stay Thy hand!
Show me no more, for I can bear no more. Oh, rather let me
ever stand and gaze upon the almighty, all-worthy, all-divine
Saviour, till my soul drinks in complete assurance that His
work undertaken for sinners is a finished work! Yes, though

the sins of all the world were on my one wicked head, still I
could not doubt that His work is complete, and that I am quite
safe when I believe in Him.

I would now plead with believers. Some of you have really
been brought by God to believe in Jesus. Yet you have no
abiding peace, and very little growing in holiness. Why is this?
It is because your eye is fixed anywhere but on Christ. You
are so busy looking at books, or looking at men, or looking at
the world, that you have no time, no heart, for looking at
Christ.

No wonder you have little peace and joy in believing. No
wonder you live so inconsistent and unholy a life. Change your
plan. Consider the greatness and glory of Christ, who has
undertaken all in the stead of sinners, and you would find it
quite impossible to walk in darkness, or to walk in sin. Oh,
what mean, despicable thoughts you have of the glorious Immanuel! Lift your eyes from your own bosom, downcast believer—look upon Jesus. It is good to consider your ways, but
it is far better to consider Christ.

I would now invite anxious souls. Anxious soul! have you
understood all the glory of Christ? Have you understood that
He undertook for guilty sinners? And do you doubt if He be
a sufficient Saviour? Oh, what mean views you have of Christ
if you dare not risk your soul upon Him!

Objection—I do not doubt that Christ has suffered and done
quite enough, but I fear it was for others, and not for me. If I
were sure it was for me, I would be quite happy.

Answer—It is nowhere said in the Bible that Christ died for
this sinner or that sinner. If you are waiting till you find your
own name in the Bible, you will wait forever. But it is said
a few verses before that, "He tasted death for every man"; and
again, "He is the propitiation for the sins of the whole world."
Not that all men are saved by Him. Ah! no; the most never
come to Jesus, and are lost; but this shows that any sinner may

come, even the chief of sinners, and take Christ as his own
Saviour. Come you then, anxious soul; say you, He is my refuge and my fortress; and then, be anxious, if you can.

II. *Consider Christ as the Apostle or Messenger of God.*

The word apostle means messenger, one ordained and sent
on a particular embassy. Now Christ is an Apostle, for God
ordained and sent Him into the world.

In the Old Testament, the name He is most often called is
the Angel of the Lord, or the Messenger of the Covenant. He
is called God's Elect, chosen for the work; He is called God's
Servant; He is called the Messiah, or the Christ, or the
Anointed, because God anointed Him and sent Him to the
work. In the New Testament, over and over again Christ calls
Himself the Sent of God. "As thou hast sent me into the world,
so have I sent them into the world, that the world may know
that thou hast sent me. . . And these have known that thou
hast sent me." All this shows plainly that it is not the Son alone
who is interested in the saving of poor sinners, but the Father
also. "The Father sent his Son to be the Saviour of the
world."

Objection—True, Christ is a great and glorious Saviour,
and able to accomplish anything to save poor sinners; but perhaps God the Father may not agree to pour out His wrath
upon His Son, or to accept of His Son as a surety in our stead.

Answer—Look here, Christ is the Apostle of God. It is as
much God the Father's work, as it is Christ's work. It occupied as much of the heart of God as ever it did of the heart
of Christ. God loved the world as much and truly as ever
Christ loved the world. God gave His Son, as much as Christ
gave Himself for us. So God the Holy Spirit is as much interested in it as the Father and Son. God gave His Son; the
Spirit anointed Him and dwelt in Him without measure. At
His baptism God acknowledged Him for His beloved Son—
the Holy Spirit came on Him like a dove.

Oh! brethren, could I lift you away to the eternity that is past—could I bring you into the council of the Eternal Three; and as it was once said, "Let us *make* man," could I let you hear the word, "Let us *save* man"; could I show you how God from all eternity designed His Son to undertake for poor sinners; how it was the very plan and the bottommost desire of the heart of the Father that Jesus should come into the world, and do and die in the stead of sinners; how the Holy Spirit breathed sweetest incense, and dropped like holiest oil upon the head of the descending Saviour; could I show you the intense interest with which the eye of God followed Jesus through His whole course of sorrow and suffering and death; could I show you the anxious haste with which God rolled away the stone from the sepulchre while it was yet dark, for He would not leave His soul in hell, neither suffer His Holy One to see corruption; could I show you the ecstasies of love and joy that beat in the bosom of the infinite God when Jesus ascended to His Father and our Father; how He welcomed Him with a fullness of kindness and grace which God alone could give, and God alone could receive, saying, "Thou art my Son, this day have I begotten Thee; Thou art indeed worthy to be called my Son; never till this day wert Thou so worthy to be called mine; thy throne, O God, is for ever and ever; sit Thou on my right hand until I make thine enemies thy footstool."

O sinner, will you ever doubt any more whether God the Father be seeking thy salvation—whether the heart of Christ and of His Father be the same in this one grand controversy? O believer, consider this Apostle of God; meditate on these things; look and look again, until your peace be like a river, and your righteousness like the waves of the sea—till the breathing of your soul be, Abba, Father!

III. *Consider Christ as the High Priest of our profession.*

The duty of the high priest was twofold: *First,* to make atonement; *second,* to make intercession.

When the high priest slew the goat at the altar of burnt-offerings, he did it in presence of all the people, to make atonement for them. They all stood around, gazing and considering their high priest; and when he gathered the blood into the golden basin, and put on the white garments, and passed away from their sight within the veil, their eye followed him, till the mysterious curtain hid him from their sight. But even then the heart of the believing Jew followed him still. Now he is drawing near to God for us; now he is sprinkling the blood seven times before the mercy seat, saying, Let this blood be instead of our blood; now he is praying for us.

Brethren, let us also consider our great High Priest.

1. *Consider Him making atonement.* You cannot look at Him on the cross as the disciples did; you cannot see the blood streaming from His five deep wounds; you cannot see Him shedding His blood that the blood of sinners might not be shed. Yet still, if God spare us, you may see bread broken and wine poured out, a living picture of the dying Saviour. Now, brethren, the atonement has been made, Christ has died, His sufferings are all past. And how is it that you do not enjoy peace? It is because you do not consider. "Israel doth not know, my people doth not consider." Consider—has Jesus died in the stead of guilty sinners, and do you heartily consent to take Jesus to be the man in your stead? Then, you do not need to die. Oh, happy believer, rejoice evermore! Live within sight of Calvary, and you will live within sight of glory; and, oh, rejoice in the happy ordinance that sets a broken Saviour so plainly before you!

2. *Consider Christ as making intercession.* When Christ ascended from the Mount of Olives, and passed through these heavens, carrying His bloody wounds into the presence of God, and when His disciples had gazed after Him, till a cloud received Him out of their sight, we are told that *they returned to Jerusalem with great joy.* What! are they joyful at parting

with their blessed Master? When He told them He was to leave them, sorrow filled their hearts, and He had to argue with them and comfort them, saying, "Let not your heart be troubled . . . it is expedient for you that I go away." How, then, are they changed? Jesus has left them, and they are filled with joy. Oh! here is the secret: they knew that Christ was now going into the presence of God for them, that their great High Priest was now entering within the veil to make intercession for them.

Now, believer, would you share in the great joy of the disciples? Consider the Apostle and High Priest of our profession, Christ Jesus. He is above yon clouds, and above yon sky. Oh that you would stand gazing up into heaven, not with the bodily eye, but with the eye of faith! Oh, what a wonderful thing the eye of faith is! It sees beyond the stars, it pierces to the throne of God, and there it looks on the face of Jesus making intercession for us, whom having not seen we love; in whom, though now we see Him not, yet believing, we rejoice with joy unspeakable and full of glory.

Oh! if you would live thus, what sweet peace would fill your bosom! And how many droppings of the Spirit would come down on you in answer to the Saviour's prayer! Oh! how your face would shine like Stephen's; and the poor, blind world would see that there is a joy which the world cannot give, and the world cannot take away—a heaven upon earth!

DUNDEE, 1836.

MESSAGE III

"As the lily among thorns, so is my love among the daughters. As the apple tree among the trees of the wood, so is my beloved among the sons. I sat down under his shadow with great delight, and his fruit was sweet unto my taste."—Song of Solomon 2:2, 3.

IF AN UNCONVERTED MAN were taken away into heaven, where Christ sits in glory, and if he overheard Christ's words of admiring love towards the believer, he

could not understand them; he could not comprehend how
Christ should see a loveliness in poor religious people whom
he in the bottom of his heart despised. Or again, if an unconverted man were to overhear a Christian at his devotions
when he is really within the veil, and were to listen to his
words of admiring, adoring love towards Christ, he could not
possibly understand them; he could not comprehend how the
believer should have such a burning affection toward One
unseen, in whom he himself saw no form nor comeliness. So
true it is that the natural man knoweth not the things of
the Spirit of God, for they are foolishness unto him.

There may be some now hearing me who have a rooted
dislike to religious people—they are so stiff, so precise, so
gloomy, you cannot endure their company! Well, then, see
here what Christ thinks of them: "As the lily among thorns,
so is my love among the daughters." How different you are
from Christ! There may be some hearing me who have no
desires after Jesus Christ, who never think of Him with pleasure; you see no form nor comeliness in Him, no beauty that
you should desire Him; you do not love the melody of His
name; you do not pray to Him continually. Well, then, see
here what the believer thinks of Him—how different from
you—"As the apple tree among the trees of the wood, so
is my beloved among the sons. I sat down under his shadow
with great delight, and his fruit was sweet to my taste." Oh,
that you would be awakened by this very thing—that you
are so different from Christ, and so different from the believer
—to think that you must be in a natural condition, you must
be under wrath!

Doctrine.—The believer is unspeakably precious in the eyes
of Christ, and Christ is unspeakably precious in the eyes of
the believer.

I. *Inquire what Christ thinks of the believer.*—"As the lily
among the thorns, so is my love among the daughters."

Christ sees nothing so fair in all this world as the believer. All the rest of the world is like thorns, but the believer is like a beautiful lily in His eyes. When you are walking in a wilderness all overgrown with briars and thorns, if your eye falls upon some lonely flower, tall and white, and pure and graceful, growing in the midst of the thorns, it looks peculiarly beautiful. If it were in the midst of some rich garden among many other flowers, then it would not be so remarkable; but when it is encompassed with thorns on every side, then it engages the eye. Such is the believer in the eyes of Christ. "As the lily among thorns, so is my love among the daughters."

1. See what Christ thinks of the unconverted world. It is like a field full of briars and thorns in His eyes. *First,* Because fruitless. "Do men gather grapes of thorns, or figs of thistles?" So Christ gets no fruit from the unconverted world. It is all one wide, thorny waste.

Second, Because, when the Word is preached among them, it is like sowing among thorns. "Break up your fallow ground and sow not among thorns." When the sower sowed, some fell among thorns, and the thorns sprang up and choked them; so is preaching to the unconverted.

Third, Because their end will be like that of thorns—they are dry, and fit only for the burning. "As thorns cut up shall they be burned in the fire." "For the earth, which is often rained upon and only bears thorns and briars, is rejected, and nigh unto cursing, whose end is to be burned."

My friends, if you are in a Christless state, see what you are in the eyes of Christ—*thorns.* You think that you have many admirable qualities, that you are valuable members of society, and you have a hope that it shall be well with you in eternity. See what Christ says, You are thorns and briars, useless in this world, and fit only for the burning.

2. See what Christ thinks of the believer: "As the lily among thorns, so is my love among the daughters." The be-

liever is like a lovely flower in the eyes of Christ. *First,* Because justified in the eyes of Christ, washed in His blood, as pure and white as a lily. Christ can see no spot in His own righteousness, and therefore He sees no spot on the believer. Thou art all fair, my love, as a lily among thorns, so is my love.

Second, A believer's nature is changed. Once he was like the barren, prickly thorn, fit only for burning; now Christ has put a new spirit in him; the dew has been given to him, and he grows up like the lily. Christ loves the new creature. "All my delight is in them." "As the lily among thorns, so is my love among the daughters." Are you a Christian? then never mind though the world despise you, though they call you names; remember Christ loves you; He calls you "my love." Abide in Him, and you shall abide in His love. "If ye continue in my word, then are ye my disciples indeed."

Third, Because so lonely in the world. Observe, there is only one lily, but many thorns. There is a great wilderness all full of thorns, and only one lonely flower. So there is a world lying in wickedness, and a little flock that believe in Jesus. Some believers are cast down because they feel solitary and alone. If I be in the right way, surely I would not be so lonely. Surely the wise, and the amiable, and the kind people I see round about me—surely, if there were any truth in religion, they would know it. Be not cast down. It is one of the marks of Christ's people that they are alone in the world, and yet they are not alone. It is one of the very beauties which Christ sees in His people, that they are solitary among a world of thorns. "As a lily among thorns, so is my love among the daughters."

Do not be discouraged. This world is the world of loneliness. When you are transplanted to yon garden of God, then you shall be no more lonely, then you shall be away from all the thorns. As flowers in a rich garden blend together their thousand odors to enrich the passing breeze, so, in the paradise above, you shall join the thousands of the redeemed, blending with theirs the odor of your praise; you shall join with the redeemed to form a garland for the Redeemer's brow.

II. *Inquire what the believer thinks of Christ.*—"As the apple tree among the trees of the wood, so is my beloved among the sons. I sat down under his shadow with great delight, and his fruit was sweet to my taste."

1. Christ is more precious than all other saviours in the eye of the believer. As a traveler prefers an apple tree to every other tree of the wood, because he finds both shelter and nourishing food under it, so the believer prefers Christ to all other saviours. When a man is traveling in eastern countries, he is often about to drop down under the burning rays of the sun. It is a great relief when he comes to a wood. When the Israelites were traveling in the wilderness, they came to Elim, where were twelve wells of water and seventy palm trees, and they encamped there by the water. They were glad of the shelter of the trees. So Micah says that God's people "dwell solitarily in the wood"; and Ezekiel promises, "they shall sleep in the woods."

But if the traveler be hungry and faint for lack of food, then he will not be content with any tree of the wood, but he will choose out a fruit tree, under which he may sit down and find nourishment as well as shade. He sees a fair apple tree; he chooses it out of all the trees of the wood, because he can both sit under its shadow and eat its pleasant fruits. So is it with the soul awakened by God. He feels under the heat of God's anger; he is in a weary land; he is brought into the wilderness; he is about to perish; he comes to a wood; many trees offer their shade; where shall he sit down? Under the fir tree? Alas! what fruit has it to give? he may die there. Under the cedar tree, with its mighty branches? Alas! he may perish there, for it has no fruit to give. The soul that

is taught of God seeks for a complete Saviour. The apple
tree is revealed to the soul. The hungry soul chooses that
evermore. He needs to be saved from hell and nourished for
heaven. "As the apple tree among the trees of the wood, so
is my beloved among the sons."

Awakened souls, remember you must not sit down under
every tree that offers itself. "Take heed that no one deceive
you; for many shall come in Christ's name, saying, I am
Christ, and deceive many." There are many ways of saying,
Peace, peace, when there is no peace. You will be tempted
to find peace in the world, in self-repentance, in self-reforma-
tion. Remember, choose you a tree that will yield fruit as
well as shade. "As the apple tree among the trees of the
wood, so is my beloved among the sons." Pray for a choosing faith. Pray for an eye to discern the apple tree. Oh! there
is no rest for the soul except under that Branch which God
has made strong. My heart's desire and prayer for you is, that
you may all find rest there.

2. Why has the believer so high an esteem of Christ?

First, Because he has made trial of Christ. "I sat down
under his shadow with great delight." All true believers have
sat down under the shadow of Christ. Some people think that
they shall be saved because they have a head-knowledge of
Christ. They read of Christ in the Bible, they hear of Christ
in the house of God, and they think that is to be a Christian.
Alas! my friends, what good would you get from an apple
tree, if I were only to describe it to you—tell you how beautiful it was, how heavily laden with delicious apples? Or, if I
were only to show you a picture of the tree, or if I were to
show you the tree itself at a distance, what the better would
you be? You would not get the good of its shade or its pleasant
fruit.

Just so, dear brethren, what good would you get from Christ,
if you only hear of Him in books and sermons, or if you see

Him pictured forth in the sacrament, or if you were to see Him with your bodily eye? What good would all this do, if you do not sit down under His shadow? Oh, my friends, there must be a personal sitting down under the shadow of Christ if you would be saved! Christ is the bush that has been burned, yet not consumed. Oh! it is a safe place for a hell-deserving sinner to rest.

Some may be hearing me who can say, "I sat down under His shadow." And yet you have forsaken Him. Ah! have you gone after your lovers, and away from Christ? Well, then, may God hedge up your way with thorns. Return, return, O Shulamite! There is no other refuge for your soul. Come and sit down again under the shadow of the Saviour.

Second, Because he sat down with great delight.

Some people think there is no joy in religion, that it is a gloomy thing. When a young person becomes a Christian, they would say, Alas! he must bid farewell to pleasure, farewell to the joys of youth, farewell to a merry heart. He must exchange these pleasures for reading of the Bible and dry sermon books, for a life of gravity and preciseness. This is what the world says.

What does the Bible say? "I sat down under his shadow with great delight." Ah! let God be true, and every man a liar. Yet no one can believe this except those who have tried it. Ah! be not deceived, my young friends; the world has many sensual and many sinful delights, the delights of eating and drinking, and wearing gay clothes, the delights of revelry and the dance. No man of wisdom will deny that these things are delightful to the natural heart; but oh! they perish in the using, and they end in an eternal hell. But to sit down under the shadow of Christ, wearied with God's burning anger, wearied with seeking after vain saviours, at last to find rest under the shadow of Christ, ah! this is great delight. Lord, evermore may I sit under this shadow!

Some people are afraid of anything like joy in religion. They have none themselves, and they do not love to see it in others. Their religion is something like the stars, very high, and very clear, but very cold. When they see tears of anxiety, or tears of joy, they cry out, Enthusiasm, enthusiasm! Well, then, to the law, and to the testimony. "I sat down under his shadow *with great delight.*" Is this enthusiasm? O Lord, evermore give us this enthusiasm! May the God of hope fill you with all joy and peace in believing! If it be really in sitting under the shadow of Christ, let there be no bounds to your joy. Oh, if God would but open your eyes, and give you simple, child-like faith, to look to Jesus, to sit under His shadow, then would songs of joy rise from all our dwellings. Rejoice in the Lord always, and again I say, Rejoice!

Third, Because the fruit of Christ is sweet to the taste. All true believers not only sit under the shadow, but partake of His pleasant fruits. Just as when you sit under an apple tree, the fruit hangs above you and around you, and invites you to put out the hand and taste; so when you come to submit to the righteousness of God, bow your head, and sit down under Christ's shadow, all other things are added unto you. Temporal mercies are sweet to the taste. None but those of you who are Christians know this, when you sit under the shadow of Christ's temporal mercies, because covenant mercies. "Bread shall be given you; your water shall be sure." These are sweet apples from the tree Christ. O Christian! tell me, is not bread sweeter when eaten thus? Is not water richer than wine, and Daniel's pulse better than the dainties of the king's table?

Afflictions are sweet to the taste. Every good apple has some sourness in it. So is it with the apples of the tree of Christ. He gives afflictions as well as mercies; He sets the teeth on edge; but even these are blessings in disguise, they are covenant gifts. Oh! affliction is a dismal thing when you are not under His shadow. But are you Christians? look on your sorrows as apples from that blessed tree. If you knew how wholesome they are, you would not wish to want them. Several of you know it is no contradiction to say, These apples, though sour, are sweet to my taste.

The gifts of the Spirit are sweet to the taste. Ah! here is the best fruit that grows on the tree; here are the ripest apples from the topmost branch. You who are Christians know how often your soul is fainting. Well, here is nourishment to your fainting soul. Everything you need is in Christ. "My grace is sufficient for thee." Dear Christian, sit much under that tree, feed much upon that fruit. "Stay me with flagons, comfort me with apples, for I am sick of love."

Promises of glory are sweet to the taste. Some of the apples have a taste of heaven in them. Feed upon these, dear Christians. Some of Christ's apples give you a relish for the fruit of Canaan—for the clusters of Eshcol. Lord, evermore give me these apples; for they are sweet to my taste.

St. Peter's, 1837.

Message IV

"A sword, a sword is sharpened, and also furbished: it is sharpened to make a sore slaughter; it is furbished that it may glitter: should we then make mirth? it contemneth the rod of my son, as every tree."—Ezekiel 21:9, 10.

FROM THE SECOND VERSE of this chapter we learn that this prophecy was directed against Jerusalem: "Son of man, set thy face toward Jerusalem, and drop thy word toward the holy places, and prophesy against the land of Israel."

We have already told you that Ezekiel, while yet a youth, was carried captive by Nebuchadnezzar, and placed, with a number of his countrymen, by the river of Chebar. It was there that he delivered his prophecies during a space of twenty-two years. The prophecy I have read was delivered in the seventh year of his captivity, and just three years before Jerusalem was

destroyed and the Temple burned. From verse 2, we learn that
these words were directed against Jerusalem; for though God
had taken Ezekiel away to minister to the captives by the river
of Chebar, yet He made him send many a message of warning
and of mercy to his beloved Jerusalem. "Son of man, set thy
face toward Jerusalem, and drop thy word toward the holy
places, and prophesy against the land of Israel."

God had already fulfilled many of the words of His prophets
against Jerusalem. He had fulfilled the word of Jeremiah
against one of their kings (Jehoiakim). "He shall be buried
with the burial of an ass: drawn and cast forth beyond the
walls of Jerusalem." He had fulfilled the word of the same
prophet in carrying another king (Jehoiachin) to Babylon with
all the goodly vessels of the house of the Lord. But still neither
prophecies nor judgments would awaken Jerusalem; so that
we are told (II Chron. 36:12) that Zedekiah, the next king,
"did that which was evil in the sight of the Lord his God, and
humbled not himself before Jeremiah the prophet, speaking
from the mouth of the Lord." Verses 14-16: "Moreover, all
the chief of the priests and the people transgressed very
much, after all the abominations of the heathen; and polluted
the house of the Lord, which he had hallowed in Jerusalem.
And the Lord God of their fathers sent to them by his messengers, rising up betimes, and sending; because He had compassion on his people, and on his dwelling place: but they
mocked the messengers of God, and despised his works, and
misused his prophets, until the wrath of the Lord arose against
his people, till there was no remedy."

It was in a time of great hardness and impenitence in Jerusalem that the prophecy before me was delivered, and just
three years before the wrath of God was poured on them to
the uttermost. *First,* All was mirth and sensuality in Jerusalem.
Second, The false prophets prophesied peace, and the people
loved to have it so. *Third,* There was no noise but that of

revelry within the devoted city. But in the midst of that din and revelry, the lone prophet by the river of Chebar heard the muttering of the distant thunder. The faithful servant of God saw God arming Himself as a mighty man for the war, and the glittering sword of vengeance in His hand, and he calls aloud to his countrymen, all at ease, with awakening thunders, "A sword, a sword is sharpened, and also furbished: it is sharpened to make a sore slaughter; it is furbished that it may glitter: should we then make mirth?"

My friends, those of you who are unconverted are in the very same situation as Jerusalem was. In the years that are now fled like the mists of the morning, how many messages have you had from God! How many times has He sent His messengers to you, rising up early and sending them! His Bible has been in your houses, a silent but most mighty pleader for God; His providence has been in your families, in sickness and death, in plenty or poverty—all, all beseeching you to flee from the wrath to come—all, all beseeching you to cleave to the Lord Jesus, the only, the all-sufficient Saviour.

All these messages have come to you, and you are yet un-converted—still dead, dry bones, without Christ and without God in the world; and you are saying, Soul, take thine ease, eat and drink and be merry. But do, my friends, hearken once more, for God does not wish any to perish. I have a word from God unto thee: "A sword, a sword is sharpened, and also furbished: it is sharpened to make a sore slaughter; it is furbished that it may glitter: should we then make mirth?"

Doctrine.—It is very unreasonable in unconverted persons to make mirth.

1. It is unreasonable, *because they are under condemnation.* —The sword is sharpened, and also furbished. It is sharpened to make a sore slaughter; it is furbished that it may glitter. Should we then make mirth? There is a common idea that men are under probation, as Adam was, and that Christless

persons will not be condemned till the judgment; but this is not the case. The Bible says, "He that believeth not is condemned already." "He that hath not the Son shall not see life, but the wrath of God abideth on him." "Cursed *is* every one [not, *shall be*] who continueth not in all things written in the book of the law to do them." Christless souls are at present in the horrible pit, every mouth is stopped, and they are guilty before God. They are in prison, ready to be brought out to execution. Therefore, when God sends us to preach to Christless persons, He calls it "preaching to the spirits in prison," that is, who are under condemnation. The sword is not only unsheathed, it is sharpened and furbished. It is held over their heads.

Should they then make mirth? It is unreasonable in a condemned malefactor to make mirth. Would it not greatly shock every feeling mind to see a company of men condemned to die, meeting and making merry, talking lightly and jestingly, as if the sword were not over them? Yet this is the case of those of you who are unconverted and yet live lives of mirth. You have been tried in the balance and found wanting. You have been condemned by the righteous Judge. Your sentence is past. You are now in prison; neither can you break out of this prison: the sword is whetted and drawn over you. And oh! is it not most unreasonable to make mirth? Is it not most unreasonable to be happy and contented with yourself and merry with your friends? Is it not madness to sing the song of the drunkard? "Eat, drink, and be merry, for tomorrow we die."

2. *Because God's instruments of destruction are all ready.*—Not only are Christless persons condemned already, but the instruments of their destruction are prepared and quite ready. The sword of vengeance is sharpened, and also furbished. When swords are kept in the armory, they are kept blunt, that the rust may not hurt their edge; but when work is to be done,

and they are taken out for the slaughter, then they are furbished and sharpened, made sharp and glittering. So it is with the sword of the executioner: when not in use, it is kept blunt; but when work is to be done, it is sharpened and made ready. It is sharpened and furbished just before the blow is struck, that it may cut clean. So is it with God's sword of vengeance. It is not sheathed and blunt, it is sharpened and furbished; it is quite ready to do its work; it is quite ready for a sore slaughter. The disease by which every unconverted man is to die is quite ready; it is perhaps in his veins at this very moment. The accident by which he is to drop into eternity is quite ready, all the parts and means of it are arranged. The arrow that is to strike him is on the string—perhaps it has left the string, and is even now flying towards him.

The place in hell is quite ready for every unconverted soul. When Judas died, the Scripture says, "he went to his own place." It was his own place before he went there, being quite prepared and ready for him. As when a man retires at night to his sleeping room, it is said he has gone to his own room, so a place in hell is quite ready for every Christless person. It is his own place. When the rich man died and was buried, he was immediately in his own place. He found everything ready. He lifted up his eyes in hell, being in torments. So hell is quite ready for every Christless person. It was prepared, long ago, for the devil and his angels. The fires are all quite ready, and fully lighted and burning.

Ah! should Christless souls then make mirth? A malefactor might perhaps say that he would be merry as long as the scaffold was not erected on which he was to die. But if he were told that the scaffold was quite ready, that the sword was sharpened, and the executioner standing ready—oh! would it not be madness to make mirth? Alas! this is your madness, poor Christless soul. You are not only condemned, but the sword is sharpened and ready that is to smite your soul; and

yet you can be happy, and dream away your days and nights
in pleasures that perish in the using. The disease is ready,
the accident is ready, the arrow is on the string, the grave is
ready, yea, hell itself is ready, your own place is made ready;
and yet you can make mirth! You can play games and enjoy
company! How truly is your laughter like the crackling of
thorns under a pot: a flashy blaze, and then the blackness of
darkness forever!

3. *The sword may come down at any moment.*—Not
only are Christless persons condemned already, and not only
is the sword of vengeance quite ready, but the sword may
come down at any moment. It is not so with malefactors;
their day is fixed and told them, so that they can count their
time. If they have many days, they make merry today at
least, and begin to be serious tomorrow. But not so Christless
persons; their day is fixed, but it is not told them. It may
be this very moment. Ah! should they then make mirth?

Some malefactors have been found very stouthearted to
the very last. Many have received their sentence quite unmoved,
and with a determined countenance. Some have even gone to
the scaffold quite unmoved; some even with a light, careless
spirit. But when the head is laid down upon the block, when
the eyes are covered, and the neck laid bare, when the glittering sword is lifted high in the air, and may come down any
moment—that is a dreadful time of suspense. It would be
very horrible to see a man in a light careless spirit at that
time. Oh! it would be madness to be merry then.

Alas! this is your madness, poor Christless soul. You are
not only condemned, and not only is the sword ready, but it
may fall on you at any moment. Your head is, as it were,
on the block. Your neck is bared before God, and the whetted
sword is held over you; and yet can you make mirth? Can
you take up your mind with business and worldly things,
and getting rich, building and planting, and this night your

soul may be required of you? Can you fill up your time with
games and amusements, and foolish books and entertaining
companions? Can you fill up your hours after work with
loose talk and wanton behavior, adding sin to sin, treasuring
up wrath against the day of wrath, when you know not what
hour the wrath of God may come upon you to the uttermost?
Can you go prayerless to your bed at night, your mind filled
with dark and horrid imaginations not fit to be named, and
yet you may be in hell before the morning? A sword, a sword;
it is furbished!

4. *Because God has made no promise to Christless souls to
stay His hand one moment.*—All the promises of God are yea
and amen, that is, they are true. He always fulfills His promises. But the same scripture says they are "yea and amen *in
Christ Jesus.*" All God's promises are made to Christ, and to
sinners that cleave to Christ. I believe that it is impossible,
in the nature of things, that God would make a promise to
an unconverted man. Accordingly, all God's promises are
made to Christ, and to every sinner that cleaves to Christ.
But unconverted persons are those who have never come to
Christ; therefore there are no promises made to them. God
nowhere promises to make them anxious. He nowhere promises
to bring them to Christ. He nowhere promises to keep them
one moment out of hell. "Should they then make mirth?"

Let me speak to Christless persons who are at ease. Many
of you hearing me may know that you are in a Christless
state; and yet you know that you are at ease and happy. Why
is this? It is because you hope to be brought to Christ before
you die. You say, Another day will do as well, and I will
hear thee again of this matter; and therefore you take your
ease now. But this is very unreasonable. It is not worthy
of a rational being to act in this way. God has nowhere
promised to bring you to Christ before you die. God has laid
Himself under no manner of obligation to you. He has no-

where promised that you shall see tomorrow, or that you shall hear another sermon. There is a day near at hand when you shall not see a tomorrow. If this be not the last, there is a sermon yet to be preached which will be the last you will ever hear.

Let me speak to Christless persons who are anxious about their souls. Some hearing me know that they are in a Christless condition, and this made them anxious; and yet it is to be feared some are losing that anxiety, and now going back to the mirth of the world. Why is this? This is most unreasonable. If you are still out of Christ, however anxious you have been, remember God has made no promises to save you. The sword is still over you, furbished and sharpened. Ah! do not then make mirth. Strive to enter in at the strait gate. Take the kingdom of heaven by violence. Press into it. Never rest till you are in the bonds of the covenant. Then be as happy as the day is long.

5. *It is a sore slaughter: "A sword! a sword!"*

Sore, because it will be on all who are Christless.—The dreadfulness of the slaughter in Jerusalem was, that all were slain, both old and young. The command which the prophet heard was (9:5, 6), "Go ye through the city, and smite. Let not your eye spare, neither have ye pity. Slay utterly old and young, both maids and little children and women; but come not near any man upon whom is the mark." Such is the sore slaughter waiting on unconverted souls. All Christless persons will perish, young and old. God will not spare, neither will His eye pity.

Think of this, *old grey-headed persons,* that have lived in sin, and never come to Christ; if you die thus, you will certainly perish in the sore slaughter.

Think of this, *middle-aged persons,* hard-working merchants and laborers, who make money, but do not sell all for the pearl of great price. Think of this, ye *Marthas,* who are care-

ful and troubled about many things, but who forget the one
thing that is needful, you also will fall in the sore slaughter.

Think of this, *young persons,* who live without prayer, yet
in mirth and jollity; you that meet to jest and be happy on
Sabbath evenings; you that walk in the sight of your own
eyes—you, too, will fall in that sore slaughter.

Think of this, *little children,* you that are the pride of your
mother's heart, but who have gone astray, from the womb,
speaking lies. Little children who are fond of your plays, but
are not fond of coming to Jesus Christ, who is the Saviour
of little children, the sword will come on you also. Oh! it is
a sore slaughter that will not spare the young, nor the lovely,
nor the kind—the gentle mother and affectionate child, the
widow and her only son. Should you then make mirth? Unconverted families, when you meet in the evening to jest and
sport with one another, ask this one question, Should we make
mirth? Is your mirth reasonable? Is it worthy of rational
beings? Unconverted companions, who meet so often for
mirth and amusement, should you make mirth together when
you are in such a case? Ah! how dismal will the contrast be
when God says, Bind them in bundles to burn them!

Sore slaughter because the sword is the sword of God.—If it
were only the sword of man that is furbished and sharpened
for the slaughter, it would not be very terrible. But it is
the sword of Almighty God, and therefore it is very terrible.
"Fear not them that kill the body, but after that have no more
that they can do. But I will forewarn you whom ye shall
fear: Fear him, who after he hath killed the body, is able
to cast body and soul into hell; yea, I say unto you, fear him."
If it were the sword of man, it could reach only to the body;
but, ah! it is the sword of God, and the iron will enter into
the soul. It is the same sword that appeared in the garden of
Eden, "a flaming sword, that turned every way to keep the
way of the tree of life." It is the same sword which pierced the

side of Jesus Christ in His agony. "Awake, O sword, against
my Shepherd, and against the man that is my fellow, saith the
Lord of Hosts: I will smite the Shepherd, and the sheep shall
be scattered." It is that sword of which Christ speaks, when
He says, "It shall cut him asunder, and appoint him his portion with hypocrites: there shall be wailing and gnashing of
teeth."

Dear brethren, it is not a few flesh wounds that that
sword will make. It will cut asunder; it will be a deathblow
—eternal death. It is a death which body and soul will be
always dying, yet never dead.

1. *Let me speak to the old.*—There may be some hearing
me in whom these three things meet, namely, that they are old,
and Christless, and full of mirth. Oh! if there be such hearing me, consider your ways, consider if your mirth be worthy
of a rational being. I have shown you plainly out of the
Scriptures what your case is: *First,* that you are condemned
already; *second,* that God's sword is ready; *third,* that it may
come down any moment; *fourth,* that God has made you no
promise to stay His hand; and, *fifth,* that it will be a sore
slaughter. Consider, then, if it be reasonable to believe a lie,
to deceive your own soul, and say, Peace, peace, when there is
no peace. In the ordinary course of things, you must soon go
the way of all living; you must be gathered to your fathers,
and then all that I have said will be fulfilled. Should you then
make mirth? Are you tottering on the brink of hell, and
yet living prayerless and Christless, and playing with straws,
telling over the oft-repeated tale of youth, and laugh-
ing over the oft-repeated jest? Alas! what a depth of meaning
was there in the word of Solomon! "I said of laughter, It is
mad; and of mirth, What doeth it? Even in laughter the heart
is sorrowful, and the end of that mirth is heaviness."

2. *Let me speak to the young.*—There may be many hearing me in whom these three things meet: They are young in

years, far from Christ, and yet full of mirth. Now, my dear friends, I entreat you to consider whether your mirth is reasonable. The sword is sharpened for a sore slaughter. Should you then make mirth?

Objection 1.—Youth is the time for mirth.

Answer.—I know well youth is the time for mirth. The young lamb is a happy creature as it springs about on the green pasture. The young kid leaps from rock to rock with liveliest glee. The young horse casts its heels high in the air, full of life and activity. But then they have no sin, and you have; they have no hell, and you have. If you will come to Jesus Christ now, and be freed from wrath, ah! then you will find that youth is the time for mirth, youth is the time for enjoying sweet peace in the bosom, and liveliest intercourse with God, and brightest hopes of glory.

Objection 2.—You would have us to be gloomy and sad.

Answer.—God forbid. All that I maintain is, that until you are come to Christ, your mirth is mad and unreasonable. If you will come to Christ, then be as happy as you will; there are no bounds to your joy there, for you will joy in God. And when you die, you will come to fullness of joy in His presence, and pleasures at His right hand for evermore.

Objection 3.—If I be Christless, it will not bring me into Christ to be sad, and therefore I may as well be merry.

Answer.—True, to be sad will not bring you into Christ; and yet, if you were really awakened to cry to God, peradventure He would hear your cry. If you were striving to enter in, you might find entrance. If you were pressing into the kingdom, you might take it by violence. Seek meekness, seek righteousness. It may be ye shall be hid in the day of the Lord's anger. If you stay where you are, you are sure to be lost. If you live on in carnal security, in mirth and jollity, while you are out of Christ, you are sure to perish.

"Rejoice, O young man, in thy youth, and let thy heart cheer

thee in the days of thy youth, and walk in the ways of thine
heart, and in the sight of thine eyes; but know thou that for
all these things God will bring thee into judgment."

Dundee, 1837.

————

Message V

"Unto you, O men, I call; and my voice is to the sons of men."—Proverbs 8:4.

THESE are the words of wisdom; and wisdom in the book
of Proverbs is none other than our Lord and Saviour
Jesus Christ. This is evident from chapter 1, verse 23, where
He says, "Behold, I will pour out my Spirit unto you"; but
it is Christ alone who has the gift of the Holy Spirit. And
again, from 8:22, where He says, "The Lord possessed me in
the beginning of his way"; and verse 30: "Then I was by
him as one brought up with him; and I was daily his delight,
rejoicing always before him." These words are true of none
but of Jesus Christ, the Word that was with God, and was
God, by whom all things were made.

Observe the places He goes to with the invitation.—*First,*
He goes to the country. He climbs every eminence, and cries
there; then He descends to the highway where many roads meet.
Second, He goes to the city. He begins at the gates, where
the people are assembled to make bargains and hear causes;
then He proceeds along the principal avenue into the city, and
cries in at every door as He passes. He first goes out into the
highways and hedges, then goes into the streets and lanes of
the city, carrying the blessed message.

Observe the manner in which He invites.—He cries aloud,
He puts forth the voice, He stands and cries, He calls and lifts
up His voice, He seems like some merchant offering his wares,
first in the market, and then from door to door. Never did
busy crier offer to sell his goods with such anxiety as Jesus

offers His salvation; verse 10: "Receive my instruction, and
not silver; and knowledge rather than choice gold."

Observe to whom the invitation is addressed.—Verse 4:
"Unto you, O men, I call; and my voice is to the sons of
men." Merchants only offer their goods to certain classes of
the people that will buy; but Jesus offers His to all men.
Wherever there is a son of Adam, wherever there is one born
of woman, the word is addressed to him: he that hath ears
to hear, let him hear.

Doctrine.—Christ offers Himself as a Saviour to all of the
human race.

I. *The most awakening truth in all the Bible.*—It is com-
monly thought that preaching the holy law is the most awakening truth in the Bible, that by it the mouth is stopped, and
all the world becomes guilty before God; and, indeed, I
believe this is the most ordinary means which God makes use
of. And yet to me there is something far more awakening
in the sight of a Divine Saviour freely offering Himself to
every one of the human race. There is something that might
pierce the heart that is like a stone in that cry: "Unto you,
O men, I call; and my voice is to the sons of men."

1. Had you lived in the days when Noah built the ark, had
you seen that mighty vessel standing open and ready, inviting all the world to come into its roomy cavities, would it not
have been the most awakening of all sights? Could you have
looked upon it without thinking of the coming flood that
was to sweep the ungodly world away?

2. Had you lived in the times when Jesus was on the earth,
had you seen Him riding down the Mount Olivet, and stopping when He came in sight of Jerusalem, lying peaceful and
slumbering at His feet, had you seen the Son of God weep
over the city, and say, "If thou hadst known, even thou, at
least in this thy day, the things which belong to thy peace!
but now they are hid from thine eyes," would you not have

felt that some awful destruction was awaiting the slumbering
city? Would He shed these tears for nothing? Surely He sees
some day of woe coming which none knows but Himself.

3. Just so, dear friends, when you see Jesus here running
from place to place, from the high places to the highways,
from the highways to the city gates, from the gates to the
doors; when you hear His anxious cry, "Unto you, O men,
I call," does it not show that all men are lost, that a dreadful hell is before them? Would the Saviour call so loud and
so long if there were no hell?

Apply this to slumbering souls.

Mark who it is that calls you—it is Wisdom! It is Jesus
Christ, in whom are hid all the treasures of wisdom and knowledge. "Unto you, O men, I call." Often, when ministers prick
your hearts in their sermons, you go home and say, "Oh! it
was only the word of a minister—shall I tremble at the words
of a man?" But here is the word of no minister, but of Christ.
Here is the word of one who knows your true condition, who
knows your heart and your history, who knows your sins done
in the light, and done in the dark, and done in the recesses of
your heart, who knows the wrath that is over you, and the
hell that is before you. "Unto you, O men, I call."

Mark in how many places He calls you.—In the high places
and the highways, in the gates, in the entries, at the coming
in of the doors. Has it not been so with you? Have you
not been called in the Bible, in the family, in the house of
prayer? You have gone from place to place, but the Saviour
has gone after you. You have gone to places of diversion,
you have gone to places of sin, but Christ has followed you.
You have lain down on a bed of sickness, and Christ has
followed you. Must not the sheep be in great danger, when
the Shepherd follows so far in search of it?

How loud He cries.—He calls and lifts up the voice. Has it
not been so with you? Has He not knocked loudly at your

door, in warnings, in providences, in deaths? Has He not cried loudly in the preached Word? Sometimes, when reading the Bible alone, has not the voice of Christ been louder than thunder?

He cries to all.—Had He cried to the old, then the young would have said, "We are safe, we do not need a Saviour." Had He cried to the young, the old men among you would have said, "He is not for us." Had he called to the good or to the bad, still some would have felt themselves excused. But He cries to you all. There is not one person hearing, but Jesus cries to you. Then all are lost—old and young, rich and poor. Whatever you think of yourselves, Jesus knows you to be in a lost condition; therefore this piercing cry, "Unto you, O men, I call."

II. *The most comforting truth in the Bible.*—When awakened persons are first told of Jesus Christ, it generally adds to their grief. They see plainly that He is a very great and glorious Saviour; but then they feel that they have rejected Him, and they fear that He never can become their Saviour. Very often awakened persons sit and listen to a lively description of Christ, of His work of substitution in the stead of sinners; but their question still is, "Is Christ a Saviour to me?" Now, to this question I answer, Christ is freely offered to all the human race. "Unto you, O men, I call." If there were no other text in the whole Bible to encourage sinners to come freely to Christ, this one alone might persuade them. There is no subject more misunderstood by unconverted souls than the unconditional freeness of Christ. So little idea have we naturally of free grace, that we cannot believe that God can offer a Saviour to us, while we are in a wicked, hell-deserving condition. Oh, it is sad to think how men argue against their own happiness, and will not believe the very word of God!

All the types show the Saviour to be free to all.

1. The brazen serpent was lifted up in sight of all Israel,

that anyone might look and be healed; and Christ Himself explains this: "So must the Son of man be lifted up, that whatsoever believeth on him should not perish, but have everlasting life."

2. The Refuge City set on a hill, with its gates open night and day, showed this. Whosoever will, may flee for refuge to the hope set before us.

3. The angels over Bethlehem repeated the same thing: "Behold, I bring you glad tidings of great joy, which shall be to all people." And the last invitation of the Bible is the freest of all: "Whosoever will, let him take the water of life freely." Mark, also, in the text before us: "Unto you, O men, I call." This shows that He is not free to devils; but to all *men,* to every one that has human form and human name the Saviour is now free. It is not for any goodness in men, not for any change in them that Christ offers Himself, but just in their lost condition as men. He freely puts Himself within their reach. There are many stratagems by which the devil contrives to keep men away from Christ.

Some say there is no hope for them. "There is no hope, no; for I have loved strangers, and after them I will go. I have committed such great sins, I have sunk so deep in the mire of sin, I have served my lusts so long, that there is no use of me thinking of turning. There is no hope, no." To you I answer, There is hope; your sins may be forgiven for Christ's sake; there is forgiveness with God. Ah, why should Satan so beguile you? True, you have waded deep into the mire of sin, you have destroyed yourself; and yet in Christ there is help. He came for such as you. Christ speaks in these words to you: you are of the human race, and Christ is free to all of the human race—"Unto you, O men, I call."

"I have not the least care about my soul. Up to this moment I never listened to a sermon, nor attended to a word in the Bible. I have no wish to hear of Christ, or God, or eternal things." To you I answer, Still Christ is quite free to you. Though you have no care for your soul, yet Christ has, and wishes to save it. Though you do not care for Christ, yet He cares for you, and stretches out His hands to you. Christ did not come to the earth because people were caring about their souls, but because we were lost. You are only the more lost. Christ is all the more seeking you. This day you may find a Saviour. "Unto you, O men, I call."

"If I knew I were one of the elect, I would come; but I fear I am not." To you I answer, Nobody ever came to Christ because they knew themselves to be of the elect. It is quite true that God has of His mere good pleasure elected some to everlasting life, but they never knew it till they came to Christ. Christ nowhere invites the elect to come to Him. The question for you is not, Am I one of the elect? but, Am I of the human race?

Some of you may be saying, "If I could see my name in the Bible, then I would believe that Christ wants me to be saved. When Christ called Zaccheus, He said, 'Zaccheus, come down.' He called him by name, and he came down immediately. Now, if Christ would call me by name, I would run to Him immediately." Now, to you I say, Christ does call you by your name, for He says, "To you, O men, I call." Suppose that Christ had written down the names of all the men and women in the world, your name would have been there. Now, instead of writing down every name, He puts them all together in one word, which includes every man, and woman, and child: "Unto you, O *men,* I call; and my words are to the *sons of men.*" So your name is in the Bible. "Go and preach the gospel to every creature."

"If I could repent and believe, then Christ would be free to me; but I cannot repent and believe." To you I say, Are you not a man, before you repent and believe? then Christ is offered to you before you repent. And, believer, Christ is not offered to you because you repent, but because you are a vile, lost sinner. "Unto you, O men, I call."

"I fear the market is over. Had I come in the morning of life—I believe Christ was offered me then, in youth, at my first sacrament—but now I fear the market day is done." Are you not still a man, one of the human race? True, you have refused the Saviour for years, yet still He offers Himself to you. It was not for any goodnes that He offered Himself to you at first, but because you were vile and lost. You are vile and lost yet, so He offers Himself to you still. "Unto you, O men, I call."

I would here, then, take occasion to make offer of Christ with all His benefits to every soul in this assembly. To every man and woman and child I do now, in the name of my Master, make full, free offer of a crucified Saviour, to be your surety and righteousness, your refuge and strength. I would let down the gospel cord so low, that sinners, who are low of stature, like Zaccheus, may lay hold of it. Oh! is there none will lay hold on Christ, the only Saviour?

III. *The most condemning truth in the Bible.*

If Christ be freely offered to all men, then it is plain that all who live and die without accepting Christ shall meet with the doom of those who refuse the Son of God. "He that sinneth against me wrongeth his own soul: all they that hate me love death." Ah! it is a sad thing that the very truth, which is life to every believing soul, is death to all others. This is the condemnation. We are a sweet savor of Christ unto God. When the ignorant heathen stand at the bar of God, Hindus, and Africans, and Chinese who have never had the offer of Christ made to them, they will not be condemned as those will that have lived and died unsaved under a preached gospel. Tyre and Sidon will not meet the same doom as Chorazin and Bethsaida, and unbelieving Capernaum.

Oh, brethren, you are without excuse in the sight of God, if you go home unsaved this day! The gospel cord has been let down very low to every one of you this day. If you go away without laying hold, your condemnation will be heavier at the last day. If Christ had not come to you, you had not had sin, but now you have no cloak for your sin.

Objection.—But my heart is so hard that I cannot believe; my heart is so set upon worldly things that I cannot turn to Christ. I was born this way.

Answer.—This does but aggravate your guilt. It is true you were born thus, and that your heart is like the nether mill-stone. But that is the very reason God will most justly condemn you; because from your infancy you have been hard-hearted and unbelieving. If a thief, when tried before the judge on earth, were to plead guilty, but to say that he had always been a thief, that even in infancy his heart loved stealing, would not this just aggravate his guilt, that he was by habit and repute a thief? So with you.

Oh, brethren, if you could die and say that Christ had never been offered to you, you would have an easier hell than you are likely to have! You must go away either rejoicing in or rejecting Christ this day; either won, or more lost than ever. There is not one of you but will yet feel the guilt of this Sabbath day. This sermon will meet you yet. See that ye refuse not him that speaketh: "How shall we escape if we neglect so great salvation?"

St Peter's, 1838

MESSAGE VI

"That which was from the beginning, which we have heard, which we have
seen with our eyes which we have looked upon, and our hands have handled,
of the Word of life (for the life was manifested, and we have seen it, and
bear witness, and show unto you that eternal life which was with the Father,
and was manifested unto us) ; that which we have seen and heard declare we
unto you, that ye also may have fellowship with us: and truly our fellowship is with the Father, and with his Son Jesus Christ. And these things
write we unto you, that your joy may be full."—I John 1:1-4.

IT WAS JESUS CHRIST and Him crucified that John
preached. "That which we have seen and heard, declare
we unto you." This was the preaching of *John the Baptist:*
"Behold the Lamb of God, which taketh away the sins of
the world." He pointed to Jesus. This was the preaching of
Philip—Acts 8:5: "Philip went down to Samaria, and preached
Christ unto them." And when he came to the Ethiopian
eunuch, "he preached unto him Jesus." This was the preaching of *Paul:* "I determined to know nothing among you, but
Jesus Christ and him crucified." This was the beginning, and
middle, and end of the preaching of Paul. This was the
preaching of *John:* To declare all that he had seen with his
eyes, heard with his ears, handled with his hands, of Immanuel
—this was the object of his life, this was the Alpha and Omega
of his preaching. He knew that Jesus was like the *alabaster
box,* full of spikenard, very costly; and his whole labor was to
break the box and pour forth the good ointment before the
eyes of fainting sinners, that they might be attracted by the
sweet savor. He knew that Jesus was *a bundle of myrrh,* and
his whole life was spent in opening it out to sinners, that they
might be overcome by the refreshing odors. He carried about
the savor of Christ with him wherever he went. He knew
that Jesus was the Balm of Gilead, and his labor was to
open out this bruised balm before the eyes of sick souls,
that they might be healed.

I. *The things John preached concerning Christ.*

1. *His eternity.*—"That which was from the beginning."
·John had often heard Jesus speak of His eternity. "In the
beginning was the Word." "Before Abraham was, I am."
He remembered how Jesus said in prayer in the garden,
"Glorify me with the glory which I had with thee before the
world was." "Thou lovedst me before the foundation of the
world." John thus knew that He was the Eternal One, that He
was before all visible things, for He made them all. By Him
God made the world. Even at the time John was leaning on
His bosom, he felt that it was the bosom of the Uncreated
One. John always declared this; he loved to make Him known.
O beloved! if you have come to lean on the bosom of Jesus,
you have come to the Uncreated One—the Eternal One.

2. *His eternal pre-existence with the Father.*—John
knew, from Proverbs 8:30, that Jesus had been with the
Father: "Then I was by him, as one brought up with him,
and I was daily his delight, rejoicing always before him." He
had heard Jesus tell many of the secrets of His Father's bosom,
from which he knew that He had been with the Father: "All
things that I have heard of my Father I have made known
unto you." He had heard Jesus plainly say, "I came forth
from the Father, and am come into the world." "Again I
leave the world, and go to the Father." John felt, even when
Jesus was washing his feet, that this was the man that was
God's fellow. Even when he saw Jesus on the cross, with
His pale lips and bleeding hands and feet, like a tortured
worm, and "no man," he knew that this was the man that
was God's fellow. He lived to declare this. Do you thus look
to Jesus? Have you beheld the glory, as of the only begotten
of the Father, full of grace and truth? O tempest-tossed soul,
this is He that comes to save thee!

3. *His eternal life.*—John knew that Jesus was the Author of
all *natural life,* that not a man breathes, no beast of the forest
roars, no bird stoops on the wing, but they all receive the

stream of life from the hand of Immanuel. He had seen
Jesus raise the ruler's daughter from the dead, and call Lazarus
from the tomb. He knew that Jesus was the Author of all
life in the soul. He had heard Jesus say, "As the Father
raiseth up the dead, and quickeneth whom he will, even so the
Son quickeneth whom he will." "My sheep know my voice,
and I give unto them eternal life." He had heard Him say,
"I am the way, the truth, and the life."

Above all, he had *felt in his own soul* that Christ was the
Eternal Life. In that morning, when he sat with his father
Zebedee in the boat, mending their nets, Jesus said, "Follow
me!" and the life entered into his soul, and he found it a never-
failing spring of life. Christ was his life; therefore did he make
Him known as the Eternal Life. Even when he saw Him give
up the ghost; when he saw His pale, lifeless body, the stiff
hands and feet, the glazed eye, the body cold as the rocky
tomb where they laid Him; still he felt that this was the
Eternal Life. O beloved! do you believe that He is the life of
the world? Some of you feel your soul to be dead—lifeless in
prayer—lifeless in praise. Oh look on Him whom John declares to you! All is death without Him. Bring your dead
soul into union with Him, and He will give you eternal life.

4. *His Being Manifested.*—O beloved, if Jesus had not been
manifested, you had never been saved! It would have been
quite righteous in God to have kept His Son in His own bosom,
to have kept that jewel in His own place upon the throne of
heaven. God would have been the same lovely God; but we
would have lain down in a burning hell. If that Eternal Life
which was with the Father had remained in His glory as the
Living One, then you and I would have borne our own curse.
But He was manifested: "God was manifest in the flesh, justified in the Spirit, seen of angels, believed on in the world, received up into glory."

John saw Him: he saw His lovely countenance; he beheld

His glory, as the glory of the only begotten of the Father, full of grace and truth. He saw that better Sun veiled with flesh that could not keep the beams of His Godhead from shining through. He saw Him on the Mount, when His face shone like the sun. He saw Him in the garden, when He lay upon the ground. He saw Him on the cross, when He hung between earth and heaven. He looked upon Him—many a time he looked upon His heavenly countenance—his eye met His eye.

He heard Him, heard the voice that said, "Let there be light!" He heard the voice like the sound of many waters. He heard all His gracious words—His words concerning God and the way of peace. He heard Him say to a sinner, "Be of good cheer, thy sins are forgiven thee."

He handled Him, he put his hands in His hands, his arms around His arms, and his head upon His bosom. Perhaps he handled His body when it was taken from the cross, touched the cold clay of Immanuel. O beloved, it is a manifested Christ we declare unto you. It is not the Son in the bosom of the Father; that would never have saved you. It is Jesus manifested in flesh. The Son of God living and dying as man in the stead of sinners; Him we declare unto you.

Learn the true way of coming to peace.—It is by looking to a manifested Jesus. Some of you think you will come to peace *by looking in* to your own heart. Your eye is riveted there. You watch every change there. If you could only see a glimpse of light there, oh, what joy it would give you! If you could only see a melting of your stony heart, if you could only see your heart turning to God, if you could only see a glimpse of the image of Jesus in your heart, you would be at peace; but you cannot, all is dark within. Oh, dear souls, it is not there you will find peace! You must *avert the eye* from your bosom altogether. *You must look to a declared Christ.* Spread out the record of God concerning His Son. The Gospels are the narrative of the heart of Jesus, of the work of Jesus, of the grace of

Jesus. Spread them out before the eye of your mind, till they fill your eye. Cry for the Spirit to breathe over the page, to make a manifested Christ stand out plainly before you; and the moment that you are willing to believe all that is there spoken concerning Jesus, that moment you will wipe away your tears, and change your sighs for a new song of praise.

II. *The object John had in view by preaching Christ.*

1. *That ye may have fellowship with us.*—To have fellowship with another is to have things in common with him. Thus, in Acts 4:32, the first Christians were "of one heart and of one soul; neither said any that aught of the things which he possessed was his own, but *they had all things in common.*" They had all their goods in common; they shared what they had with one another. This is what John desired in spiritual things —that we should share with him in his spiritual things, share and share alike.

In Forgiveness.—Some people think it impossible to have the same forgiveness that the apostles had, that it would be very bold to think of tasting the same. But is it not far bolder to say that John is a liar, and that the Holy Spirit is a liar? For he here says plainly, that all his preaching, and all his desire was, that you should have fellowship with Him. Yes, sinner, forgiveness is as open to you as it was to John. The blood that washed him is ready to wash you as white as snow. John had the same need of Christ that the vilest of you have. Only look to a declared Immanuel; clear your eye from unbelief, and look at a freely-revealed Jesus, and you will find the same forgiveness is as free to you as it was to John.

In the same love of Jesus.—John was the disciple whom Jesus loved. Just as Daniel was the prophet whom He greatly loved, "a man greatly beloved," so John was the disciple whom Jesus loved. At the Last Supper which Jesus had in this world, John leaned upon His bosom. He had the nearest place to the heart of Christ of any in all the world. Perhaps you think it is impossible you can ever come to that. Some of you are trembling afar off; but you, too, if you will only look where John points you, if you will only believe the full record of God about Jesus, will share the love of Jesus with John, you will be one of His peculiarly beloved ones. Those that believe most, get most love; they come nearest to Jesus—they do, as it were, lay their head on His breast; and no doubt you will one day really share that bosom with John. If you believe little, you will keep far off from Jesus.

In the same fatherly dealings as John.—John experienced many wonderful dealings of God. He experienced many of *the prunings* of the Father. He was a fruitful branch, and the Father pruned him that he might bring forth more fruit. When he was very old, he was banished to Patmos, an island in the Ægean Sea, and, it is supposed, made a slave in the mines there. He was a companion in tribulation; but he had many sweet shinings of the Father's love to his soul. He had sweet revelations of Christ in the time of his affliction; and he was joyfully delivered out of all his troubles. He experienced peculiarly the fatherly dealings of God. And so may you do, believer. Look where John looked, believe as John believed; and, like him, you will find that you have a Father in heaven, who will care for you, who will correct you in measure, who will stay His rough wind in the day of His east wind, who will preserve you unto His heavenly kingdom.

2. *That ye may have fellowship with the Father.*—O beloved, this is so wonderful, that I could not have believed it, if I had not seen it! Shall a hell-deserving worm come to share with the holy God? Oh the depth and the length of the love of God, it passeth knowledge!

In His holiness.—A natural man has not a spark of God's holiness in him. There is a kind of goodness about you. You may be kind, pleasant, agreeable, good-natured, amiable people; there may be a kind of integrity about you, so that you are above stealing or lying; but as long as you are in a natural state, there is not a grain of God's holiness in you. You have not a grain of that absolute hatred against all sin which God has; you have none of that flaming love for what is lovely, pure, holy, which dwells in the heart of God. But the moment you believe on a manifested Christ, that moment you receive the Spirit, the same Spirit which dwells in the infinite bosom of the Father dwelleth in you; so you become partakers of God's holiness, you become partakers of the divine nature. You will not be as holy as God; but the same stream that flows through the heart of God will be given you. Ah! does not your heart break to be holier? Look then to Jesus, and abide in Him, and you will share the same spirit with God Himself.

In His joy.—No joy is like the divine joy. It is infinite, full, eternal, pure unmingled joy. It is light, without any cloud to darken it; it is calm, without any breath to ruffle it. Clouds and darkness are round about Him, storms and fire go before Him; but within all is peace ineffable, unchangeable. Believers in some measure share in this joy. We might mention some of the elements of God's joy. *First,* All things happen according to the good pleasure of His will. He has foreordained whatsoever comes to pass. Nothing comes unprepared upon God. Many things are hateful in His sight, yet, looking on the whole, He can delight in all. If you have come to Christ, you will have some drops of His joy. You can look upon all events with a calm, holy joy, knowing that your Father's will and purposes alone shall stand. *Second,* The conversion of souls. There is joy in the presence of the angels of God over one sinner repenting, more than over ninety-nine who need no repentance. I have no doubt that this is one of the great elements of His joy —seeing souls brought into His favour. He loves to save; He delighteth in mercy; He delights when He can be a just God and a Saviour. If you are come to Christ, you will have the same joy.

3. *That ye may have fellowship with the Son.*

We share with the Son in His justification.—Once Jesus was unjustified; once there were sins laid to His charge—the sins of many. It was this that occasioned His agony *in the garden, on the cross.* His only comfort was, "He is near that justifieth me." He knew the time would be short. But now the wrath of God has all fallen upon Him. The thunderclouds of God's anger have spent all their lightnings on His head. The vials of God's wrath have poured out their last drops upon Him. He is now justified from all the sins that were laid upon Him. He has left them with the graveclothes. His fellow men and devils laid all sins to His charge; He was silent. Do you believe this record concerning the Son? Do you cleave to Jesus as yours? Then you have fellowship with Him in His justification. You are as much justified as Christ is. There is as little guilt lying upon you as there is upon Christ. The vials of wrath have not another drop for Christ, nor another drop for you. You are justified from all things.

In His adoption.—When Jesus went up to heaven, He said, "I go to my Father." When He entered heaven, the word of God was "Thou art my Son; sit thou on my right hand until I make thine enemies thy footstool." Oh, it was a blessed exchange, when He left the frowns and curses of this world for the embrace of His Father's arms; when He left the thorny crown for a crown of glory; when He came from under the wrath of God into the fatherly love of God! Such is your change, you that believe in Jesus. You have fellowship with the Son, you share in His adoption. He says, "I ascend to my Father and your Father." God is as much your Father as He is Christ's Father, your God as Christ's God. Oh, what a change! for an heir of hell to become an heir of God, and joint-heir with Christ; to inherit God; to have a son's interest in God! Eternity alone will teach you what is in that word, "heir of God."

4. *That your joy may be full.*—Other joys are not filling.

Creature joys only fill a small part of the soul. Money, houses, lands, music, entertainments, friends, these are not filling joys; they are just drops of joys. But Christ revealed makes the cup run over. "Thou anointest my head with oil, my cup runneth over." Believing in a manifested Christ fills the heart full of joy. "In thy presence is fullness of joy." Christ brings the soul into God's presence. One smile of God fills the heart more than ten thousand smiles of the world.

You that have nothing but creature joy, hunting after butterflies, feeding upon carrion, why do you spend money for that which is not bread? You that are afflicted, tempest-tossed, and not comforted, look to a manifested Jesus. According to your faith so be it unto you. Believe none, and you will have no joy. Believe little, and you will have little joy. Believe much, and you will have much joy. Believe all, and you will have all joy, and your joy will be full. It will be like a bowl running over, good measure, pressed down, and running over. Amen.

St. Peter's, 1839.

Message VII.

"A garden enclosed is my sister, my spouse; a spring shut up, a fountain sealed."
—Song of Solomon 4:12.

THE NAME here given to believers is "my sister, my spouse," or rather, "my sister-spouse." There are many sweet names from the lips of Christ addressed to believers: "O thou fairest among women" (1:8); "My love" (2:2); "My love, my fair one" (2:10); "O my dove" (2:14); "My sister, my love, my dove, my undefiled" (5:2); "O prince's daughter" (7:1). But here is one more tender than all, *"My sister, my spouse"* (4:9); and again, verse 10, and here, verse 12. To be spoken well of by the world is little to be desired; but to hear Christ speak such words to us, is enough to fill our hearts with heavenly joy. The meaning you will see by what Paul says,

I Corinthians 9:5: "Have we not power to lead about a sister, a wife, as well as other apostles?" He means power to marry one who is likeminded—a sister in the Lord; one who will be both a wife and a sister in Christ Jesus—a *wife* by covenant, a *sister* by being born of the same Father in heaven. So Christ here says of believers, "My sister, my spouse," that they are not only united to Him by choice and covenant, but are likeminded also.

I. *These two things are inseparable.*—Some would like to be *the spouse* of the Saviour, without being the sister. Some would like to be saved by Christ, but not to be made like Christ. When Christ chooses a sinner, and sets His love on the soul, and when He woos the soul and draws it into covenant with Himself, it is only that He may make the soul a sister, that He may impart His features, His same heart, His all, to the soul. Now, many rest in the mere forgiveness of sins. Many have felt Christ wooing their soul, and offering Himself freely to them, and they have accepted Him. They have consented to the match. Sinful and worthless and hell-deserving, they find that Christ desires it; that He will not be dishonored by it; that He will find glory in it; and their heart is filled with joy in being taken into covenant with so glorious a bridegroom. But why has He done it? To make you partaker of His holiness, to change your nature, to make you sister to Himself, of His own mind and spirit. He has sprinkled you with clean water, only that He may give you a new heart also. He brings you to Himself and gives you rest only that He may make you learn of Him His meekness and lowliness in heart.

1. You cannot be the spouse of Christ without becoming sister also. Christ offers to be the bridegroom of sin-covered souls. He came from heaven for this; took flesh and blood for this. He tries to woo sinners, standing and stretching out His hands. He tells them of all His power, and glory, and riches, and that all shall be theirs. He is a blood-sprinkled bridegroom; but

that is His chief loveliness. The soul believes His Word, melts
under His love, consents to be His. "My beloved is mine, and
I am his." Then He washes the soul in His own blood; clothes
it in His own righteousness; takes it in with Him to the presence
of His Father. From that day the soul begins to reflect His
image. Christ begins to live in the soul. The same heart, the
same spirit, are in both. The soul becomes sister as well as
spouse—Christ's not only by choice and covenant, but by likeness also. Some of you Christ has chosen; you have become
His justified ones. Do you rest there? No; remember you must
be made like Him, reflect His image; you cannot separate the
two.

2. *The order of the two.*—You must be first the spouse before you can be the sister of Christ, His by covenant before His
by likeness. Some think to be like Christ first, that they will
copy His features till they recommend themselves to Christ.
No, this will not do. He chooses only those that have no comeliness—polluted in their own blood, that He may have the
honor of washing them. "When thou wast in thy blood,"
Ezekiel 16:6. Are there any trying to recommend themselves to
Christ by their change of life? Oh, how little you know Him!
He comes to seek those who are black in themselves. Are
there some of you poor, defiled, unclean? You are just the
soul Christ woos. Proud, scornful? Christ woos you. He offers you His all, and then He will change you.

II. *To what Christ compares believers:*

1. *"A garden enclosed."*—The gardens in the East are always enclosed; sometimes by a fence of reeds, such are the
gardens of cucumbers in the wilderness; sometimes by a stone
wall, as the garden of Gethsemane; sometimes by a hedge of
prickly pear. But what is still more interesting is, they are often
enclosed out of a wilderness. All around is often barren sand;
and this one enclosed spot is like the garden of the Lord. Such
is the believer.

Enclosed by election.—In the eye of God, the world was one great wilderness, all barren, all dead, all fruitless. No part was fit to bear anything but briers. It was nigh unto cursing. One part was no better than another in His sight. The hearts of men were all hard as rock, dry and barren as the sand. Out of the mere good pleasure of His will, He marked out a garden of delights where He might show His power and grace, that it might be to His praise. Some of you know your election of God by the fruits of it, by your faith, love, and holiness. Be humbled by the thought that it was solely because He chose you. Why me, Lord, why me?

Enclosed by the Spirit's work.—Election is the planning of the garden. The Spirit's work is the carrying it into effect. "He fenced it" (Isa. 5:2). When the Spirit begins His work, it is separating work. When a man is convinced of sin, he is no more one with the careless, godless world. He avoids his companions—goes alone. When a soul comes to Christ, it is still more separated. It then comes into a new world. He is no more under the curse—no more under wrath. He is in the smile and favor of God. Like Gideon's fleece, he now receives the dew when all around is dry.

Enclosed by the arms of God.—God is a wall of fire. Angels are around the soul. Elisha's hill was full of horses of fire. God is round about the soul, as the mountains stand round about Jerusalem. The soul is hid in the secret of God's presence. No robber can ever come over the fence. "A vineyard of red wine: I the Lord do keep it; I will water it every moment: lest any hurt it, I will keep it night and day" (Isa. 27: 2, 3). This is sung over thee.

An Eastern garden was watered in three ways: by a hidden well—it is the custom in the East to roll a stone over the mouth of a well, to preserve the water from sand; by a fountain of living water—a well always bubbling up; by streams from Lebanon.

2. *"A spring shut up."*—This describes the Spirit in the heart, in His most secret manner of working. In some gardens there is only this secret well. A stone is over the mouth. If you wish to water the garden, you must roll away the stone, and let down the bucket. Such is the life of God in many souls. Some of you feel that there is a stone over the mouth of the well in you. Your own rocky heart is the stone. Stir up the gift of God which is in thee.

3. *A well of living water.*—This is the same as John 4—a well that is ever full and running over. Grace new every moment; fresh upsprings from God. Thus only will you advance.

4. *Streams from Lebanon.*—These are very plentiful. On all sides they fall in pleasant cascades, in the bottom unite into broad full streams, and on their way water the richest gardens. The garden of Ibrahim Pacha, near Acre, is watered with streams from Lebanon. So believers are sometimes favored with streams from the Lebanon that is above. We receive out of Christ's fullness—drink of the wine of His pleasures. Oh, for more of these streams of Lebanon! Even in the dry season they are full. The hotter the summer, the streams from Lebanon become the fuller, because the heat only melts the mountain snows.

III. *The fruit.*—The very use of a garden is to bear fruit and flowers. For this purpose it is enclosed, hedged, planted, watered. If it bear no fruit nor flowers, all the labor is lost labor. The ground is nigh to cursing. So is it with the Christian. Three remarkable things are here:

1. *No weeds are mentioned.*—Pleasant fruit trees, and all the chief spices; but no weeds. Had it been a man that was describing his garden, he would have begun with the weeds—the unbelief, corruption, evil tempers, etc. Not so Christ. He covers all the sins. The weeds are lost sight of. He sees no perversity. As in John 17: "They have kept thy word; they

are not of the world." As in Revelation 2:2: "I know thy works."

2. *The fruit was the very best—the pomegranate.* All were pleasant fruits, and all His own. "From me is thy fruit found", "His pleasant fruits" (v. 16). The graces that Christ puts into the heart and brings out of the life are the very best, the richest, most pleasant, most excellent that a creature can produce. Love to Christ, love to the brethren, love to the Sabbath, forgiveness of enemies, all the best fruits that can grow in the human heart. Unreasonable world! to condemn true conversion, when it produces the very fruits of paradise, acceptable to God, if not to you. Should not this make you stand and consider?

3. *There were spices in this garden.*—These spices do not naturally grow in gardens. Even in the East there never was such a display as this. So the fragrant graces of the Spirit are not natural to the heart. They are brought from a far country. They must be carefully watched. They need the stream, and the gentle zephyr. Oh, I fear most of you should hang your heads when Christ begins to speak of fragrant spices in your heart! Where are they? Are there not talkative, forward Christians? Are there not self-seeking, praise-seeking, man-pleasing Christians? Are there not proud-praying Christians? Are there not ill-tempered Christians? Are there not rash, inconsiderate ones? Are there not idle, lazy, bad-working Christians? Lord, where are the spices? Verily, Christ is a bundle of myrrh. Oh to be like Him! Oh that every flower and fruit would grow! They must come from above. Many there are of whom one is forced to say, "Well, they may be Christians; but I would not like to be next them in heaven!" Cry for the wind: "Awake, O north wind; and come, thou south; blow upon my garden, that the spices thereof may flow out."

MESSAGE VIII.

"Who is this that cometh up from the wilderness leaning upon her beloved? I raised thee up under the apple tree: there thy mother brought thee forth, there she brought thee forth that bare thee. Set me as a seal upon thine heart, as a seal upon thine arm: for love is strong as death; jealousy is cruel as the grave: the coals thereof are coals of fire, which hath a most vehement flame. Many waters cannot quench love, neither can the floods drown it: if a man would give all the substance of his house for love, it would utterly be contemned."—Song of Solomon 8:5-7.

WE ARE INTRODUCED to the great Redeemer and a believing soul, and are made to overhear their converse.

I. *The posture of the church.*

1. *From the wilderness.*—To a child of God this world is a wilderness. *First, Because everything is fading here.* Here is nothing abiding; money takes wings and flees away; friends die. All are like grass; and if some are more beautiful or more engaging than others, still they are only like the flower of the grass—a little more ornamented, but withering often sooner. Sometimes a worldly comfort is like Jonah's gourd; it came up over his head to be a shadow to deliver him from his grief. So Jonah was exceeding glad of the gourd. But God prepared a worm, when the sun rose the next day, and it smote the gourd that it withered. So our worldly comfort sometimes grows up over our head like a shadow, and we are exceeding glad of our gourd; but God prepares a worm, we faint, and are ready to die. Here we have no continuing city; but we seek one to come. This is a wilderness: "Arise, depart, this is not thy rest, for it is polluted." An experienced Christian looks upon everything here as not abiding; for the things that are seen are temporal, but the things that are not seen are eternal.

Second, Because everything is stained with sin here. Even the natural scenery of this world is stained with sin. The thorns and thistles tell of a cursed earth. Above all, when you look at the floods of ungodly men.

"We are of God, and the whole world lieth in wickedness."

The world does not know a Christian, and does not love him. Though you love them, and would lay down your body that they might pass over to glory, yet they will not hear. Above all, the sin in our own heart makes us bend down under our burden, and feel this to be a valley of weeping. Ah! wretched man, if we had no body of sin, what a sweet glory would appear in everything; we would sing like the birds in spring.

2. *Coming out of it.*—Unconverted souls are going down into the wilderness to perish there. All Christians are coming up out of it. Sabbath days are like milestones, marking our way; or rather they are like the wells we used to come to at evening. Every real Christian is making progress. If the sheep is on the shoulder of the shepherd, it is always getting nearer the fold. With some the shepherd takes long steps. Dear Christians, you should be advancing, getting higher, nearer to Canaan, riper for glory. In the south of Russia, the country is of vast plains, rising by steppes. Dear friends, you should get on to a higher place; up another step every Sabbath day.

In traveling, you never think of making a house in the wilderness. So, dear friends, do not take up your rest here; we are journeying. Let all your endeavors be to get on in your journey.

3. *Leaning upon her beloved.*—It is very observable that there is none here but the bride and her Beloved in a vast wilderness. She is not leaning on Him with one arm, and upon somebody else with the other; but she is leaning on Him alone. So is it with the soul taught of God; it feels alone with Christ in this world; it leans as entirely upon Christ as if there were no other being in the universe. She leans all her weight upon her Husband. When a person has been saved from drowning, he leans all his weight on his deliverer. When the lost sheep was found, He took it upon His shoulder. You must be content then to lean all your weight on Christ. *Cast the burden of temporal things on Him. Cast the care of your soul on Him.* If

God be for us, who can be against us? They that wait upon the Lord shall renew their strength. The eagle soars so directly upward, that poets have fancied it was aiming at the sun. So does the soul that waits on Christ.

II. *Christ's word to the leaning soul.*

1. *"I raised thee up."*—He reminds the believer of his natural state. Every soul now in Christ was once like an exposed infant (Ezek. 16), cast out into the open field. "Behold, I was shapen in iniquity." Do not forget what you were. If ever you come to forget what you were, then you may be sure you are not right with God. Observe when the contrition comes. When you are leaning on Christ, then He tells you of your sin and misery (Ezek. 36:31).

2. He reminds you of His love: "I raised thee up." *He Himself* is the apple tree, open on all sides, affording shadow and fruit. *I raised thee.* Christ not only shelters, but draws into the shelter. *"To Him be glory."* Are there not some who feel like an infant—cast out? Turn your eye to Christ, He only can raise up your soul under the apple tree.

III. *The leaning soul cries for continued grace.*

Set me as a seal.—It is a sure mark of grace to desire more. The high priest had a beautiful breastplate over his breast, adorned with jewels—make me one of these. He had also a jewel on each shoulder—make me one of these. These were bound with chains of gold, but the believer with chains of love. This is a true mark of grace. If you be contented to remain where you are, without any more nearness to God, or any more holiness, this is a clear mark you have none. Hide me deeper, bind me closer, and carry me more completely.

1. *The love of Christ is strong as death.*—Death is awfully strong. When he comes upon a stout young man, he brings him down. So is the love of Christ.

2. *Cruel, or stubborn, as the grave.*—The grave will not give up its dead, nor will Christ give up His own. Oh! pray that

this love may embrace you. Vehement as hell—unquenchable
fire. You have your choice, dear friends, of two eternal fires.
"Who shall separate us from the love of Christ?" (Rom. 8).
Floods cannot drown it, afflictions cannot.

3. *It cannot be bought.*—"If a man would give all the substance," etc. You must accept it free or not at all.

DUNDEE, 1840.

MESSAGE IX.

"After this I beheld, and, lo, a great multitude, which no man could number,
of all nations, and kindreds, and people, and tongues, stood before the throne,
and before the Lamb, clothed with white robes, and palms in their hands;
and cried with a loud voice, saying, Salvation to our God which sitteth upon
the throne, and unto the Lamb. And all the angels stood round about the
throne, and about the elders and the four beasts, and fell before the throne
on their faces and worshiped God, saying, Amen: Blessing, and glory, and
wisdom, and thanksgiving, and honor, and power, and might, be unto our
God for ever and ever. Amen. And one of the elders answered, saying unto
me, What are these which are arrayed in white robes? and whence came
they? And I said unto him, Sir, thou knowest. And he said unto me,
These are they which came out of great tribulation, and have washed their
robes, and made them white in the blood of the Lamb. Therefore are they
before the throne of God, and serve him day and night in his temple: and
he that sitteth on the throne shall dwell among them. They shall hunger no
more, neither thirst any more; neither shall the sun light on them, nor any
heat. For the Lamb, which is in the midst of the throne, shall feed them,
and shall lead them unto living fountains of waters: and God shall wipe
away all tears from their eyes."—Revelation 7:9-17.

I T IS ONE THING to read these words with a poet's eye, and
another thing to read them with the eye of a Christian. Oh
pray, dear friends, that the Spirit may tear away the veil from
our hearts, and show us the grand realities that are here! It is
sweet and profitable—

1. *For the awakening of the ungodly,* that you may see what
are the exercises of the heavenly world, and how unfit you
would be for them. I suppose many of you feel that you have
not washed your robes, and that you could not sing their song.
Then you must be on the road to hell.

2. *For the instruction of believers.*—It shows you what are

the chief employments of that happy world, where we shall so
soon be; it gives you the keynote of the heavenly song; it
teaches you to spend much of your time in the same exercises
in which you shall spend eternity.

3. *For comfort to afflicted believers.*—It shows you how short
your trials will be. These light afflictions are but for a moment;
you need not murmur nor grieve. A little while, and we shall be
with Christ, and God shall wipe away all your tears. For this
end it was given to John.

I. *What John saw and heard.*

1. *A great multitude of all nations.*—When John was on
earth he saw but few believers: "We are of God, and the whole
world lieth in wickedness." The church was like a lily in a field
of thorns, lambs in the midst of wolves; but now quite different—thorns are plucked away, the lilies innumerable. *"Out
of all nations."* Perhaps he could discern his fellow apostles,
his own brother James, and holy Paul, and angel-faced Stephen;
the dark Egyptian, the swarthy Ethiopian, the wooly-headed
Negro, the far distant Chinese, the Burman, the Hindu, the
blue-eyed German, the dark-eyed Italian, and multitudes perhaps from a distant island of the sea. Every country had its
representatives there, some saved out of every land. All were
like Christ, and yet all retained their different peculiarities.

Learn that Christ will have a glorious crown.—He shall see
of the travail of His soul, and be satisfied. Often, when I look
at a large town like Dundee, and see so few converted to
Christ, my heart sickens within me; I often feel as if we were
laboring for nought and in vain. Although there has been so
much blessing, yet such masses of ungodly families! But oh,
cheer up, Christ shall have His full crown! Though there
should not be another saved out of this place, Christ will have
His full reward. We shall be quite satisfied when we see the
whole. He hath mercy on whom He will have mercy. Learn
the power of His blood. It blots out the sins of all that multi-

tude, sins of every name and dye. Why not yours? Oh! when such a glorious company are saved, why should you be lost? When so many are going out of this place, why should you keep back?

2. *Their position.*—They stood before the throne—yea, nearer than the angels, for they stood round about. The redeemed stood next the throne, the angels round them. This marks their complete righteousness. But the ungodly cannot stand in the judgment. If God were only to bring an ungodly man into His presence, he would die. You greatly mistake if you think God needs to put out great strength to destroy you. As a cloud is dried up by being in the light of the sun, so you would perish at the presence of God as a moth in a candle. But this great company stand next the throne, God's eye full upon them. In Christ they stand, not in themselves. Nearer than angels: the angels have only creature-righteousness; these have on Creator-righteousness. The righteousness of Christ is a million times more lovely than that of the highest angel, therefore they stand nearer. The righteousness of God is upon them all—who shall condemn? If you are ever to be near God, you may come freely to Him now. Why keep so far away?

3. *Their dress; white robes and palms.*—They have all the same dress, there is no difference. It is the garment of Christ. One was a far greater believer than another—made far greater advances in holiness—yet the same dress. *Whiter than the angels,* verse 13. The angels also are represented as dressed in white; yet it would appear that their robes were far outshone by the bright shining raiment of the redeemed. The angels have on creature-righteousness, the redeemed the righteousness of God. This is what is now offered to you, sinners. Awakened persons are sometimes led to cry, "Oh that I had never sinned!" but here is something better than if you had never sinned. *Palms* are signs of victory. The Jews used to take branches of palms at the feast of tabernacles, or ingathering, which was a

type of heaven. The angels have no palms, for they have fought no fight, they have gained no victory. Everyone that has a white robe has a palm. Everyone that is in Christ shall overcome. Be not afraid of your enemies.

4. *Their song. The substance of it—salvation.*—They give God all the glory. On earth, there are many that cannot believe in an *electing* God—that God chose them for no good in them; but in heaven they all feel it, and give Him all the praise. On earth, many speak of making themselves willing; but in heaven they sing "Salvation to God." On earth, many go about to establish their own righteousness; in heaven, "glory to the Lamb." On earth, many take Christ as part of their righteousness, and their duties as part; in heaven, all give glory to the Lamb. What say you to this song? Does it find an echo in your heart? Remember you must begin it now, if you are to sing it afterwards.

The effect of it—it stirs up the hearts of the angels (vv. 11, 12). Often on earth, when one believer begins to praise God for what He has done for his soul, it stirs up the hearts of others. So in heaven, when the angels hear the voice of redeemed sinners—brands plucked out of the fire—standing near the throne, they will obtain a ravishing view of the glory of God, His mercy and grace, and they will fall down and worship God. They will not envy the redeemed their place; but, on the contrary, be filled with intense praise by hearing of what God has done for their souls. How do you feel when you hear of others being saved and brought nearer to God than you? Do you envy and hate them, or do you fall down and praise God for it?

II. *Their past history* (vv. 13, 14).

Two particulars are given. Each had a different history; still in these two they were alike:

1. *They had washed their robes.*—This leads us back to their conversion. Once every one of that company had filthy

garments. They were like Joshua, their garment was spotted by the flesh. It was like a garment with the leprosy in it. Some stained with blood, spots of blood upon their garments; some with adultery; some with disobedience to parents; some with pride, falsehood, evil speaking—all, all were stained. Everyone was convinced that he could not make himself clean; he could not wash his garments nor throw them off; he was brought to see himself lost and helpless. Jesus was revealed to him, and His precious blood shed for sinners, even the chief, saying to the heavy-laden, "Come to me." Of all that company, there is not one stands there in any other way. All are washed in blood. It is their only way of standing. Have you been washed in blood? You will find not one in heaven who went there in any other way. You think to go to heaven by your own decency, innocency, attention to duties. Well, you would be the only such one there: all are washed in blood. Come and let us reason together.

2. *They came out of great tribulation.*—Every one that gets to the throne must put his foot upon the thorn. The way to the crown is by the cross. We must taste the gall if we are to taste the glory. When justified by faith, God led them into tribulations also. When God brought Israel through the Red Sea, He led them into the wilderness; so, when God saves a soul, He tries it. He never gives faith without trying it. The way to Zion is through the Valley of Baca. You must go through the wilderness of Jordan if you are to come to the Land of Promise. Some believers are much surprised when they are called to suffer. They thought they would do some great thing for God; but all that God permits them to do is to *suffer*. Go round everyone in glory; everyone has a different story, yet every one has a tale of suffering. One was persecuted in his family, by his friends and companions; another was visited by sore pains and humbling disease, neglected by the world; another was bereaved of children; another had all these afflictions.

Mark, all are *brought out of them.* It was a dark cloud, but it passed away; the water was deep, but they have reached the other side. Not one of them blames God for the road He led them: "Salvation" is their only cry. Are there any of you, dear children, murmuring at your lot? Do not sin against God. This is the way God leads all His redeemed ones. You must have a palm as well as a white robe. No pain, no palm; no cross, no crown; no thorn, no throne; no gall, no glory. Learn to glory in tribulations also. "I reckon that the sufferings of this present time are not worthy to be compared with the glory that shall be revealed in us."

III. *Future history.*

1. *Immediate service of God.*—Here, we are allowed to spend much of our time in our worldly callings. It is lawful for a man to win his bread, to plough, sow, reap, to spin and weave. Then, all our strength will be put forth in the immediate service of God. We shall stand before Him, and He shall dwell among us. It will be a perpetual Sabbath. We shall spend eternity in loving God, in adoring, admiring, and praising God. We should spend much of our present time in this. Some people imagine that they are not serving God unless they are visiting the sick, or engaged in some outward service; whereas the highest of all service is the love of adoration in the soul. Perhaps God gets more glory by a single adoring look of some poor believer on a sickbed, than from the outward labors of a whole day.

2. *Not in the wilderness any more.*—At present we are like a flock in the wilderness, our soul often hungry, and thirsty, and sorely tried. Often we feel as if we could go no farther, but must lie down and die. Often we feel temptations too much for us, or persecutions too strong for us to bear. When we are with Christ we shall hunger no more, all our pains shall be ended. Learn to glorify Him in the fires, to sing in the wilderness. This is the only world where you can give God that glory.